CAMBRIDGE STUDIES IN LINGUISTICS

General Editors : W.SIDNEY ALLEN, B.COMRIE
C.J.FILLMORE, E.J.A.HENDERSON, F.W.HOUSEHOLDER
R.LASS, J.LYONS, R.B.LE PAGE, F.R.PALMER, R.POSNER
J.L.M.TRIM

On explaining language change

In this series

ON EXPLAINING
LANGUAGE CHANGE

ROGER LASS

Reader in Linguistics, University of Edinburgh

CAMBRIDGE UNIVERSITY PRESS

CAMBRIDGE

LONDON   NEW YORK   NEW ROCHELLE

MELBOURNE   SYDNEY

CAMBRIDGE UNIVERSITY PRESS
Cambridge, New York, Melbourne, Madrid, Cape Town, Singapore, São Paulo, Delhi

Cambridge University Press
The Edinburgh Building, Cambridge CB2 8RU, UK

Published in the United States of America by Cambridge University Press, New York

www.cambridge.org
Information on this title: www.cambridge.org/9780521117166

First published 1980
This digitally printed version 2009

A catalogue record for this publication is available from the British Library

Library of Congress Cataloguing in Publication data

Lass, Roger.
On explaining language change.

(Cambridge studies in linguistics; 27)
Bibliography: p.
Includes index.
1. Linguistic change. I. Title. II. Series.
P142.L3   410   79-51825

ISBN 978-0-521-22836-7 hardback
ISBN 978-0-521-11716-6 paperback

Contents

FOR JAIME

'We have got to the deductions and the inferences,' said Lestrade, winking at me. 'I find it hard enough to tackle facts, Holmes, without flying away after theories and fancies.'

'You are right,' said Holmes demurely; 'you do find it very hard to tackle the facts.'

The Boscombe Valley Mystery

Deus enim omnibus providet secundum quod competit eorum naturae: est autem naturale homini ut per sensibilia ad intelligibilia veniat: quia omnis nostra cognitio a sensu initium habet. Unde convenienter in sacra scriptura traduntur nobis spiritualia sub metaphoris corporalium . . .

St Thomas, *Summa Theol.* Ia, q.1, a9R

Let us now assume that for certain remarkable facts I have no alternative explanation. Of course, that alone does not dictate acceptance of whatever theory may be offered; for that theory might be worse than none. Inability to explain a fact does not condemn me to accept an intrinsically repugnant and incomprehensible theory.

Nelson Goodman

Preface

Any discipline whose main concerns are explanation and the justification of hypothesized unobservables must make its points by argument, not ostension. For this reason the quality of its argumentation crucially determines the quality of the knowledge it delivers, and the validity of its claims on the credence of outsiders. I take it that this is a reasonably uncontroversial, even trivial, point. I also take it that linguistics (synchronic or historical) is one of these argument-based subjects, and that just about anything interesting that linguists come up with is the result of a complex interaction between argumentative strategies and (ultimately largely theory-defined) 'data'. And that because of this, the data are largely neutral with respect to most interesting conclusions – in the sense that they in no way 'determine' them, but at most, in conjunction with accepted argument types, suggest directions in which one might look for adequate solutions to problems.

Given this, it would seem that questions both about ontology in the widest sense (the nature of data and theoretical constructs) and methodology (the force and epistemic status of arguments) should be of pressing concern to linguists. But there are, within the profession, two attitudes toward this. One is that 'metaworries' (to use a term of Kiparsky's, 1975: 204) are clearly a central concern, and that we are in something of a state of 'crisis' until we dispose of some of the worst ones. The other is that we should forget about them, rejoice in the 'paradigm' that a superficial reading of Kuhn (and generally none of late Popper, Lakatos, or Feyerabend) has convinced some of us that we have, and get on with the serious business of doing linguistics. Let the philosophers (if any are interested) worry.

In what might be called the 'mainstream' of linguistics (a place I seem, happily or not, not to inhabit), the second attitude prevails: at least this is a reasonable inference from the general apathy that seems to have greeted the work of Botha, Derwing, Anttila, Jon Ringen, Itkonen, and others concerned with these things (though the number of 'practising' linguists involved in the symposia reported in Cohen (1974) and Cohen & Wirth (1975) is a hopeful sign). I suggest that this attitude is unacceptable: if we don't identify and get rid of some of the worst metaworries, there will be precious little serious linguistics to do.

But linguists by and large are a rather inbred lot, and often seem not to worry about much except their intradisciplinary self-images, their positions *vis-à-vis* current orthodoxies and heresies, and the like. This is (apparently) what enables many to claim, for instance, to be 'empirical scientists', to pay lip- (or footnote-) service to philosophy of science (an occasional approving reference to Popper, or a self-congratulatory one to Kuhn) – all the while cheerfully practising axiomatics (Ringen 1975; Itkonen 1976b), hermeneutics (Itkonen 1974, 1976a, b) or some other non-empirical discipline (Lass 1976a: epilogue). It is also what enables them (and here I do not exclude myself from 'them') often to base major claims on arguments so weak, shoddy or confused that they would surely not pass muster outside the hermetic confines of the subject (cf. the discussions in Botha 1971; Botha & Winckler 1973; Linell 1974).

Since I am a practising linguist by profession, this book is to be taken as an insider's critical report: specifically on the status of some aspects of argumentation in one area of current historical linguistics – attempts at the explanation of linguistic (mainly phonological) change. I here disarm at least one type of criticism in advance by admitting that I have been guilty, in print, of most of the errors I attempt to anatomize. (Though except for a few relatively brief references I will stick, through modesty and a distaste for festivals of recantation, to the work of others. I see no reason why sinners should be denied the pleasure of casting the first stone, provided they identify themselves in advance.)

My conclusions will in general be both unfavourable to current practice, and pessimistic – at least for the positivistically inclined. I will try to show that the hitherto most popular explanatory argument types in this area are empty or fallacious, or at the very least seriously flawed; and that certain domains that are generally assumed to be amenable in principle to positivist (in this case deductive) explanation are in principle not so; and that certain weaker but still 'respectable' explanatory strategies (notably probabilistic explanations and explanations by 'natural tendency') are not in fact explanatory. And because of this, that most (if not all) of the objects that currently pass for explanations are not – in the light of standard metascientific orientations anyhow – acceptable. I will further try to show that the failures mentioned above lead directly to the collapse of what has recently (and at various times in the past) looked like a promising avenue for research: the provision of 'functional' explanations for language change. The discussion will also lead to a sharper focus on the vacuity of notions like 'naturalness' and 'markedness' (a point I have made elsewhere in a more preliminary way: Lass 1975).

I conclude that given current approaches to scientific and even semiscientific epistemology, there are at present no intellectually respectable strategies for explaining linguistic change: the supposed explanations reduce either to taxonomic or descriptive schemata (which, whatever their merits – and they are considerable: cf. §5.6 – are surely not explanations), or to rather desperate and logically flawed pseudo-arguments. Whether this is due to our (contingent?) shortcomings as linguists ('gaps in our knowledge') or to the nature of language and language change is of course debatable; though I will suggest that the latter is the case, and outline some tentative paths toward an alternative epistemology, and some rather different goals from those we usually accept.

A number of my colleagues have suggested, along the lines of the second of the two attitudes toward 'metaworries' detailed above, that the kind of thing I am trying to do here is counter-productive, obscurantist, and inappropriate for anyone who actually 'does' linguistics. But this separation between 'real' linguistics and 'metalinguistics' (the latter being a distraction) is surely untenable. To put it at its simplest, how do you go about practising your discipline if you're convinced that much of the practice rests on shaky foundations? (Imagine a doctrinaire generative phonologist trying to give a convincing lecture on the validity of taxonomic phonemics.)

On a more sophisticated level, this attitude is rather Philistine. Surely it can only be healthy (in an amateur but not dilettante way anyhow) to be one's own 'philosopher'. That is, all the while one is thinking about language, to be thinking about thinking about language ... etc. (Cf. Collingwood 1946: 1 on the value of this attitude for the historian: his remarks apply here as well.)

This seems to me a reasonable position. At the very least it can grant an occasional parole from the prison of one's own conceptions and metaconceptions. It can also help deflate some forms of pretension and high seriousness, and provoke a bit of self-satire and scepticism about the whole enterprise of knowing things. This is often (though of course not always) a good cure for the worst kinds of humourless pomposity and the *hubris* of expertise. I would even assert programmatically that one of the major obstacles to 'progress' in any field is taking oneself or the things one is most interested in and committed to fully seriously, and getting ego-involved in one's own theories. Whatever the substantive results of this enquiry, I take the informing attitude as one of its justifications.

Most of the more trenchant critics of current linguistic argument and theory approach the subject from one of two points of view: (a) as positivists (good old-fashioned, neo-, or crypto-) trying to show linguists how to be 'good' empirical scientists (Botha 1971; Derwing 1973; Ohala 1974; Sampson 1975b); or (b) as non-positivists trying to show that positivist approaches are either failures (Anttila 1976a, b) or frauds (Itkonen 1974, 1975; Ringen 1975): i.e. that those crypto- or neo-positivists who say they are empirical scientists or whatever are hermeneuticians without admitting it, or mathematicians or analytical philosophers.

My approach here will be somewhat different. I will try to avoid the 'what is linguistics?' gambit, which is by now rather a bore (the right-minded know, and few of the Heathen are likely to be converted). I am more interested in looking at assertions and arguments, especially central and subject-defining ones, and trying to determine their logical and/or empirical validity, and their epistemic status. Or at least in raising questions for others to try and answer.

I would like to thank all of my colleagues whose work and conversation has deepened or otherwise interfered with my understanding of the issues I treat here. In particular, John Anderson, Richard Coates, and Jim Hurford, who commented in detail on an earlier draft of this work; as well as the following, all of whom have read parts of this or other work of mine bearing on similar themes, or have listened to oral presentations, and have given freely of their time and energy to discuss things with me: Kristján Árnason, Gill Brown, Paul van Buren, Gaberell Drachman, Steve Harlow, David Lightfoot, Lachlan Mackenzie, H. H. Meier, Jim Miller, Suzanne Romaine, and Nigel Vincent. I am also indebted to Cambridge University Press' anonymous reader for helpful comments, and for sharpening my perception of some major philosophical issues, and to Mary Hesse for a useful and pleasant afternoon of tutorial assistance. All these and the many I have forgotten are to be congratulated on whatever share they may have in anything good in this book, and absolved from blame for the rest: I am after all responsible for knowing when my friends and colleagues talk nonsense.

And finally, my deepest gratitude to my wife, Jaime, who put up with the long periods of abstraction and surliness that seem to go with writing, and is still willing to speak to me.

Edinburgh

1 *What does it mean to explain something?*

Christianae religionis reuerentiam plures usurpant, sed ea fides pollet
maxime ac solitarie quae cum propter uniuersalium praecepta regularum,
quibus eiusdem religionis intellegatur auctoritas, tum propterea, quod
eius cultus per omnes paene mundi terminos emanauit, catholica uel
universalis uocatur.

Boethius, *De Trinitate* I

1.1 The historical mode: prologue

Historical linguists, like other historians, engage in two basic types of
activities: we usually call them 'reconstruction' and 'explanation'. Non-
linguistic historians might use terms like 'chronicle' or 'plain story' for
the first, and 'interpretation' for the second. But the distinction is clear:

(i) What happened (and/or how?)
(ii) Why did it happen?

There is (particularly for linguists) a hierarchical ranking: type (i)
questions are about mere matters of fact ('natural history', 'bug-
collecting'); type (ii) questions involve general principles, matters of
theoretical interest, etc., and answering them represents a higher mode of
achievement – more or less on the same grounds as Aristotle's ranking of
history and poetry. They are also extremely complex, and my purpose in
this study is to consider some of the difficulties we get into trying to
answer them, and the nature of some of the answers we get.

There are two opposed (and superficially reasonable) views of what it
is that an explanatory historian really ought to do. One, which we may
call the 'positivist' or 'unified science' view, is that there is only one
'real' kind of explanation, and that historical explanation – if there is
such a thing, and if there is, if it's worth anything – belongs to that type:
'the historical concept of explanation is subject-neutral' (Dray 1964: 5).
Thus Hempel (1959: 348–9):

Historical explanation, too, aims at showing that the event in question was not a

1

'matter of chance', but was to be expected in view of certain antecedent or simultaneous conditions. The expectation referred to is not prophecy or divination, but rational scientific anticipation which rests on the assumption of general laws.

The other view is that historians (of all kinds) are in essence myth-makers. History is mythopoesis in the highest sense, where (ideally) *mythos* is *vera narratio*. The historian wades into the mass of disorder left by the past, and by an inspired and disciplined rooting about imposes some kind of order and intelligibility on it, through the construction of exemplary narratives. These, like the questions they are designed to answer, are of two kinds: (i) genetic myths, and (ii) explanatory myths. (Genetic myths are the province of reconstruction, and I will not consider them here: but cf. the methodological remarks in the appendix to chapter 2.) The mythological view[1] may be exemplified by these remarks of Abelson's (1963: 168):

> In his *History of the Russian Revolution*, Trotsky writes that 'the revolution made its first steps toward victory under the belly of a Cossack's horse'. This statement ... is in fact brilliantly explanatory, for it provides the reader with a clear vision of an infinitely complex pattern of events, attitudes and purposes. Trotsky's description is explanatory in the way that art, not science is explanatory, in the way of illumination rather than of deductive inference.

The following preliminary questions arise: will historical explanation in linguistics turn out to be more like Hempel's 'rational scientific expectation' or Abelson's 'clear vision'? If it should be the case that Hempel's desiderata can't be achieved, is there a case to be made for the mythological view as either rational or intellectually satisfying, or acceptable in any other way?

The first three chapters will be concerned with the first question: whether there are any satisfactory examples of 'subject-neutral' explanatory strategies in historical linguistics. In chapter 4 I will explore the problem of 'causality' (which is intimately linked to Hempel's type of explanation), and sketch out some reasons why I suspect that such explanatory strategies can't exist. Finally in chapter 5 I will attempt to come to grips (rather tentatively) with the implications of an essentially mythological view of explanation, or perhaps better, present some idea of what may have to be substituted for explanation in the usual sense

[1] I am using 'mythological' here not in the sense in which it is opposed (as 'false') to (the 'true') historical, but in the more classical sense suggested above, both in the reference to *vera narratio* (which does not mean HISTORICALLY true narrative), and in the sense of the Aristotelian poetry/history hierarchy.

(which turns out to be what IS in fact – though silently – usually substituted).

1.2 Preliminary pessimism

By way of introduction and warning I will expand a bit on why I am doubtful of the existence of Hempelian explanations in historical linguistics, why I do not think there can be deductive answers to 'why?' questions about language history. The deductive paradigm with its emphasis on 'laws' (which I will discuss in some detail below) seems to offer the strongest and most generally satisfying kind of explanation; but it is appropriate only to certain subject matters (cf. chapter 4), and this set includes neither linguistics nor any form of history, and thus *a fortiori* excludes historical linguistics. Further, a slightly weakened form of this strong paradigm, the so-called 'probabilistic' explanation, which is often taken to be useful in the social sciences, biology, and other slightly woolly domains, is not in fact 'explanatory' in any useful sense.

Very simply, deductive explanations (except in some rather uninteresting cases) are not available in the domain of linguistic history, because 'laws' of the relevant type do not exist. The enterprise of seeking them is doomed to failure, because the history of language (whatever its physiological, physical, and perceptual substrates) is in essence culture history. And cultures are not 'law-governed' because they are symbolic constructs, not 'natural objects'; they are norm-governed and rule-governed, which is quite a different thing (cf. Itkonen 1974). Explanation by law applies to objects in the natural world; if cultures and their artefacts (like languages) are 'in' any world at all, it is Teilhard's (1965) 'noösphere', which is very different from the biosphere, or something like Popper's 'World 3' (Popper 1973; Popper & Eccles 1977; and cf. §§4.8–9). And even the biosphere, when it comes to history (i.e. evolution) is only weakly law-governed (cf. §4.11).

The assumption that cultures and their histories are controlled by laws is a venerable positivist error, the root fallacy of Marxism and all other forms of what Popper (1961) calls 'historicism'. The basic problem in any historical explanation involving human beings is ultimately the problem of intention (or crudely, 'free will'); and this leads to a second and related one, that of 'principled indeterminacy', which I will treat in detail in the following chapters. Chapters 2–5 will be, I hope, an adequate expansion and justification of these introductory *ex cathedra* remarks. It is only fair, I think, to warn the reader what to expect.

This general pessimism will not be very much offset by any positive suggestions of great moment (though I will make a few). But in the present climate of opinion it is perhaps necessary to defend the practice of making negative and carping remarks without offering much in the way of positive alternatives. It is a commonly held, and erroneous and counter-productive belief, that in order to be justified in criticizing something, you have to have something better to substitute for it.[2] If there is such a thing as 'progress' in knowledge in the Popperian sense (a debatable claim, but a reasonable starting point), then this belief is untenable; since one of the main ways that progress comes about is by criticism, which is well served by destruction or attempted destruction. If a totally negative assessment causes the babies to be thrown out with the bath-water, this is no great loss; if the babies are really worth keeping and raising to maturity, someone is bound to fish them out again. (As long as we retain a sense of tradition, and are not too hard-nosed about discarding apparently 'refuted' or 'superseded' theories.) As Norman Macbeth says in the introduction to his brilliant (and too little known) *Darwin retried* (1974: 5): 'The proponents of a theory, in science or elsewhere, are obligated to support every link in the chain of reasoning, whereas a critic or skeptic may peck at any aspect of a theory, testing it for flaws. He can be purely negative if he so desires ... The winner in these matters is the skeptic who has no case to prove.' (Cf. the rather similar remarks in Popper 1976: 149.) This is in part the spirit in which I will approach my subject here.

1.3 Definitions and contexts

Explaining what explanation is has become a major subsidiary of the metascience industry. As with any other well-trodden field, there is always a danger that another *noch einmal* will merely induce nausea and

---

[2] It is certainly not held by philosophers in general that this is so; but I am responding here to a common attitude among linguists (commoner perhaps in spoken argument than in writing), at least with respect to global claims or to theories (especially fundamental or 'paradigm'-defining ones) – not an attitude with respect to individual arguments within the framework of a theory. I am also not referring to the Lakatosian idea that in order to be justified in rejecting a GOOD theory you ought to have a replacement; I am (as will become clear later) talking about BAD theories, or untenable global claims related to (possibly good, possibly bad) fashionable theories. I do not recommend scrapping serviceable theories because of anomalies, but I do worry about accepted but in my view unacceptable theories.

inattention. But I will take the risk, because there are interesting (and unsettled) questions involved, and because a certain amount of stage-setting is needed.

My interest here is in the epistemological status of certain kinds of explanation in linguistics; but in order to attack this problem we need a general context to work in. In particular, we must have at least a preliminary approach to the question of where explanations live. That is, are they World 3 phenomena (in the sense of Popper 1973: 106 ff) or do they live somewhere else?[3] Is an explanation something objective, or is it contextually relative?

In a stimulating and useful study, Peter Achinstein (1971) has suggested that explanation should be construed essentially as an 'illocutionary act': the notion 'explanation' is not to be taken as separate from either 'explaining' or its desired result, 'understanding' (ch. IV). An act of explaining (and therefore an explanation) is to be defined in terms of some kind of Austin-type felicity conditions or sets of Searlean speech-act rules (65); and this definition ultimately includes (though Achinstein doesn't state it in these terms) the adoption by the explainee of the explainer's (Gricean) 'propositional attitude'. While admitting (65) that the concept of explanation 'has an act-content ambiguity', he nonetheless stresses the importance, throughout, of the 'act' factor. Thus (105 ff) he criticizes Hempel's contention that an explanation should provide good grounds for believing that something occurred (cf. §1.5 below), and instead attempts to relativize explanations to sufficiency-criteria for particular contexts.

Thus, to take one of his examples, say that 2 per cent of people who are injected with penicillin develop a rash, and Jones is injected with penicillin and develops a rash. According to Achinstein (105) it is therefore reasonable to explain Jones' rash by saying that he was injected with penicillin.[4] But the adequacy of this explanation is defined

---

[3] Popper's three worlds are (1973: 106): (1) 'the world of physical objects or ... states'; (2) 'the world of states of consciousness, or of mental states, or perhaps of dispositions to act'; and (3) 'the world of *objective contents of thought*, especially of scientific and poetic thoughts and of works of art'. The critical point in the definition of the third world is that it consists of 'objective knowledge': 'Knowledge in the objective sense is *knowledge without a knower*; it is *knowledge without a knowing subject*' (*ibid.*, 109. Emphasis Popper's). For a more detailed exposition of the theory, especially that of the World 2/World 3 distinction, cf. Popper & Eccles (1977; especially chapters P1–P6).

[4] On the problem (or perhaps pseudo-problem) of causes that normally do not have their proper effects, but still may be causes of a sort, cf. Scriven (1959) and the discussion in §4.5.

situationally: i.e. given only the simple question 'Why did Jones get a rash?', the explanation is adequate.

What, however, if we give an explanation specifying precisely what it was about Jones that made him get a rash while 98 per cent of people who get penicillin don't? For Achinstein, this is an answer to a different question; it is not suitable for the situation where someone merely asks why Jones got a rash, but only for the one where 'someone wants to know in what sort of physiological condition Jones is'.

I find this distinction hard to follow: but more to the point, it focusses clearly on the kind of definition of explanation I think it necessary to avoid. As a starting position, I suggest that it is wrong to say that 'Jones was injected with penicillin' is ever a satisfactory answer to 'Why did Jones get a rash?'. Just because some people might accept it is no criterion. (I am reminded of the character in a Graham Greene story who decided that celibacy was the key to immortality, because everybody he knew who had sexual intercourse eventually died.) I can't legitimately criticize a claim about the nature of scientific explanation, in other words, on the grounds that I can think of other kinds of explanation that someone sufficiently muddled or uninterested would find acceptable.[5]

If we are not to give up in advance any hope of determining what an

---

[5] This criticism may be uncharitable. In this case it would of course be possible to define 'Jones was injected with penicillin' as 'elliptical' rather than inadequate (and therefore as salvageable in the sense that the ellipsed material could be recovered if it were appropriate to do so, and the explanation made to approach deductive form: cf. §1.5). But this is still, at this stage in the argument, an excessive relativization.

Another salvage-operation for this kind of explanation is suggested by Hilary Putnam (1978: 41ff). He claims that explanation is an 'interest-relative' notion, and hence partly 'pragmatic' (42), in that the concept itself can't be divorced from (extralogical) criteria of goodness. Putnam's particular kind of relativism (conceived in terms of 'ranges of interests') would allow Achinstein's explanation to be good if and only if it corresponded to the structuring of the explainee's 'explanation-space' (43). Hence (presumably) a dumb explanation is good if it's a response to a dumb question, or corresponds to the structuring of a dumb person's explanation-space. This may be all right in everyday life, but that's not where we are at the moment.

To be fair, Putnam doesn't go as far as this in practice, though he is open to this objection in principle. Given his definition of philosophy (of science) as 'normative' (47), it then follows that we're allowed to define goodness in terms of pre-set goals (e.g. stating truths, discovering laws, finding out what's possible and what's not, etc.). But this in turn implies that only CERTAIN 'interests' or 'structurings of the explanation-space' are to count as good ones; and this gets us back to a worse position than we were in before, since these judgements of goodness (if 'pragmatic' or whatever) can't be fully principled, but must reflect the philosopher's *a priori* commitment.

explanation is, we should not subscribe to Achinstein's assertion (108) that 'independently of contextual considerations it is not possible to classify a set of statements as an explanation, let alone determine whether it is a satisfactory one'. I think in fact that the traditional acceptance of some pretty awful specimens of bad explanation is due precisely to the unwillingness of scholars in a particular field to bring general, field-independent considerations to bear on explanations that seem, without reflection, to be satisfactory within their own hermetically sealed boundaries.

The proper initial approach, if we assume that claims to epistemic validity may not be solely field-internal, is to assume something like a 'universal' definition (epistemological criticism is not analytic philosophy or conceptual explication). I therefore assume that there exist objects called explanations, and that these can be defined abstractly, in non-contextual terms. In an ideal world (which is where we should begin), questions of illocutionary effect,[6] situational appropriateness, etc. can't be allowed to be relevant to the problem of defining the adequacy of explanations within a particular discipline, or generally. I will adopt the view that criteria of adequacy for explanation should be defined in advance in terms of the nature of human rationality (which I assert metaphysically is not culture-specific); and this in turn may or may not mirror the nature of the world (but that is a larger question, and not strictly relevant here).

1.4 Explanation and understanding

Despite my strictures against Achinstein's situational account of explanation, it is still clear that the only reason we seek explanations for things is because we don't understand them, and because we assume that after they are (properly) explained we do understand them – at least more than we did before. The basic explanatory schema, then, would seem to involve (in a simple-minded way) a pair of sentences like these (cf. Wunderlich 1974: §3.6):

(1) (a) Why X ?
     (b) X because Y

---

[6] It may turn out to be necessary to admit PERLOCUTIONARY effect at least as part of the definition of adequacy. That is, 'understanding' must in the end be taken as a perlocutionary, not an illocutionary effect: since there are no efficacious conventions (e.g. performatives) to define 'making one understand' as an illocutionary effect in Austin's sense (*'I hereby make you understand X'). For more discussion see chapter 5.

But there are many kinds of answers to 'why?' questions that do not come under the heading of the kind of explanation relevant in the local context of linguistics or any other science or science-like field: e.g. answers of the form 'X because there is a convention that says X', or 'X because I'll break your jaw if not-X', and the like. In the particular area of explaining linguistic change, there seem to be three types of clauses generally introduced by 'because', which lead to three (partially distinct) types of understanding:[7]

(i) Causal: we understand X because we know the (lawful) mechanisms that brought it about.
(ii) Functional (or Teleological): we understand X because we know what function it serves.
(iii) Genetic: we understand X because we know what came before it, i.e. how it originated.

(I will return to the question of causality in chapter 4; function will be the subject of chapter 3, and the problem of understanding will be treated in more detail in chapter 5.)

Curiously, even though type (iii) would seem *prima facie* the crucial type for any historical field, in its pure form it isn't. By and large purely genetic explanations are both non-rigorous and shallow, i.e. they essentially involve trivial plain story sequences rather than principles of any depth or interest (history as chronicle). I am thinking here of particularistic anecdotal explanations like those accounting for pairs like *cow/beef, sheep/mutton*, etc., or an explanation of why *church* and *kirk* both exist in Scotland with different meanings.[8] We might say roughly that type (iii) serves at best as a 'factual' input to (i)–(ii), i.e. it is generally the genetic sequences that prompt us to look for explanations, or allow explanations to be based on them, rather than being themselves explanatory in any interesting way.

Though there is a sense in which certain phenomena that are claimed to be 'interesting' under one theoretical interpretation can be shown to be rather less so under another, by allowing genetic explanation priority, where it is possible, over synchronic explanation, and insisting that only

---

[7] Cf. Eysenck (1970: 388–9) who follows Nagel (1961). A fourth type of explanation, the 'probabilistic', mentioned by Nagel and Eysenck, will be dealt with in detail below (§§1.6, 2.1–4).

[8] This is not to say that principles of some interest can't be involved in such explanations; only that if they are, the explanation is no longer purely genetic, but approaches (i) or (ii). The point is the epistemological difference between 'genetic and systematic problems' (Cassirer 1944: 118).

one of the two is allowed: thus the so-called 'synchronic vowel shift' phenomena in English, like the *divine/divinity* alternation, can be shown to be explicable genetically – they are leftovers from a set of processes that once happened. And on methodological grounds this can be taken to disallow any synchronic 'abstract' origin or 'derivation' for them, under the assumption that if something can be explained in one simple way, it is otiose to add a second, more complex explanation: cf. the enunciation of this view under the rubric 'one fact needs one explanation' in Sampson 1975a.

We will see in what follows that the distinction between (i) and (ii) is really not as clear as it seems: that there is at least a strong temptation to look for type (i) regularities as meta-explanations for object-explanations of type (ii). This of course involves a preference, on non-empirical grounds, for a certain type of explanation. We will also see, I think, that there are very serious problems with both types.

1.5 Deductive-Nomological explanations

From the explainee's point of view, the most satisfactory explanation must surely be the one that automatically excludes all possible competitors. The 'best' explanation is 'X, because it couldn't have been otherwise (because Y)'. Whether this is attainable or not is a moot point, but it is clear that at least one important 'school' or aggregation of philosophers of science has thought for some time that it is, and considerable energy has been expended on debate and discussion.

The explanation type that seems to come closest is the now familiar 'Hempel-Oppenheim' or 'Deductive-Nomological' schema, which characterizes the physical sciences (or a particular vision of them).[9] It is based on deductive inference and, as its name implies, 'laws', and is 'ideal' in the sense that a well-formed explanation has the form of a deduction, and is in principle equivalent to a prediction.[10] Psycho-

[9] Cf. Hempel & Oppenheim (1948); Rescher (1963); Hempel (1966a, b); Achinstein (1971: 99ff). For some discussion in the general context of linguistic theory see Wunderlich (1974: ch. 3); Ringen (1975); and the papers in Cohen (1974).

[10] It is actually a matter of dispute whether prediction and explanation differ only 'pragmatically' (in terms of the temporal locus of the act) or in actual structure. Scheffler (1963: 43) adduces some arguments to the effect that there is a genuine 'structural divergence', but Hempel's 'requirement of explanatory relevance' (see below) may help to counter this. The question is in any case open, but this raises no problems for my discussion here. There are however certainly some cases where, leaving aside the question of whether an explanation must be predictive, it is clear that there are predictions that are not explanatory: cf. §§ 1.7, 5.5.

logically at least this is a good thing, because it makes the explanation approach necessity (any other outcome would be illegal).

In the deductive-nomological (henceforth D-N) schema we have an EXPLANANDUM (the observation to be explained, or – on another interpretation – the observation-sentence to be explained), and an EXPLANANS, which is a conjunction of statements specifying certain antecedent conditions and a set of 'general laws', i.e.:

$$(2) \qquad \left. \begin{array}{l} C_1, \dots \\ L_1, \dots \end{array} \right\} \text{Explanans}$$

$$\overline{E \qquad \text{Explanandum}}$$

Given the set of conditions $(C_1, \dots)$ and the laws $(L_1, \dots)$, the observed state of affairs (or the sentence representing it) follows logically. The schema (2), that is, represents explanation as a special case of deductive inference, whose premises are particular statements and general laws, and whose conclusion is the thing to be explained. The explanandum follows from the explanans by *modus ponens*:

$$(3) \qquad \begin{array}{l} p \supset q \\ \underline{ p} \\ \therefore q \end{array} \quad , \text{i.e.} \quad \begin{array}{l} (C \,\&\, L) \supset E \\ \underline{ (C \,\&\, L)} \\ \therefore E \end{array}$$

To take a trivial and informal example, let E = 'John died after being decapitated'. A D-N explanation for this might run:

$$(4) \qquad \begin{array}{ll} C_1 & \text{John's head was cut off.} \\ L_1 & \text{The heart will not beat if it is disconnected from the brain.} \\ L_2 & \text{Persons whose hearts don't beat die.} \\ \hline E & \text{John died} \end{array}$$

Note that this is 'historical' in the loose sense that it accounts for what happened and does it chronologically; but it is also ahistorical in that it serves as a uniformly valid prediction: we can assert that anytime someone's head is cut off he will die. Even though the 'laws' and the explanandum are empirical, the explanans–explanandum relation is purely logical.

The most important property of this kind of explanation is that if it adheres to certain conditions, it cannot possibly be denied. If it is the case that (a) the argument from explanans to explanandum is correct, (b) that the explanans has empirical content, and (c) that the explanans is true, the only circumstance under which one can deny the validity of the explanation is if one refuses to accept *modus ponens* as a valid argument-schema. And I assume that if you accept it, there is no very effective way of communicating with someone who doesn't.

The 'empirical content' of the explanans can be a problem, even in a strict D-N framework. Thus it may be the case, as Achinstein has argued, that it is possible for 'laws' to be invoked in a well-formed D-N explanation which lead to deductively sound but 'irrelevant' explanations. His example (1971: 101f) is:

(5)   C : At time *t* physician P examined the patient and declared that he
        would be dead within the time *t* + 24. Physician P has many
        years of training and experience.

      L : Whenever a physician with many years of training ...
        examines a patient and declares that he will be dead within
        some time span the patient does die within that time-span.

      E : The patient died within the time span *t* + 24.

Achinstein claims that this, within the D-N framework, meets all the requirements for being a satisfactory explanation; but yet (104) that it would 'under no circumstances ... be an acceptable explanation' of the patient's death.

This is on the face of it true; but Hempel does require something more of a good D-N explanans. He invokes a 'requirement of explanatory relevance' (1966a: 48), which is 'that the explanatory information adduced affords good grounds for believing that the phenomenon to be explained did, or does, indeed occur'. By 'good grounds' Hempel means, it would seem, 'good grounds – on the basis of the totality of our knowledge and assumptions about the structure of the universe, cause and effect, etc.'. Even if this is imprecisely formulated by Hempel, it is still enough to defuse Achinstein's argument. He claims (104) that Hempel gives no real argument for this requirement – which is true; but neither does Achinstein give any argument for why he won't accept (5) as a 'relevant' explanation. Presumably his reason is in fact a good reflection of Hempel's relevance requirement.[11] Another way of

---

[11] This could be related to Achinstein's earlier definition (71) of 'understanding' as involving 'not only knowledge of a correct answer but also knowledge that this answer is consonant with one's other beliefs'. This criterion alone, given a framework of beliefs in which (5) is not a proper causal explanation, would suffice to define it as unsatisfactory. In a later discussion of explanation (1975), Achinstein returns to the question of relevance, and dismisses the doctor-type cited above because 'they don't answer the questions most likely to be asked when explanations are demanded in these cases' (1975: 35). Cf. also the examples of 'terrible' explanations given by Putnam (1978: 42f).

putting this might be to insist that D-N explanations be (strictly) 'causal'. I will assume this in what follows, as well as assuming that explanation without empirically motivated causal connections is defective.

1.6 Probabilistic explanations

Unfortunately, we often don't have 'laws' of the requisite precision to allow us to obtain D-N explanations, and this prevents us from attaining our ideal. In these cases, we have to rely instead on what are called 'statistical laws' or 'probabilistic laws'. There is a weaker (but in principle similar) explanatory schema which Hempel calls a 'probabilistic explanation' (1966a: §§5.4–5.6). Here the explanandum will not follow deductively from the explanans, but rather with 'high likelihood'. To use an example of Hempel's (1966a: 58–9), Jim's getting the measles can be explained by saying that he caught it from his brother, who had it a few days earlier. The 'statistical law' here is that there is a very high probability of people exposed to measles catching it. (Hempel incidentally neglects to mention one necessary antecedent condition for this explanation: that the person exposed not be immune. In the case of immunity we would have a D-N explanation for Jim's NOT getting the measles.) The probabilistic schema looks like this (1966a: 67):

(6) p (O, R) is close to 1

$$\frac{i \text{ is a case of R}}{i \text{ is a case of O}} \text{ [makes highly probable]}$$

In this specific instance (69):

(7)   The probability for persons exposed to the measles to catch the disease is high.

$$\frac{\text{Jim was exposed to the measles.}}{\text{Jim caught the measles.}} \text{ [makes highly probable]}$$

(The double line signifies that the explanans–explanandum relation is not deductive but probabilistic.) Hempel comments as follows (*ibid.*):

... a probabilistic explanation of a particular event shares certain basic characteristics with the corresponding deductive-nomological ... explanation. In both cases, the given event is explained by reference to others, with which the explanandum event is connected by laws. But in one case, the laws are of universal form; in the other, of probabilistic form. And while a deductive explanation shows that, on the information ... in the explanans, the explanandum was to be expected with 'deductive certainty', an inductive explanation [like this] shows only that, on the information ... in the explanans, the explanandum was to be expected with high probability, and perhaps with 'practical certainty'; it is in this manner that the latter argument meets the requirement of explanatory relevance.

I think there is an equivocation here, ultimately an important and damaging one. The 'requirement of explanatory relevance' (cf. §1.5 above), says Hempel, is what allows us, when it is met, to say 'That explains it – the phenomenon ... was indeed to be expected under the circumstances' (48). We will see in the next chapter that this requirement is not in fact normally met in probabilistic explanations (except those of a very special type); nor does the kind of satisfied expectation that Hempel mentions arise, if we consider things carefully. And if it does, it does not mean what Hempel thinks, but is far more mysterious and less convincing. The fact that 'explanations' like (7) give us only inductive likelihood, not deductive certainty, makes them not only 'weaker' than D-N explanations, but makes them non-explanatory. I will suggest that – at least in the form in which they commonly occur in linguistics – they fail to make sense.

Let us assume for the moment that there is something problematical about probabilistic explanations: at least that they are, as Scheffler says (1963: 35) 'a case of pragmatically incomplete deductive explanation' (a point I will return to), and that they are 'less satisfying than their fully deductive counterparts'. This would be a problem to seekers after 'perfect' explanations in historical linguistics only if it were the case that D-N explanations were not available. And this, I will argue, is the actual state of affairs.

1.7 The asymmetry between explanation and prediction

In the (ideal) model of explanation considered above, explanation implies prediction: an event is not explained unless we could have predicted it. There is, however, an important asymmetry here. Just because an event can be predicted does not mean it can be explained; while any (correct) explanation involves correct prediction, not every correct prediction involves explanation.

Perhaps the simplest kind of non-explanatory prediction is the kind that stems from inductive generalization over 'normal' properties and event-sequences in the everyday world. Thus we 'predict' that today's sunset will be followed by tomorrow's sunrise, that physical objects will retain their shapes, that centipedes (in well-ordered houses) will not come out when we turn the hot-water tap, that water will not become wine without special (divine or human) interventions, etc. On a more sophisticated level, perhaps, a physician, on seeing the so-called 'Koplick spots' in a patient's pharynx, will predict the onset of the symptoms of measles. In at least some of these instances it is in fact possible to produce a D-N explanation; but in everyday life, at any rate, this is irrelevant. And in any case the correctness of our informal (often ignorant) predictions does not lend them any explanatory value. The reason of course is that while the predictions may be correct, they do not involve any laws with 'explanatory relevance' in Hempel's sense.

The same can also be said of many perfectly correct predictions in science, especially those based simply on observed mathematical relationships – regardless of how sophisticated they may be. An example (discussed by Achinstein 1968: 131) is Balmer's formula for the wavelengths of lines in the spectrum of hydrogen. This formula derives the relationships between successive lines of the spectrum by an equation involving (among other things) an 'axiomatic' constant $R = 109{,}677 \, \text{cm}^{-1}$, and by certain substitutions it is possible to predict the wavelengths of further lines – unobserved by Balmer, but later found to exist. An equation of this type gives us an axiomatic system in which predictions of empirical events are provable as theorems: but, as Achinstein points out, 'it provides no explanation whatever of the existence of the observed lines, of why the wavelengths are what they are . . . and so forth. At most, it organizes the data in such a way that we are in a better position to seek a theory to explain the initial phenomena.' That is, a taxonomic generalization – no matter how formalized and 'fruitful' – is not an explanation. (But cf. §5.5.)

The confusion, however, is often made, especially perhaps by linguists; and it is an important confusion to watch out for. We will see some particularly egregious examples in the following chapter.

2 *Why 'naturalness' does not explain anything*

Nomina si nescis, perit et cognitio rerum.

Linnaeus

2.1 On 'natural' sound changes: generalities[1]

A number of years ago I came to the conclusion that notions like 'markedness' and 'naturalness', in spite of the fuss that has been made of them in recent linguistic theory, really mean very little. Not many people seem to have agreed with me. I published the first results of my discontent in 1972 (revised version: Lass 1975), and have since become, if anything, more convinced that I was on the right track. This chapter is a rather more elaborate attempt to develop some of those earlier ideas, and to consider their relevance to the problem of explaining language change.

Let us begin the investigation proper with a type of explanation in historical phonology that looks at first as if it might just be D-N, but really is probabilistic; and then let us observe how it deteriorates under scrutiny. My first example will be the attempted 'phonetic explanation' of sound changes or cross-language synchronic distributions. The entry to the field is the notion of 'naturalness' as it occurs in our intuitive reactions to processes of change; we can then look at how this notion might be deployed in a specific explanation.

I will start off by looking at a fairly characteristic definition of naturalness, so that we can be sure just what we are talking about. The following passage (Schane 1972: 206) comes after a discussion and

---

[1] This chapter grows in part out of conversations with Jim Hurford, who is largely responsible for my taking some of the issues here seriously, and getting interested enough in the subject to take it up again after a rest of nearly six years. See Hurford (1977) for some relevant views of his.

listing of some 'obviously natural' types of rules, both synchronic and historical (e.g. nasalization of pre-nasal vowels):

> Why are natural rules 'natural'? So far I have been relying heavily on intuitive feelings for determining which rules are natural. It goes without saying that such intuitions exist. I would feel confident ... that a group of phonologists would agree fairly well as to which phonological processes are natural ones. We hopefully look for them in the languages we study. NATURAL RULES, THEN, HAVE A UNIVERSALITY — WE EXPECT THEM ... in languages of diverse type. Why should such rules recur in language after language while OTHER RULES — THAT IS, THE UNNATURAL ONES — MAY HAVE AN EXTREMELY LIMITED DISTRIBUTION? One would hope to find something in the structure of the natural rules which would explain their universal popularity. [Emphasis mine]

This passage raises a whole set of issues that I will deal with later in this chapter: e.g. the status of our 'expectations' (I of course generally share Schane's: I only interpret them differently), the problem of 'limited universality', and the basic issue of the significance of 'significant' distributions.

Phenomena seem to become 'interesting', and thus subject to judgements of significance and attempts at explanation, mainly insofar as they depart from randomness of distribution (presumably science is in the end about 'order'). As everyone knows, the generalizations that science (for the moment including linguistics) is interested in are the 'significant' ones; and significance, to be intelligible, is assumed to have some kind of statistical interpretation (cf. Hurford 1977).

An example: consider a sound change C and five possible distributions of this change in the histories of known languages:

(1)　　　Histories showing C (%)

D_1	50
D_2	45
D_3	90
D_4	0
D_5	100

D_1–D_2 are uninteresting with respect to the naturalness question; they provoke no judgements, because they represent the kind of distribution we might expect in any case, if no principle of interest were involved.[2] D_4 is usually the reflex of a 'boring universal' (I owe this

---

[2] John Anderson has suggested to me that a 50 per cent distribution in this case is not really 'chance level' or 'random', since the chances that any history should contain any particular change should be minute, given the number of possible changes and

term to Geoff Pullum): e.g. 'no language has a change [+ segment] →
[+ ingressive]' (or one did, but all the speakers died of anoxia). This also
holds for distributions of segment types, e.g. 'no language has
apico-uvular stops'. D_5 is the special case of the 'universally necessary
change', which is a fake: since if there were such a thing, its input would
be illegal and we would never know that it occurred. But in principle
both D_4 and D_5 would be candidates for D-N explanation.

The kind that usually interests linguists, however (cf. the passage
from Schane above) is D_3, which leads to theories and attempted
explanations based on notions like 'naturalness', 'markedness', and the
like. It is this kind which has generally been most widely discussed, and
is supposed to have the most significant implications for general
linguistic theory.[3]

2.2 An attempt at a phonetic explanation

Let us take a fairly transparent D_3 type – though without real numbers.
The lack of 'genuine' statistics is in any case not a real problem (what are
the real numbers for the percentage of people exposed to measles who
get it?); what counts is the existence of massive (intuitively above
chance) disparities in distribution. It seems to be generally true that if a
language has nasal + obstruent clusters, the chances are very great that
they will be homorganic. Overall we can say:

(i)   We expect NC clusters to be homorganic (at least within the
      morpheme).
(ii) We expect them to become homorganic if they aren't already.

That is, assimilation of nasals to following consonants (especially
obstruents) is both a natural (synchronic) rule and a natural sound
change.

There is of course a simple and well-known 'phonetic explanation' for
this, which might be schematized as follows:

---

histories. This is true: though the number of changes that do appear is of course more
restricted than the set of (theoretically) possible ones. But given the existence of SOME
change, which is not at issue, it would seem that equal frequency of occurrence and
non-occurrence would count for most linguists' purposes as 'random'. In any case the
basic point is unaffected, even if the figures are not fully appropriate. Certainly the
general statement about linguists' characteristic intuitions of 'interest' still holds.

[3] Markedness theory of the Chomsky & Halle variety is not explicitly statistical, but it is
     clearly implicitly so (cf. Lass 1975).

(2)

	[n]	[b]
{Articulation	apical	labial
{Velic attitude	down	up

	[m]	[b]
{Articulation	labial	labial
{Velic attitude	down	up

That is, it takes two separate gestures to get from [n] to [b], and only one to get from [m] to [b]. There is therefore 'less effort' involved if NC clusters are homorganic.[4] And in Schane's taxonomy (1972: 207), a change [nb] > [mb] would come under one of the three 'categories of natural rules': assimilations.

Now observe that if we leave the explanation this way, the form is not D-N:

(3) C_1 a sequence [nb]
     L_1 [mb] is 'easier than' [nb]

    E   [nb] > [mb]

E does not follow deductively of course; and L_1 isn't really a 'law'. Or if it is, it does not fulfil Hempel's 'explanatory relevance' requirement, at least in this form.

We can now attempt to weaken the explanation, by casting it in a probabilistic form. In order to do this, we must introduce, in addition to the notion of 'ease', a 'statistical law' of this type:

(4) L_2 It is overwhelmingly (very, quite, etc.) probable that, given a choice, speakers will choose 'easier' articulations over 'harder' ones.

(Jespersen's principle of 'ease', Curtius' *'Bequemlichkeit'* (Jespersen 1964: 261), Zipf's 'law of least effort', etc. Cf. also Paul 1920: 56, and the discussion in Weinreich, Labov & Herzog 1968: 111–12.)

With the new 'law' (4) incorporated, the full probabilistic explanation will look like this:

---

[4]   This is reasonably traditional, though not following any one particular account. The principle has been enunciated in various ways: thus Bloomfield (1933: 370) says that 'the general direction of a great deal of sound change is toward a simplification of the movements which make up the utterance of any given linguistic form'. For some theoretical background and discussion of earlier literature on the 'ease theory' see Jespersen (1964: ch. xiv, §6).

(5) C_1 a sequence [nb]

   L_1 [mb] is 'easier than' [nb]

   L_2 it is (overwhelmingly, ... etc.) probable that, given a choice, speakers will choose 'easier' articulations over 'harder' ones

E   [nb] > [mb]

This appears to say (a) that we ought to be surprised if [nb] fails to go to [mb]; (b) that we ought not to be surprised if [nb] does go to [mb]; and (c) that – apparently – the reason we ought not to be surprised at the explanandum-observation, if we make it, is that there is a 'law' which says in essence that we ought not to be surprised. And, one ought to admit, a law that seems, given a certain rather simplistically unreflecting view of human nature and its relation to language, to meet something approaching Hempel's 'relevance' criterion. (For some discussion of the problem of 'surprise' and 'expectation' cf. §2.3.)

But any failure of this law to apply IN A PARTICULAR INSTANCE raises difficulties; difficulties which, to be fair, did not escape some earlier proponents of 'ease' explanations, like Jespersen. But the way they were forced to cope with failures raises some interesting questions about the explanatory force of 'ease', which in turn raise further questions about the status of probabilistic explanations and 'tendencies' in general (a point I will return to in the following section, and in a wider context in chapter 3).

Jespersen, for instance (1964: 262f) realized quite clearly the problem inherent in the usual formulation of the ease-theory as embodying tendencies rather than being an absolute predictive hypothesis, and he was critical of those scholars (like Sütterlin 1913) who took singular counter-examples (especially developments of 'harder' articulations) as global falsifications. Now he was surely correct in pointing out a conceptual error on their part: singular counter-instances do not falsify probabilistic theories. Though he failed to see that this is an epistemological difficulty that threatens to reduce all 'tendency' explanations to vacuity (if in fact it doesn't succeed, as I would claim: cf. the following section).

Jespersen was also, with his usual acuteness, aware of another consequence of 'historicist' claims of this kind: that since the direction of change is supposed by and large to have been toward greater ease, there must have been a time when language in general was 'more difficult' than it now is. And his attempt to cope with this problem led him to a rather desperate move, which effectively undermines the ease-theory in its usual form. He says (1964: 263f):

> It is, of course, no serious objection to this view that if this has always been the direction of change, speaking must have been uncommonly troublesome to our earliest ancestors – who says it wasn't? . . . as if people at a remote age had been able to compare consciously two articulations and to choose the easier one! Neither in language nor in any other activity has mankind at once hit upon the best or easiest expedients.

Aside from the fact that such a claim presupposes a methodologically inadmissible shift in language typology over time (cf. the appendix to this chapter, §3), and the fact that the notion of 'conscious choice' is merely a red herring (since 'ease' must, as Jespersen's own earlier discussion implies, have a physiological basis), there is another difficulty. And this is that the scenario suggested in the passage cited above undermines the entire case for 'ease' being a naturalistically explicable notion. (The same problem arises when we consider the propagation of putatively 'functionally motivated' changes through a speech community: cf. the appendix to chapter 3, §4.)

Leaving aside the questions, which will be focussed more clearly later on, let us rather turn to the more basic epistemological difficulties raised by probabilistic schemata in general.

2.3 On the status of probabilistic explanations

The achievement of 'inductive probability' raises problems about the status of something like (5). Because it is a necessary property of such explanations that they are (in the strict sense) non-empirical: unlike D-N explanations THEY CAN NEITHER PREDICT PARTICULAR STATES OF AFFAIRS (in the sense of singular spatio-temporal occurrences) NOR COUNTER-PREDICT THEIR OPPOSITES. (Except of course in the unachievable limiting case of generalizations over sequences of infinite length: but see below.)

This is really obvious, of course: statistical generalizations (except for the extreme cases where the predicted frequencies are either 100 per cent or zero) hold only for distributions over an aggregate or sequence. They cannot predict for individual members of the aggregate or sequence. We find ourselves then in the following difficulty: insofar as we are concerned in any given explanatory attempt with a particular instance of something happening or not happening, a probabilistic explanation has no empirical content, because NO INDIVIDUAL FAILURE OF THE 'STATISTICAL LAW' CAN EVER BE A COUNTER-INSTANCE. Thus only a sequence of failures of some length deemed by investigators in a field to invalidate the generalization can lead to its being scrapped: and then only globally, i.e. it is determined to be a false generalization. The problem of individual cases remains unresolved.

So if the aim of explanation is to account for particular singular instances (as in our case anyhow I presume it is: but cf. p. 137, fn. 17), then probabilistic explanations are non-empirical, since no singular instance can falsify them. They are, strictly speaking, not even rational, since they are not subject either to 'nonempirical falsification' (Itkonen 1976a) or rational counter-argument (cf. Popper 1968a: 146).[5] Though within a 'personalist' theory of probabilistic confirmation, there are ways of assessing the worthiness of a generalization for 'rational belief' (cf. Hesse 1974).

In what sense then can the notion of 'ease' be said to explain either a change [nb] > [mb] or the cross-language distribution of homorganic NC clusters? My answer would be: in no sense. What we have in (5) is merely a semi-formalized paraphrase of an observed distribution, which incorporates a non-empirical (ultimately invulnerable) causal (or perhaps better 'pseudo-causal') hypothesis. The formalization produces an illusion of informativeness, but nothing is really 'explained': neither the distribution itself (which the probabilistic schema in fact brings to our attention as the REAL explanandum, a problem we skirt by invoking a 'probabilistic law'), nor of course the particular instance we were trying to explain in the first place. Causality, for any instance or for the aggregate, is still as opaque as it was before, and we are left only with what in any case we already know we had: a taxonomic generalization.[6] It seems then that it makes very little sense to use probability statements

---

[5] I am talking here only in terms of theoretical explanation, which presumably makes rather high claims, not everyday living: there of course RELIANCE ON inductive generalizations is of practical use (e.g. getting your umbrella when you see dark clouds). But this is simply response to 'constant conjunction', and doesn't involve explanation. The fact that I get my umbrella when I see clouds because I know that clouds usually bring rain doesn't imply any explanation of why this is the case, or – in the absence of further information – any knowledge on my part of a causal or other relation. (This note was evoked by a comment by Richard Coates, involving clouds and umbrellas.)

[6] In the framework of the first three chapters of this book, I am assuming (traditionally) that deductive explanation is the *Summum Bonum*, and that 'mere taxonomy' is at best a poor substitute. I will have occasion to challenge this view later on (chapter 5).

as 'laws' in any enterprise that claims to be explanatory (as opposed to merely predictive: cf. §1.7).[7] Certainly not if the concept of explanation includes anything like Hempel's criterion of relevance.

There is clearly something peculiar about probabilistic laws; their status (as indeed the nature of probability itself) has been the subject of much discussion. Interpretations have ranged from various kinds of subjectivism (e.g. the 'Laplacean' view that statistical distributions are merely pseudo-indeterminisms due to lack of omniscience: cf. Popper & Eccles 1977: 25), 'subjective logical' or 'personalist' interpretations (Popper 1968a: 148f; Hesse 1974), or Polanyi's 'personal' interpretation (1958: see below) – to doctrines of 'objective probability' or 'propensity' (Popper 1968b: 59f, 119; 1973: §34; Popper & Eccles 1977: 25f).

Polanyi's view (which is non-Laplacean but still subjectivist) is interesting, if only for what it shows us of the problems that statistical distributions can cause, and those raised by the particular way out he chooses. Polanyi appears to think that probabilities (of any sort?) are essentially 'epistemic', not empirical facts. If for instance we accept that 'probability statements can never be strictly contradicted by experience' (Polanyi 1958: 21), then they might appear to reduce to statements not about 'the world' but about our relation to it (our 'personal knowledge', in his terms). Thus (22):

If I accept the probability statement that the chances of throwing three double sixes in succession are one in 46656, I shall entertain a correspondingly small expectation of doing so; while if it should happen, I shall be surprised, to a degree corresponding to the reciprocal of this numerical probability. Such is my participation in the event to which a probability statement refers, and this I regard as the proper meaning of its probability ... I ascribe universal validity to my appraisals of probability, in spite of the fact that they make no predictions which could be contradicted by any conceivable events.[8]

It is however probably necessary to abandon such a strong subjectivist view; there seems little doubt that – however much one's

---

[7]   This does not imply any denial of the validity or interest of statistical laws in microphysics, etc. – though it does assert that they are non-explanatory. I will return to this below. We will see that in any case the microphysics analogy is not an apt one for language change or synchronic distribution of properties.

[8]   There is of course a conventionalist sense in which a statistical law or generalization can be regarded as 'refuted by experience': an investigator (or a discipline) can set a threshold beyond which, if the distribution fails to work out satisfactorily, the 'law' can be dropped (suggested to me by Ruth Clark). There are also rather more detailed and rational possibilities: cf. Popper (1968a: §§65, 68), and Hesse (1974).

personal RELATION to statistical distributions may be an epistemic fact – there are such things as 'objective probabilities' or 'propensities' (i.e. that the probability of some event occurring represents 'a real disposition – though not a deterministic state of affairs': Popper 1976: 155). It does not seem possible, given the arguments of Popper and others, to revert completely to a Laplacean subjectivism, or to any other kind – even in microphysics. Statistical distributions apparently represent in some cases 'real properties' of the world (but cf. §2.4): at least they do if one assumes a 'realist' (if not naïve realist) interpretation of what science and subjects like linguistics are about. What is at issue here, though, in the context of a discussion of explanation, is their possible link with causality (in fact the causation of single occurrences); and it is here that probabilistic explanation seems to me not to explain anything (cf. further the discussion of 'tendencies' in chapter 3).

Let us return for a moment to causality. This is not a simple matter, even in the case of Humean 'constant conjunctions', much less in the case of statistical correlations. Given two events (A, B) such that there is spatio-temporal contiguity between A and B, and A precedes B, it is tempting to argue for causal connection; or given a statistical correlation between A and B which is constant and non-random, it is tempting to assume, for instance, that there is a 'common cause' C which is connected to both A and B. But even this is not always possible, and whether it can be theoretically justified is a matter of debate (for the positive view see Salmon 1975; for arguments against this, and for the claim – which I find sympathetic – that only 100 per cent correlations can be causally explanatory, see Mellor 1975).

When however we are faced not with a pair of events, but the frequency of a phenomenon or state of affairs, the problem is quite different. It is possible to take the statistical distribution (say in Polanyi's dice example) as an empirically established, formalizeable, but 'self-contained' property, i.e. simply a predicate of the 'series' in which the event or state occurs (cf. Hacking 1976: ch. 1; this is presumably closely related to the notion of propensity). Thus in the dice example there is obviously no sense in which one throw of the dice has any causal relation to a succeeding one; the individual throws are in principle independent, and the overall distribution is a property of the long-run series of throws itself. This has been taken by some to suggest connection with an 'acausal' or 'synchronistic' principle in nature (Jung 1955; Koestler 1974). At any rate, it certainly tends to throw suspicion on any attempt to connect non-trivial statistical distributions (i.e. other than totality or zero) with 'causes'. More on this below.

2.4 Further epistemological considerations: the 'stochastic factor'

Despite problems like this, many people still insist that probabilistic explanations are both useful and genuinely explanatory. One strong attempt to justify them has been made by Rescher (1963). He begins by making an important distinction between two domains in which what he calls 'the stochastic factor' can appear. Statistical explanation, he says (45), is strictly involved only where the stochastic factor enters into the LAWS. When it enters into the DATA (e.g. through imprecision of measurement, etc.), the explanation can still be deductive. Our example here is obviously of the first type, and so should be a genuine candidate. Further, the homorganic nasal example comes under Rescher's definition of a 'strong statistical explanation', which is one in which, given the explanans, the explanandum is 'rendered *more likely than not* (i.e. is more probable than all its alternatives put together; has a conditional probability greater than one-half)' (45; emphasis Rescher's).

His defence of statistical explanations, even when, because of the nature of the laws, 'it is in principle impossible to move from' explanans to explanandum (45), is divided into two parts. The first is a 'theoretical' reason (46): '... *given stochastic rather than deterministic laws, the pattern of reasoning involved ... is, except for the differences in the type of laws, strictly parallel to the pattern of reasoning involved in D*[eductive] *explanations. We continue to get plausible and intellectually helpful answers to questions of the type "Why did X rather than Y occur?"* ' (emphasis Rescher's). I will suggest below that this is not generally true. There are other problems as well, as we will see. Rescher's other justification is 'pragmatic': '... in contexts where stochastic laws alone are operative, S[tatistical] explanation is the only type of explanatory reasoning which is possible in the very nature of things'. Therefore, to exclude it is to limit scientific explanation unnecessarily by 'a fiat of definition buttressed solely by fond memories of what explanation used to be in 19th-century physics' (46). Again, I think this is not necessarily true. For one thing, it skirts the question of what statistical laws can possibly MEAN, as well as special problems having to do with 'exceptions', i.e. the residue (of whatever size) of instances excluded from the workings of the 'law' for no apparent reason other than the statistical distributions stated by the law. There may be cases where Rescher's 'pragmatic' move is justified, but I don't think linguistics is one of them.

Let me focus this problem with reference to theories of 'markedness' and the like. On the face of it, the claims they make are very difficult to understand. For instance (cf. Lass 1975: 486), it seems to be the case that roughly 15 per cent of the world's languages have front rounded vowels, while 85 per cent don't. This leads to the claim (in Chomsky & Halle-type markedness theory) that it is an 'intrinsic' property of front round vowels that they are 'marked', i.e. 'unnatural', 'complex', etc. (Cf. my discussion of the logic of markedness arguments, 1975: 485–8 and §2.8 below). This, it would seem to me, leads to two questions, which I would like to see answered:

(i) How can it be a property of something that only N per cent of the world's languages have it?[9]
(ii) How can it be a property of languages that only N per cent of them have something?[10]

Until someone comes up with an acceptable (or at least intelligible) answer, I shall assume that notions like markedness and naturalness have no explanatory significance, but are merely taxonomic cover-terms for observed distributions, or instances of the 'naming fallacy'. (I will return to this problem below.)

Now one could argue that the way out of this particular bind might be through a notion of probability like that in modern microphysics, where 'physical events are directed toward states of maximum probability, and physical laws, therefore, are essentially "laws of disorder", the outcome

[9] John Anderson has suggested to me (personal communication) that this is not in fact the claim made by markedness theory: 'the distribution is a statistical reflection of a property'. But surely my version is what the theory boils down to: the property itself is an unobservable, and is merely (circularly) asserted in order to account for the distribution. (For an analysis of a similar argument type, see my discussion of the Jakobsonian arguments for 'tenseness', Lass 1976a: ch. 1, appendix).

[10] The same confusion about what distributions mean occurs in the work of non-generative linguists as well. Thus Weinreich, Labov & Herzog (1968: 126f), under the heading of 'generalizations about how languages are constructed', talk about it being 'possible to make ... statistical generalizations about existing languages', and thus 'to show whether a given change produces a language state that violates, or more significantly, conforms with the statistical norms'. Why should it be 'significant' that something 'conforms' in this way?

of unordered, statistical events' (von Bertalanffy 1968: 30). This could save probabilistic explanations by allowing for genuine 'stochastic laws' in Rescher's sense. But this raises two fundamental problems. The first is the general one of whether it is appropriate to consider languages to be 'objects in the natural world', and thus responsive to (external) 'laws' rather than merely organized in terms of (internal and not strictly spatiotemporal) 'rules' (on this distinction cf. Itkonen 1974). I will return to this question in chapter 4. The second problem is more local, but related; and it may also be more serious. It is this: the metaphorical leap from domains like enclosed volumes of gases or other collections of particles in random motion, etc., would be immense, and as far as I can see completely unjustifiable.

The difficulty here would be to justify a framework in which the percentage distributions of characteristics of natural languages represent reflexes of 'macrophysical' laws, derived from generalizations over the 'microphysical' domain of the histories of individual languages. Among other things, this would demand some motivation (other than the mere observation that characters appear to be statistically distributed) for the 'micro-'/'macro-' distinction: this is clearly motivated in physics, but is at least obscure for a domain like the pan-chronic set of all languages and their histories. Even if, for instance, we could develop some 'system' concept (in the mathematical sense) that could effectively treat individual languages as 'organisms', the jump from there to the set of all languages as a 'supersystem' or 'superorganism' would (at least in the state of our knowledge, and given the evidence available) be arbitrary. The implication of such a move would be that the set of all languages constitutes, in relation to its members, something like an 'epiorganism', in the way human or animal communities can be seen as epiorganisms (emergent or near-emergent wholes) with respect to the individuals that constitute them. This seems to me utterly implausible: but it also seems to be a necessary assumption for making any sense of markedness and similar notions, i.e. for interpreting the distributions of characters as being the reflexes of genuine stochastic laws like those of microphysics. Until something like this can be achieved, however, arguments like Rescher's cannot be used (at least in linguistics) to justify probabilistic schemata as being in any way explanatory.

This is not however tantamount to asserting that stochastic laws do not exist in the domain of linguistics; only that they do not exist as defined over the pan-chronic set of all languages, and that they are not of the general 'naturalness' or 'markedness' type. I shall outline the conditions under which a pan-chronic distribution could count as a genuine stochastic law (and thus make 'naturalness' statements genuinely nomic – even if unintelligible); and then I will give an example of what a genuine stochastic law in linguistics looks like.

At an oral presentation I gave of some of this material at the University of York, Steve Harlow made an intriguing suggestion, which can be paraphrased (I hope accurately) as follows: there is one way in which a statistical distribution could be shown to reflect a 'law', rather than merely the irrational contingencies of historical development. This would be if the distribution remained constant over long periods of time, but NOT IN THE SAME LANGUAGE FAMILIES. For instance: at present the 15 per cent or so of languages (according to figures in Sedlak 1969) with front rounded vowels are disproportionately clustered in a very small group of families: Indo-European (especially Germanic, with a scatter in Romance and elsewhere), Ural-Altaic, and Sino-Tibetan. Since in these instances the front rounded vowels are fairly ancient possessions, it is reasonable to attribute their continued presence (and frequent new development) to a parochial contingency, i.e. a family habit or 'family universal' (Lass 1975). If it were to turn out that front rounded vowels got lost in a large number of families or languages now possessing them; and if in this eventuality they were then to arise (*ex hypothesi* 'compensatorily') in other families or languages, so that the ratio stayed around 15 per cent regardless of genetic affiliations or geographical location: then we would have evidence for some 'inherent' property, i.e. a 'statistical law'. This would constitute a genuine empirical (rather than simply transcendental) argument for markedness being conceptually meaningful. Though it would still leave us with the problem of trying to determine what the empirical reasons for this constancy were; i.e. as I suggested in the previous section, the distribution itself is still the primary explanandum, and has no explanatory force *per se*.

The time-span involved in testing this would of course involve burying our predictions in a time-capsule; but at least this is a genuine (if pragmatically difficult) test-implication deducible from the theory of markedness. This seems to be about the only one that hasn't failed yet. Nevertheless – despite its present high degree of falsification – it remains one of the few empirical hypotheses that can be extracted from generative 'universalism'.

Now to genuine stochastic laws. These are exceedingly mysterious (in that for the most part their mechanisms are at present quite unintelligible), but well documented. The classic instance is the Labovian 'index score' for a phonological variable. This is a sociologically/ stylistically varying distribution for (say) a given phonetic exponent of a variable category, which has all the characteristics of a genuine probabilistic law, e.g. prediction over a sufficiently large corpus of tokens, but no prediction for single instances, etc. Examples in the literature are legion: I will cite just one here.

It is well known that the implementation of /t/ as [ʔ] in certain positions is an important sociolinguistic marker in Scots (as well as other forms of English). In a Labov-type study of linguistic stratification in Glasgow, Macaulay & Trevelyan (1973: 61) investigated 'tokens of post-tonic potential [t]' from samples of running speech, and found distributions of the following type: in Social Class I (professional/ managerial), the average occurrence of [ʔ] for /t/ was 30·9 per cent; in Social Class III (upper working class), the average was 90·4 per cent. What this means is that any class I or class III informant might, at any given time, produce [bʌtər] or [bʌʔər] for *butter*; but given a large enough corpus, the class I informant will have about 70 per cent [t], and the class III informant about 10 per cent (p. 63, table 10). This is exactly the kind of result we expect from genuine stochastic laws in the natural sciences, e.g. those of genetics or gas dynamics.

It is important to note that this kind of 'law' can never be explanatory of change; though it can, of course, under certain conditions be diagnostic (i.e. there are distribution types that seem to be symptomatic of change in progress: cf. Labov 1966; Trudgill 1974, etc.).

There is an interesting point about the existence of these (non-universal) 'laws', which could tie in with cross-language distributions, I suppose, but does not appear to. And this is that it suggests the existence of some kind of mysterious statistical 'control mechanisms' governing speech production. On the face of it, it looks distinctly odd: can we really believe that properties of utterance-tokens are controlled in some way merely by 'propensities'? (Cf. Macaulay 1976: 269: 'Something that has always worried me about the evidence uncovered in urban dialect surveys is how a speaker knows how to produce the appropriate percentage of, say, glottal stops for his particular station in life.' Macaulay then, however, goes on to say that if a speaker's articulatory setting in some way acts as an overall control on utterance, as suggested by Trudgill and others, 'then the situation becomes much less mysterious'. I fail to see why: the empirical problem of what kind of mechanism could control the averaging out of percentages over long periods of time and great numbers of utterances is still there.)

At any rate there is a problem here, and a serious one: the data merely present a mystery, and talk of 'variable rules' and the 'influence' of social factors merely covers it up. One interesting line of research in this area (or perhaps better, of speculation) would be along the lines of whether these distributions are in fact controlled from inside speakers or from the outside.

2.5 The status of exceptions, 1: the null strategy problem

I can see one obvious objection to what I've said so far. That is, it could be the case that the problem is not inherent in the mode of explanation itself; it is rather the case that the statisticalness is spurious. That is, we simply don't know, for a given generalization, the precise conditions under which it will fail. In other words, the need for inductive reasoning like this is merely a symptom of ignorance; the domain of the generalization will in fact turn out to be fully deterministic when we finally discover the relevant laws in their true form.[11]

But note that this will only work in one type of case: the situation cited by Rescher where it is the DATA that are stochastic, not the laws; in other words, subsumability under a deductive or 'covering-law' schema will be possible only where our present analysis of the data is defective. (This would, as a principle, exclude microphysics as a domain for deductive prediction: properly, as this seems to be the case empirically.)

So as long as we are dealing with a situation where – if my argument above is correct – we are not concerned with genuine stochastic laws of the microphysical type, my contention that probabilistic explanations are defective still holds: 'when we know enough' the explanation will be properly D-N, i.e. we will get the laws and conditions right. Probabilistic explanations in these cases are only as it were provisional, and their explanatory unsatisfactoriness (if that's what it is) is merely a sign of our ignorance, as Scheffler says.

Here the difficulty is of course that we have no idea whether there are

[11] Cf. Scheffler (1963: 75): 'We may . . . wish to construe statistical explanation as a special case of pragmatically incomplete deductive explanation, where needed elements are missing through ignorance.'

in fact special conditions operative in any given case that would determine whether the generalization would hold for it. That such conditions do exist is a matter of faith, not reason.

If we wanted the best of both worlds, as well as an explicit statement that that's what we wanted, we would need an explanatory strategy like the one below, which is I suspect what many (most?) linguists actually operate with. At least it puts all the relevant cards on the table:

(6) C_1 a sequence [nb]
    L_1 [mb] is easier than [nb]
    L_2 speakers will – *ceteris paribus* – prefer easier articulations

---

    E   [nb] > [mb]

Proviso: 'ceteris paribus' stands for a set of fully determinate but as yet undiscovered conditions.
Assumption: when the conditions covered by 'ceteris paribus' are discovered, it will be the case that $(C_1 \& L_1 \& L_2) \supset E$.

The assumption is a metaphysical assertion (= *confessio fidei*) that linguistics is a deterministic domain; it is not an empirical principle (though it may be a methodological one: see below). The defective schema (6) falls, given the current state of our knowledge, somewhere between a probabilistic explanation and an 'explanation sketch' or what has been called an 'explanation in principle'.[12] But as of now we have no warrant for accepting 'ease of articulation' as an explanation of the assimilation in any particular case. All that (6) says really is that it MAY be the case, when (and if) we unpack *ceteris paribus*, that this schema will serve as the skeleton of a D-N explanation. But until that unpacking is accomplished, we have no right to claim that the phenomenon 'is explained': (6) is only a token of faith.[13]

---

[12] Cf. von Bertalanffy (1968: 35): 'Theoretical economics is a highly developed system, presenting elaborate models for the processes in question. However, professors of economics, as a rule, are not millionaires. In other words, they can explain economic phenomena well "in principle" but they are not able to predict fluctuations ... with respect to certain shares or dates. Explanation in principle, however, is better than none at all.' It is this last notion that I find hard to swallow.

[13] Cf. Scheffler (1963: 35) on the statistical explanation (based on actuarial data) of Smith's getting cancer: 'To say that there is a high incidence of cancer in Smith's age, occupational, and geographical group is compatible with saying we do not understand why Smith was afflicted with cancer.'

The difficulty, then, is accounting for the N per cent of cases in which the 'law' doesn't apply (i.e. those that make it statistical). In the case of the simple rule of homorganic nasal-assimilation we have been considering, the problem can be put this way: while it is true that there are whole language families that seem to take the easy way out (e.g. Dravidian, Bantu), there are others that allow non-homorganic NC clusters quite freely (Germanic, Slavic). Even in these latter languages, to be sure, speakers will sometimes assimilate in rapid speech,[14] which suggests at least a Stampean sort of 'naturalness' (speakers fail to suppress 'natural' processes in fast speech: cf. Dressler 1975). But even here, with the added 'support' given to the naturalness idea by allegro phenomena, it seems that we must still admit either the intentions of speakers (which I assume are non-deterministic: though this is of course arguable under metaphysical assumptions different from mine),[15] or ignorance of the (putative) 'real' determining factors.

Does this mean that we should abandon the search for D-N explanations? The answer is no. The very attempt to formulate them is of course a prerequisite to serious explanation (or serious theory), and is often exceedingly fruitful: deductive schemata or something of the sort are a necessary heuristic, because (a) they allow us to discover hidden determinancies that we didn't suspect before, and (b) they simultaneously uncover the residue of non-deterministic instances. And this is true even in a domain – like language change – where there seem to be no 'laws' of any interest. At least I claim there aren't, and that in the nature of things there can't be; I will defend this in more detail later on.

But before proceeding, let me introduce a distinction – which I may seem to have overlooked – between looking for explanations in terms of 'general laws' and attempting to refine DESCRIPTIONS by purging exceptions from general RULES. That is, Verner's (1877) programme and its descendants have nothing to do with what I am talking about here. This is because, to take Verner as an example, the 'exceptions' to Grimm's Law are not exceptions to a general law, but to a contingent (culture-determined) rule. A *Lautgesetz* of course is not a 'law' in the D-N sense, but a (singular) contingent fact, which happens to generalize

---

[14] At least when the clusters occur across a boundary: cf. the examples from German in Kohler (1974: 89). I have never heard of cases within the morpheme, e.g. German *Amt* as *[ant].

[15] For some good arguments against the determinism of intention and other mental states see Popper & Eccles (1977: chs. P1, P4, E7 and Dialogue X), and Polyani & Prosch (1975: chs. 2, 3, especially 48–51).

over sequences of cultural artefacts; there is nothing 'lawful' about the effect of accent-placement on fricatives.[16]

To return: it is not only impossible to establish any necessary conditions for homorganic nasal-assimilation; it is not even possible to establish a sufficient condition (except, trivially, the sequence NC). At least it is not possible to establish any except vacuous ones like the 'essence' of Slavicness on the one hand or Dravidianness on the other (this is the old ploy of attributing the soporific properties of opium to its *virtus dormativa*).

Those languages that do not have homorganic nasal-assimilation illustrate what I call the 'null strategy problem': given a 'function' (like minimization of energy-expenditure or whatever), a language may simply refuse to do anything about it. The question then is: what is the status of a 'strategy' when it may not be used to solve a problem? Or, what is the status of a problem if some languages appear not to consider it one? (I will return to this in detail in chapter 3.) The somewhat animistic view of languages suggested above by 'consider', etc., is not unintentional: but if it smacks too much of the Romantic *Sprachegeist* you are free to substitute some harmless periphrasis like 'speech community'.

We seem at this point to be getting further and further away from 'laws' of any kind, and into a domain where instead of explanation all we have is *post hoc* identification. This may be a matter of necessity, as I will try to show below.

2.6 The status of exceptions, 2: optimization and null strategy

The area we have been wandering about in is what may loosely be called 'optimization' ('loosely', because as we will see it's a very loose notion). I will look in this section at a process-type that has typically been placed under this heading, and at the notion itself. I will try to show that the arguments normally used to define it are flabby and unconvincing.

But first an example. It has been asserted (notably by Schane 1972) that open syllables are in some sense 'optimal'; languages change so as to maximize CV structures, and rules that produce CV are therefore 'natural'. Now if we start with (say) CVC, there are, obviously, two ways of achieving CV:

[16] There may be a 'natural tendency' involved, but this is something quite different. Cf. chapter 3 below.

(7)   (a) CVC > CV
       (b) CVC > CVCV

Option (7a) was that chosen historically by Polynesian (cf. Hale 1971), and (7b) that chosen by Dravidian (in general: but see below). This raises the problem of 'multiple strategies', which I will look at in more detail in the next section: i.e. even if you can predict that a language will maximize CV (which you can't, as I will show), you still don't know which way it will do it. And this also has to be predicted if the explanation is to be convincing.[17]

Now Schane's optimality argument (1972) is based mainly on a handful of examples from French, plus a general assertion that CV is a 'preferred syllable structure'. He gives no basis for this assertion of 'preference', but as far as I can tell it is based on one of the now canonical *obiter dicta* in Jakobson & Halle (1956), plus an implicit argument on the relation of 'implicational universals' to 'optimality'.

Optimality arguments are often based on the fact that no language LACKS a certain kind of structure or segment. It is worth looking at this kind of argument, because it is so frequently employed, and so fundamentally confused. What we have to start with is an implication: that CVC ⊃ CV, but not *vice versa* (cf. Jakobson & Halle 1956: 37: 'Since many languages lack syllables without a pre-vocalic consonant and/or with a post-vocalic consonant, CV . . . is the only universal model of the syllable').

The difficulty is that there are few if any really clearly worked out examples of the argument, since it is 'traditional';[18] what follows is in part, therefore, a 'rational reconstruction' of what the argument would look like if anyone worked it out clearly, and my criticism is a criticism of that reconstruction. But I suspect that I am not being unfair;

---

[17] According to Lightfoot (1979) it is only the fact of change that has to be predicted (on the grounds of some general grammatical theory), not the particular change. I find this unsatisfactory.

[18] Cf. Hooper's criticism of one of the Chomsky & Halle marking conventions on the grounds that it does not distinguish in markedness between open and closed syllables, which is bad because 'it is generally agreed that CV is the unmarked syllable' (1975: 539). Cf. also her comments on what is 'known' to be marked or unmarked (1976: 58): 'We know . . . that [−nasal] is not a conditioned value, but rather the natural or unmarked value for the feature when no environmental conditions are affecting it.' She discusses two competing formalizations of a rule and opts for one on the sole grounds that it 'captures this fact' (*ibid.*).

virtually any standard discussion of markedness or naturalness has some of this in it.[19]

The first problem is this: the mere fact that all languages happen to have a particular syllable type (if it's even true), is taken to have historical (and ultimately, in the now familiar way, 'cognitive' or 'psychological') implications. But this is surely a *non sequitur*: such a 'universal' distribution IN ITSELF is meaningless in historical or developmental terms. The leap from universal presence to 'preference' in terms of development (i.e. making a goal out of a mere distribution) is not given any warrant in the usual type of argumentation. Just because all languages happen to have something does not mean that an increase of that something automatically constitutes an 'optimization': maybe the feature is neutral, or maybe languages are deteriorating by doing silly and harmful things. At least it doesn't constitute an optimization unless we assert this to be true by definition: 'Optimization = *df* increase of things that lots of/all languages have anyway'. I can't see that this means anything.[20]

Further, even if the 'universal' holds, this clearly fails to predict for any given case that the other type(s) will be eliminated. Once again we have a probabilistic type of what might best be called 'pseudo-prediction': the claim that CV is 'optimal' is either analytic, or substantial but unfalsifiable. Because of this, it cannot be used to explain, e.g., deletion of final consonants in Polynesian or the development of the so-called 'euphonic' vowels in Dravidian. And, of course, it will be unable to account for another type of language, one that not only 'fails to optimize' by increasing CV syllables, but one whose history is peppered with changes that effectively MINIMIZE CV – even within a family that has tended by and large to maximize it. Here I am thinking of Toda, which has adopted the 'counter-Dravidian' strategy of deleting final vowels in disyllabic words and dropping vowels in affixes and postpositions, so that it not only ends up with CVC where cognate languages have (original or derived) CVCV, but with CVCC, CVCCC, etc.[21] Similar examples can be multiplied almost at will, e.g.

---

[19] For one fairly clear example see Postal (1968: 165ff). For some discussion, Lass (1975: 476–8).

[20] Cf. Cassirer (1944: 66) on the use of the notion 'instinct' in human and animal psychology, which he describes as 'at best an *idem per idem*, and in most cases ... an *obscurum per obscurius*'. I think this applies nicely here.

[21] On Toda see Emeneau (1958) and the Toda examples from the various cognate sets in Emeneau (1970).

loss of certain final unstressed vowels in Germanic (OE *dæg*, ON *dagr*, OHG *tag* < PG **dagaz*, etc.), loss of final unstressed *-e* in Middle English (*throat* < ME *prǫte*, etc.), the fall of the *jers* in Slavic producing clusters from former open syllables, various losses of case-endings in Indo-European, and the like. Not to mention production of clusters by epenthesis, e.g. insertion of stops in nasal environments in English (*thunder* < OE *punor*, etc.).[22] Many of these cases, of course, can be argued away by 'competition' with some other tendency, as Schane does (1972; especially 216f); but it doesn't seem possible to predict which tendency will win when two come face to face.

In general then 'optimization' can't be predicted; it can only be recognized when, given the prior definition, something occurs that can be said to be an optimization. If it fails to occur, then 'things weren't equal'. This doesn't leave optimization – for all the fuss that has been made about it, including its deification in King (1969) – a very exciting notion. Languages are apparently quite free not to optimize. This unruliness underlines the absurdity of notions like optimal and non-optimal LANGUAGES, which at one time at least could apparently be talked about with a straight face (e.g. Chomsky & Halle 1968: 410–11; cf. Lass 1975: 491). The problem of 'refusal to optimize' will continue to haunt us; I will draw out more of its implications later on.

2.7 Multiple strategies and a 'law of assimilation'

Given a definition of naturalness in terms of frequency and expectability, it is clear that one paradigmatically natural rule type is assimilation (cf. Schane 1972). But if we continue along the lines I have been suggesting, even the naturalness of assimilation becomes either boringly analytic or mysterious.

Consider for instance this change that occurred in many Austrian dialects (Keller 1961: ch. VI; cf. Chen 1974: 53):

(8)
$$\begin{bmatrix} i \\ e \\ \varepsilon \end{bmatrix} \rightarrow \begin{bmatrix} y \\ \o \\ \oe \end{bmatrix} / \underline{\quad} \textltail{l}$$

(That is, non-low front vowels round before a 'dark' /l/.) This change, incidentally, follows the unrounding of historical /yøœ/ in these

---

[22] Though this one could be explained away by a 'competing' tendency to maximize certain 'felicity conditions' or 'interludes': Jones (1973: 79). On 'competing tendencies' see chapter 3 below.

dialects, thus replacing a 'marked' vowel type that had been optimized out of existence (cf. Lass 1975: 480–5 for similar examples from English).

How can we explain a change like (8)? There seems to be no superficially obvious motivation, but since it is contextually determined, the usual heuristic assumption is that the context should be 'naturally' related to the change in some way – ideally as a 'cause'. If we look at the process in articulatory terms, we do not appear to find anything particularly relevant: the environment is unround, coronal, back, lateral, voiced, etc.; but none of these properties appear to have any reasonable connection with rounding of an unround vowel. If for example we formulated the change in terms of Chomsky & Halle features, we would get something of this sort:

$$(9) \qquad \begin{bmatrix} V \\ -\text{back} \\ -\text{low} \end{bmatrix} \rightarrow [+\text{round}] / \underline{\hspace{1cm}} \begin{bmatrix} -\text{obs} \\ +\text{cons} \\ +\text{ant} \\ +\text{cor} \\ +\text{high} \\ +\text{back} \\ +\text{lat} \\ +\text{voice} \end{bmatrix}$$

None of these feature specifications appear to be connected with the rounding: we might expect raising of /e ɛ/ because of [+high], retraction of the whole set because of [+back], or even alveolarization because of [+ant, +cor] – but not what we do get.[23]

If however we look at the rule in terms of (Jakobsonian) acoustic features, we find that a change of [−flat] to [+flat] occurs before a [+grave] segment. The specifications themselves don't tell us anything yet, but the acoustic correlates are interesting. Grave segments have low second formants, and flat ones have low second and third formants, with the transition from a previous segment characterized by a sharp downshift of these two formants (Jakobson, Fant & Halle 1951: §2.42; cf. Lass 1976a: 203–5). That is, we have two low-tonality features

---

[23] Alveolar vowels (vowels whose point of maximum stricture is opposite the alveolar ridge, not the palate) cannot be ruled out in Germanic on typological grounds: they occur for instance in some forms of Belfast speech (the 'r-diphthongs' described by Milroy 1976). Elsewhere in Indo-European they occur in some dialects of North Welsh (David Abercrombie, personal communication) and they are common in other language families, like Sino-Tibetan (cf. Chen 1976).

involved. Lip rounding, as is well known, produces an acoustic effect similar to velarization. We might suggest then that the change (8) is not an articulatory assimilation, but a 'perceptual' one, involving low-tonality transitions.

And we could describe it, in Henning Andersen's (neo-Piercean) terms (1973) as an ABDUCTION: the acoustic effect is as it were 'misinterpreted'. The low transition between the front vowel and the back consonant is taken as a property of the vowel, and the high-tonality vowel is adjusted accordingly: the transition is 'displaced', and read back into the vowel. Diagrammatically:

(10)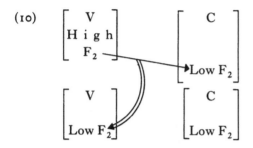

But now there is a problem: there are other equally (or more) typical effects that velars (or velarized coronals, which can count as velars) have on preceding front vowels. Let us look first at the effects of [ɫ], and then the other velars.

(i) *Retraction.* In many Central Scots dialects, /ɛ/ > /ʌ/ before [ɫ], e.g. [hʌɫ] 'hill'/'hull'.[24]

(ii) *Diphthongization* (epenthesis of a back vowel or [ə]). Old English breaking before [ɫC]: PrOE *ell > *æull > æall, *selx > *seulx > seolx (orthographic *eall, seolh* – cf. Lass & Anderson 1975: ch. III); Middle English diphthongization before [ɫ]: /al/, /salt/ > /aul/, /sault/, hence NE /ɔ:/ in *all, salt*, etc. rather than expected /æ/; epenthesis of [ə] in many NE dialects (including my own), e.g. [bɪəɫ] 'bill', [fɫɪəɫ] 'feel', etc.[25]

So [ɫ] has at least three possible effects on a preceding front vowel: retraction, diphthongization, and rounding. (Not to mention no effect at all, or the things it can do itself, like vocalizing to [u], etc.)

[24] From my own observations (Aberdour Parish, Fife). This is a mirror-image rule: the same thing happens after [ɫ] as well, e.g. [ɫʌft] 'lift'. The 'normal' value can be seen in [hɛ̂ʔt] 'hit', etc.

[25] This goes back at least to the seventeenth century: cf. Cooper's comment (1687: ch. 1, §4) to the effect that the vowel 'e lingual' before *l* takes an epenthetic satellite: 'but in *sale, tale*, it is sounded as if it was writ *sa-ul, ta-ul*'.

If we look at the larger class of velars other than (or including) [ɫ], we get at least the following array:[26]

(iii) *Raising*. OE (Anglian) /æ/ > /e/ before liquid + velar, and /æ:/ > /e:/ before velars: *merg* 'marrow', *hēh* 'high' vs. WS *mearg, hēah* (where *e* in the digraph spellings = [æ]: Lass 1976a: 178); OE (WS) raising of /æ(:)/ > /e(:)/ before velars in 'Late West Saxon Smoothing': *seh* 'saw', *ēge* 'eye' < *sæx, *æge < *seah, ēage* (Lass 1976a: 178); OE (WS) raising of /eo/ > /i/ ('Palatal Umlaut'), e.g. *cneoht* 'servant' > *cniht* (Lass 1976a: 179); ME raising of /eo/ in *English* < OE *englisc, wing* < ON *vengr* (with raising of /o/ attested mainly in rhyme (Jordan 1934: §31 and Anm.; Lass 1976a: 180); U.S. raising of /æ/ before /ŋ/ (Lass 1976a: 183); Belfast /a/ > /ɛ/ before velars (Milroy 1976).

(iv) *Diphthongization*. OE breaking before /x/, e.g. *eoh* 'yew' < **ex-* (Lass & Anderson 1975: ch. III); ME diphthongization before /x/, e.g. *heigh* 'high' < lOE *hēh, plough* < OE *plōh* (Lass 1976a: 180–1); ME diphthongization before [ŋC], e.g. *leinþe* 'length' < OE *lengðu* (Jordan 1934: §§102–3; Lass 1976a: 181); U.S. diphthongization before velars, e.g. [bæɪg] 'bag', [sũɪŋ] 'sing' (Lass 1976a: 183).

Of the diphthongizations detailed under (ii) and (iv), some, like OE breaking, involve epenthesis of a back vowel; others, like the ME diphthongization before /x/, involve epenthesis of a vowel agreeing in backness with the original one; while still others (before [ɫ]) produce an inserted vowel that is neither front nor back. These three types of diphthongization suggest different interpretations: in OE breaking, etc., the assimilation could be said to be to backness, since the inserted vowel is always back;[27] in the ME diphthongization, the assimilation is to highness, since the backness of the epenthetic (high) vowel is determined by that of the original vowel; and in cases like the insertion of [ə] before [ɫ], the conditioning can be taken as involving some feature like vocalicness, i.e. copying of the 'vocalic element' of [ɫ] (cf. Harms 1968: 70–1; Anderson & Jones 1974a; Sigurd 1975: 205–6).

Of the other changes, we have already seen that low-tonality assimilation seems to be a reasonable explanation for the Austrian rounding; and clearly all cases of raising can be taken as assimilation to

---

[26] In many of the changes that follow, other classes of segments are implicated as well; but this does not detract from the fact that velars – whatever else is involved – are doing something.

[27] Note that in Old English a very similar change ('velar umlaut') is triggered by the presence of a back vowel in the following syllable (Lass & Anderson 1975: ch. III).

highness. And, just to set things in perspective, we might add that there are many cases (perhaps a majority) in which nothing at all happens before any velars.

This is of course only one example of the multiple strategy problem (which is usually paired with null strategy); we could take any number of others, e.g. the effect of post-vocalic nasals (raising, lowering, diphthongization, nasalization, nothing), retroflex consonants (retraction, retroflexion, lowering, nothing), and so on.[28]

Before drawing any more general conclusions, I want to look at another example, where the 'explanation' of a sound change in phonetic terms seems very clear-cut. Ohala (1974) discusses the problem of explaining a change that occurred in some Norwegian dialects, where /s/ > [ʃ] before /l/, but not before other sonorants or other dentals. His object is a criticism of the account given by Foley (1973), who tries to show (51) that 'there is no phonetic explanation for this', but rather only a 'phonological' (i.e. abstract, Foleyan) one. Foley says (*ibid.*) that 'the conversion of *s* to *š* cannot be attributed to phonetic influences since *l* and *n* are both dentals, and in any case conversion of dental *s* to palatal *š* looks more like dissimilation than assimilation'. The 'real' answer, according to Foley, is that '*l* is phonologically stronger than *n*, and *s* is strengthened by proximity to *l* but not by proximity to the relatively weaker *n*: the strengthened *s* then manifests itself as *š*'.

Ohala objects to this on two grounds (1974: 254–6): first, that 'the notion of "strength" ... is undefined and must be so in order to serve Foley's cryptotaxonomic goals'. And second (256), that there is a 'genuine' phonetic (though not articulatory) explanation, which had in fact already been proposed in the literature. This is that 'in all likelihood the [l] in the [sl] clusters became partially devoiced yielding [sl̥l]'. Then:

[l̥] is acoustically a fricative – in fact, it is very much like ... [ʃ], as we can see from the spectra of the fricatives [s], [ʃ], [l̥] ... [which Ohala presents in an illustration on p. 255]. This is true even though [ʃ] and [l̥] are very different in articulation. Thus, auditorily [sl̥l] could also appear to be [sʃl]. Probably there was then an acoustic assimilation of the [s] to the following fricative, yielding either [l̥l] or [ʃl] ... The reason [s] didn't become [ʃ] before [n] is because if the

---

[28] The multiple strategy problem is not of course to be formulated as 'anything can happen anywhere'. There are certainly constraints on what can happen in certain environments, and even more certainly constraints on the size (and possibly the direction) of changes. But these operate, as the evidence above suggests, within pretty wide latitudes, i.e. they are rather loosely determined by physiological or perceptual 'boundary conditions' (cf. §4.9).

same partial devoicing of the [n] had occurred in the [sn] clusters it would not yield a fricative sounding anything like [ʃ], and the fricative it would yield, [n̥] has extremely low intensity and wouldn't cause [s] to assimilate to it.

Ohala further adds that the hypothesized intermediate stage [l̥] is in fact attested in some other dialects.

Now this is all very nice, and seems to rest on firmer grounds than Foley's explanation. And it is indeed plausible, especially when bolstered by the convincing spectrograms Ohala provides, where [ʃ] and [l̥] show two maximal amplitude spikes at the same point on the time axis, differing in virtually nothing but absolute intensity. But there are some possible objections, which if they don't support Foley over Ohala, certainly point up a serious problem in the credibility (if not the plausibility) of the latter's account.

First, let us remember that spectrographic similarity or even acoustic similarity (to a phonetician) does not necessarily equal perceptual similarity. A case in point is the range of interpretations that English speakers give to the Welsh voiceless lateral fricative /ɬ/, which is if anything more fricative than [l̥] (unless Ohala's [l̥] is in fact [ɬ]). Given Ohala's argument, one would expect the characteristic English rendering of /ɬ/ (in *Llandudno, Llewelyn*, etc.) to be [ʃl]. But it isn't: in the case of names borrowed into English, the typical interpretation is either [l] (*Lloyd*) or [fl] (*Floyd*, from the same source; and cf. Shakespeare's *Fluellen*). One might argue that the reason for [fl] rather than [ʃl] is that the latter isn't a permissible English cluster; but this won't do, since [ʃl] wasn't permissible in Norwegian either, before the change. If one can judge, for instance, from the pronunciations of BBC newsreaders, [ɬ] is often interpreted and produced as [θl] and [xl] – which are also non-English. Impressionistically I should say that [ʃl] is rather rare. And my experience in teaching [ɬ] to phonetics students suggests that [[θl], [xl], [çl] are ar least as common as first approximations as [ʃl].[29]

Second, many English dialects – my own included – devoice /l/ after initial /s/; and there is to my knowledge no dialect of English that has

---

[29] A possible objection to the use of English speakers' reactions to Welsh sounds in this context is this (due to John Anderson): that while Ohala's example involves a change within the native language, my evidence involves speaker-judgements of a foreign segment-type. But I think one could answer that if a new segment arises in a language (however it does), it too is 'foreign' until fully 'nativized'. The two situations, both involving judgements on novelties, seem to me perceptually parallel enough for the purposes of this argument.

turned [sl] to [ʃl]. English initial [ʃ] < /s/ seems always to be articulatory in origin, e.g. before retracted affricated /t/ produced by a following /r/, as in New York [ʃtʃɹɪit] 'street' or before a palatized /t/: various British [ʃtʃuːd̥n̥t] 'student', etc.

So even if Ohala's case is plausible on the face of it (as one possibility), he has given us no particular reason to believe it. That is, he has adduced neither a necessary nor a sufficient condition for the transition from [l̥l] to [ʃl]; he has provided no reason why anything at all should happen, or if something did, why it should be just that. I conclude that Ohala has not in fact provided a 'phonetic explanation' of the change, to be preferred to Foley's simply because it IS a (fairly concrete, empirically interpreted) phonetic rather than an (unmotivated, abstract, empirically unin-terpreted) 'phonological' one. If Foley's explanation is vacuous, and Ohala's is more plausible and methodologically better, since at least some of it depends on measurable (if open-ended) data, this still does not amount to a justifiable claim that Ohala's version is in fact what happened. All he has shown is that given a particular theory, it could have happened, maybe.[30]

With this kind of uncertainty, it is clear that it is impossible to make any useful predictions about assimilations: either that they will occur, or if they do, precisely what form they will take. They appear to have no nomic necessity. We seem to end up with a 'law of assimilation' that can be stated this way:

(11) Universal Law of Assimilation:
      If there is an assimilation (which there may not be: null strategy),
      then it will be to some property, acoustic or articulatory, of the
      segment assimilated to (multiple strategy).[31]

---

[30] The same confusion between an explanation WHY and a statement of a possible mechanism HOW shows up in Catford's account (1974) of the development of ejectives in Armenian and implosives in Sindhi. Catford specifies ways in which (given properties of the vocal tract, airstreams, etc.) these segments might have originated; but he invokes no genuinely causal factors that might have led to these properties being capitalized on in particular ways in particular cases.

[31] Attempts have been made to constrain the direction of assimilations, etc., but these merely end up as taxonomies with evaluative terms attached to the commonest and least common types (e.g. Batliner 1975). All statements of 'laws', 'universals', etc. of course founder on insufficient data anyhow – regardless of the conceptual confusions involved. (For examples of attempted universals on a very restricted data base, cf. Schachter 1969; Schane 1972.) My job is easier in a way: since all I have to do is cite counter-examples to ANY universal claim, and demand an explanation.

This is of course analytic: any 'prediction' we can make about assimilation is merely definitional. The upshot of this is that NO PHONETIC EXPLANATION WHICH IS NOT NOMICALLY NECESSARY IS AN EXPLANATION. Or, more simply, phonetic explanations of sound changes in the strict sense do not exist.[32]

2.8 Is there a distinction between markedness and naturalness?

It may be objected that in the preceding discussion I have been confusing two rather different concepts: 'markedness' and 'naturalness', and that the objections to one do not hold for the other. The argument might run this way: while 'markedness' (in the Chomsky & Halle sense) is a theoretical term, which has its full meaning only within a complex, highly articulated formal theory, 'naturalness' belongs rather (in a quasi-Carnapian sense) to our 'observation language'. That is, markedness derives its substance from its position in a specific set of definitions and other theoretical terms (including binary coefficients, rules of certain types, a specific phonological theory, an evaluation metric, etc.), whereas naturalness is an 'everyday language' concept.

This is not in fact the case. In an earlier paper on this subject (Lass 1975) I attempted to reconstruct the logic of markedness arguments and the structure of the theory; I made no real distinction between the two notions there, and I will restate some of my arguments here in an abbreviated form, with some additional comment, since the matter is relevant.

The theory of markedness in its canonical formulation (Chomsky & Halle 1968: ch. 9) is a set of interlocking statements ('marking conventions') which assign 'marked' and 'unmarked' values to particular coefficients of particular (binary) features in lexical representations. It also incorporates (though this is less relevant here) a projective device ('linking') which ties marking conventions, as conditions on lexical representations, to the outputs of phonological rules. If a value u(nmarked) is assigned to some specification $[\alpha F]$ for some feature $[F]$ and m(arked) to $[\beta F]$ (where α and β are variables over

---

[32] These conclusions may seem excessively general, given the highly particular instances they're based on. But at least my knowledge of the literature suggests that ALL attempts at phonetic explanation suffer from the same defects, and that the conclusions I have come to are fair, given my argumentative stance and what has been done in the field. (For some account of what the preliminaries to a predictive phonetic theory might look like, cf. Lindblom 1978.)

the values + and − and α ≠ β), then a representation containing [αF] is 'cost-free' with respect to [F], 'while a 'cost' is attached to [βF]. An inventory approaches 'optimality' as the number of m specifications approaches zero. Marking theory is thus a 'cost'-assigning algorithm, which defines 'highly valued' as against 'less highly valued' configurations.

An examination of the literature (especially the discussion in Postal 1968: ch. 8) shows clearly that markedness is traditionally equated with 'abnormality' (cf. Postal, 166 on the 'non-normal' status of glottalized consonants, and Chomsky & Halle 1968: 400 on 'naturalness'). The fairest reconstruction I can make of the reasoning behind the assignment of m and u values is the following (cf. Lass 1975: 486–7):

(i)   Some phonological phenomena (segment-types, configurations of feature-specifications, etc.) are relatively common in the world's languages, and others are not.

(ii) Therefore 'common' = 'unmarked' and (relatively) 'uncommon' = 'marked': i.e. what is not expected is more noticeable than what is expected.

(iii) Since what is commonest must (in an unreflecting way) be considered the 'natural' state of things, 'unmarked' = 'natural' and 'marked' = (relatively) 'unnatural'.

This leads to a set of projections to the likely behaviour of marked and unmarked configurations, unfortunately based almost entirely on purely theoretical criteria, as I showed in my earlier paper, and not sufficiently tested in advance. (This is not to deprecate deductions from a theory, merely to suggest that it's a good idea to do some preliminary testing before making public pronouncements.) These projections go this way:

(iv) The very commonness of the common is evidently a sign that it has a higher degree of viability than the uncommon (otherwise it wouldn't be so common); therefore what is less common is less stable, and will tend to be superseded by what is common (mergers will go in the direction of unmarkedness, etc.).

(v)   This means that the common is in some sense 'optimal'; and since the theory says that 'optimization' is to be defined in terms of increasing 'simplicity', then 'common' = 'natural' = 'optimal' = 'simple'.

If the above reconstruction is fair (it is at least as fair as I can make it, considering what there is to work with), what it expresses is the blinding tautology that nature tends toward the natural; and as far as I can tell markedness theory in its formal dress is simply an alternative (actually pseudo-mathematical) representation of this intuitive judgement. There is therefore no difference (except the trivial formal one) between the two notions: they both make the same predictions, have the same conceptual content, and may be regarded as the same thing in two different languages, i.e. as translations of each other. The only slight difference seems to be that the term 'natural' implies some physiological, acoustic or perceptual substrate for the phenomena, while 'marked' does not seem to make the same suggestion.

This however is again very superficial. Since e.g. Chomsky & Halle's feature-system is supposed to represent 'the phonetic capabilities of man' (1968: 295), and since markedness captures the 'intrinsic content' of features (*ibid.*, 400), it would seem that there is no fundamental difference. Therefore I would claim that all arguments against the explanatory utility of one notion hold for the other as well, and that an instance of the naming fallacy is an instance of the naming fallacy no matter what kind of language it is expressed in.

APPENDIX TO CHAPTER 2

Naturalness, 'uniformitarianism', and reconstruction

Das Höchste wäre: zu begreifen, daß alles Faktische schon Theorie ist.

Goethe

1 The problem of historical knowledge

I have argued that there is no justification for attributing 'theoretical signifance' to statistically widely distributed but non-nomic properties of languages. This holds, I would claim, even when the particular properties can be reasonably (i.e. without excessive ingenuity) associated with empirical domains like anatomy, physiology, perception, etc. That is, I find no compelling reason to believe that mere frequency of occurrence over the pan-chronic set of languages, or even 'motivated' frequency (in terms of reasonable association with empirical properties) could be significant in any of the senses dear to the harder-line generativists, among others. I am aware of no evidence that justifies attributing to these distributions 'cognitive' or 'psychological' content. It is certainly clear that there exist no explicit warrants for arguing from distributions to anything else; any claim that such argument is meaningful or valid is an assertion of belief, not the invocation of any traditionally justified or publicly acknowledged principles of inference. The necessary empirical connections (not to mention the theoretical ones) are missing. Theories of naturalness and markedness are at present uninterpreted calculi. (I doubt that the requisite evidence for producing such inferential warrants will ever be forthcoming: but this also is an assertion of belief, based if you like on a failure of pre-cognitive imagination, not an argument: though cf. chapter 4 below.)

So I see no reason for allowing naturalness considerations to have any bearing on linguistic metatheory, e.g. in terms of rewarding rule types as 'highly valued' because they are 'natural'. Indeed, as I have argued elsewhere (Lass 1975), notions like 'cost' and 'value' have no content, since they refer not to any known empirical properties of languages or their users, but merely to linguists' transcendental assumptions or the formal artefacts ('grammars') that partly derive from them.[1]

But even if this is true, there is still reason to pay attention to naturalness, and a way in which it can be a useful notion, even if it is in itself of no particular theoretical interest. It can have a pragmatic, 'technological' value as part of the quasi-conventionalist armory of (non-explanatory) genetic linguistics, i.e. reconstruction. And because reconstruction is so central to historical linguistics, and because the theory of history is so important to all procedures in historical linguistics, I shall treat the relationship between naturalness considerations and theory of history in some detail.

To begin with, it is clear that reconstruction is not strictly an 'empirical' procedure, but at least partly a conventionalist one (though as we will see below this does not make it vacuous). Reconstructions of genuine interest and importance are not testable (against what they are supposed to be reconstructions of), since the cases where reconstruction is most necessary and most informative are precisely those where there is nothing to test it against (cf. Lass 1977, 1978). A reconstruction which merely mirrors a documentary record tells us nothing about history, in the crucial sense of supplying the missing pieces we need; at best it merely gives us some hope that our normal techniques may be reliable.

This means that reconstruction in general must be justified, not by direct confrontation with some independent reality, but at least in part according to methodological criteria. These are of two kinds: purely conventional ones like Occam's Razor and the like, and partly empirical, partly conventional ones like an overall 'uniformitarian' bias (see below). The latter means in particular, as we will see, that the outputs of

---

[1]   The use of 'naturalness' – especially 'phonetic naturalness' – as an argument in attempts to justify (pre-phonetic) synchronic rules in generative phonologies is equally invalid, but on different grounds. Namely that the use of phonetic (which must mean physical) criteria in 'mental' derivations is a category mistake (leaving aside the question of whether the idea of a 'mental derivation' is motivated or even intelligible). The notion of a synchronic derivation of alternants from unique 'underlying forms' probably also involves a category mistake, but a different one: the confusion of 'relations' (e.g. those holding over a pair or n-tuple of alternants) with 'things' (e.g. common underliers). For discussion of this problem in generative phonology cf. Linell (1974), Coates (1977). But this is merely by the way here.

reconstructive technologies must be constrained by the best-informed judgements available as to what constitutes a possible (or likely) segment (language, process, etc.), either in universal or language-specific terms.

Justification of this requires some consideration of the general principles of historical enquiry. The excursus to follow may seem wildly irrelevant at first, but it will eventually home in on both the problem of naturalness and the basic issue of 'historical truth' and 'historical knowledge' – which is after all what we are really interested in.

To begin with, it is obvious that all forms of historical enquiry have in common some attempt at 'recovery of the past' or 'time-reversal' (historians are makers of time-machines). The aim of any historical (or more precisely historiographic: see below) operation is to produce 'knowledge of the past': to recover information that has been lost or obscured through the passage of time, i.e. that is not directly available, or available at all, when the operation begins. The material recovered can be in the general nature of 'facts' (history as reconstruction, or if you like 'genetic myth': cf. §1.1 above) or interpretations of facts (history as explanation, or as 'explanatory myth').[2] These are both important goals, but the second presupposes the first.

A history may be taken broadly as a set of sentences purporting to contain information about some aspect of the past in some domain (with an implicit claim to our acceptance of and trust in it). This raises two important questions: (a) How do we arrive at such statements? and (b) Can they be said to have any truth-value, or at least to be 'justifiable' (if not, as we might prefer, falsifiable)?

These questions derive their seriousness primarily from the simple fact that the past is where it is in relation to us; and, secondarily, because of the 'directionality' or 'irreversibility' of time in the usual way

---

[2] By insisting that the products of reconstruction (filled gaps in records, or states antecedent to all known records) are as much part of 'history' as records and their interpretations, I dissociate myself emphatically from a chronicle-bound or document-bound notion of history like Croce's. Croce argues (1921: ch. 1) that history must be verifiable, and that its reality inheres precisely in its ultimate verifiability; this means that true history is nothing but 'critical exposition' of documents. This would rule out much of what is of interest in linguistic or, say, biological history, since the gaps and pre-'documentary' stages are often of crucial importance. (And I think the same is true, *pace* Croce, for cultural or political history as well.) In any case, Croce's notion of what constitutes a 'historical fact' seems rather naïve: cf. Becker (1955) and the discussion below.

of looking at things.[3] The past is not an observable; it can be an object of intellectual contemplation only by virtue of some human act that makes it so. In fact, as I shall argue, by virtue of some (hopefully principled and rationally justifiable) act that creates it as an 'objective' past. This is a problem that tends to be skirted, because the term 'history' is often used, as the saying goes, with a 'systematic ambiguity': it can mean either a historian's account purporting to represent past events, or the events themselves. In everyday language we don't normally bother to distinguish the two senses, and indeed we treat the 'history' we learn from historians' accounts (e.g. the histories of our nations) as equivalent to the thing itself. If we want to make the distinction clear, we can refer to the historian's products as 'historiography', and reserve the term 'history' for their purported subject matter.

The ambiguity is convenient, as equivocations usually are: but too much reliance on it can lead us away from central questions and difficulties. The most important are: how far are we justified in making the tacit equation involved in accepting the ambiguity? Are history and historiography really the same thing, or even similar? The answers to questions like this (whether or not they are attainable) are clearly of the first importance, because the fact that we are willing (even informally) to make the identification implies a considerable trust in what are at least to begin with purely historiographic procedures (reconstruction techniques, standard explanatory strategies): i.e. a tacit faith in their ontological pretensions.

The main point is that the 'leap of faith' involved in accepting the ambiguity is unavoidable, and not to be deprecated in principle – as long as we are reasonably vigilant, and try our best to develop both logical and empirical or quasi-empirical checks on our procedures. This does not mean, however, that reconstructive techniques, for instance, can ever be algorithms that generate 'historical truth' (except in a special sense: cf. §§3–4 below), or that historical linguistics will ever be 'empirical' (in a Popperian sense). No history is empirical science,[4] and

---

[3] Even if time is not 'directional' in this sense, i.e. if the past and future could be 'directly experienced' (in the manner of J. W. Dunne's famous 'experiment with time' (1929)), this does not really help the historian. At least not in the matter of testing historical claims, since the results of a procedure like Dunne's (involving disciplined recall of apparently trivial details in dreams) seem to be too closely linked to the investigator's own personal past and future. If 'time travel' is possible, it would seem, according to Dunne's evidence, to be so mainly along one's own 'world line'.

[4] Cf. the principled (if excessive) separation of the 'sciences' (*Wissenschaften*) into the *Empiricisch-Analytisch* and *Historisch-Hermeneutisch* proposed by Habermas (1968;

historical knowledge is even more flawed and provisional than knowledge in the so-called 'hard sciences' – or even the 'softer' synchronic ones like biology. To set ourselves in a reasonable frame of mind, I suggest that we give up in advance any hope of attaining 'final' or 'absolute' truth, or 'proving' historical conjectures; this will free us of one set of unprofitable illusions.

2 The central paradox

The claim that the past only exists insofar as it is mediated by a historiographic act seems on the face of it perverse. After all, the monuments of the past surround us, the evidence for it is apparently collected in buildings, archaeological sites, documents, traditions, works of art, fossils, the configurations of the earth and the universe. Let us call these things collectively 'witnesses'.

But now observe that the witnesses themselves are neither 'history' nor 'the past'. It is only human intellectual acts that gather these *disjecta membra* into coherent sequences and produce rational accounts of them. By themselves, in the absence of theory, they are obtuse and unenlightening, not parts of anything in particular. It is only when we interpret them, on the basis of theories of what they might mean, and supply, also through theory, the more important missing ones, that a rational past comes into existence. I am claiming that historiography is essentially CONSTITUTIVE, and that 'history' or 'the past' is what it constructs.[5]

---

critically discussed by Wunderlich 1974: §1.5). Whether historical linguistics in its explanatory aspect can or should be 'hermeneutic' is a separate problem: this depends on whether it is possible to 'understand' change in a human sense, and this depends in part on the validity of teleological views of change. For discussion of claims of this type, and a negative appraisal, see chapters 3 and 4 below, and §5.5. For a positive appraisal see Itkonen (1978).

[5] For some arguments against this view, and in favour of a rather naïve realism, which transcendentally asserts the 'reality' of historical events and the possibility of getting at 'the truth' about them in a fairly simple sense, see Elton (1969: 17–86). Elton argues that a constitutive view of history leads to total relativism, and a reduction of the study of history 'itself' to the study of historiography. As I will try to show, the first problem can be avoided by a suitably constrained historiographic technology; the second is not a problem, since the very act of 'studying history' is historiographic. (None of this of course absolves the investigator from responsibility for mastery of the techniques in his field, good scholarship, etc.) For some further arguments in favour of a constitutive view of language history, see Lass (1978); for a treatment of this problem in a different field, with conclusions in large part similar to mine, see Steinberg (1977: especially chs. 1, 15); this is an elegant case-study in the history of art which shows clearly the extent to which our actual 'experience of the past' may be in part a historiographic artefact.

Let us look at the consequences of accepting such a view (the arguments for it will come shortly). If it is tenable, we're faced with the following problem: say that (however we did it) we've come up with something that looks or feels like an independently known past. How do we know if we're knowing the real thing? How can we tell if any account of the past (reconstructive or explanatory) represents 'what really happened' or whether it's a total or partial fiction?

That is, if I am right so far, it is impossible in principle to compare something that purports to be a true account of the past with the object that it purports to be a true account of: since it is only by constructing some account that we have a past to consider at all. The claim that historiography is past-creating does not of course mean that an independent past never existed; only that whether it did or not we can't know it independently, and therefore can't compare it directly with the construct we have made on the basis of what we assume to be its witnesses. This means that we need some principles: in short, something like a general theory of history. This will ultimately force us to introduce a certain element of conventionalism into the historical enterprise: whether to an intolerable degree or not depends on the reader's judgements as to whether (a) I have made my case persuasively, and (b) his metaphysics will allow the discipline to retain its credibility in case of (a) being true.

Let us look briefly at what such a theory will have to be like: this will bring us back with a vengeance to the problem of unknowability. What follows is not to be taken as a theory, but merely a sketch of some of its more important properties.

First, we must be able to identify potential witnesses. Second, we must be able to evaluate their testimony (witnesses can lie or be mistaken). This means that we must have rules of evidence that will tell us what kind of testimony is admissible, and how it should be weighed; and we must also have rules of interpretation in case the testimony (as so often happens) is obscure or ambiguous;[6] and we must have a set of publicly agreed canons of inference, preferably of a sort that are acceptable in other fields as well (this is obviously one of the major concerns of this book). It is clear that the actual shape of what we imagine to be history will often be determined by the efficacy of these

---

[6] Much of this cannot of course be formalized, and will always remain in the area of 'art' or 'connoisseurship' (Polanyi 1958). This is what is usually thought of as 'philological skill', 'interpretive tact', etc.

strategies: think of the 'history of man' before the unmasking of the Piltdown fraud or the 'history of the settlement of America' before the Kensington Stone was shown to be a nineteenth-century forgery.

These (explicit or implicit) rules of evidence for any field are an important part of its theory of history. The general principles of interpretation, etc., not bound by specific subject matters, those which govern all historical enquiry, are the theory of general history. I will have little to say about this (except in a crude way below); though much that I have to say will bear on it at least indirectly.

The most important relationship, however, is that between the theory of history for a given domain, and the (non-historical) general theory of that domain. In matters of substance, the latter will always be at least a local constraint (which is not necessarily to say that the theory of linguistic history is totally constrained by general linguistic theory, as argued by Lightfoot 1979: but this is an independent issue).

To return to our subject: the theory of history in linguistics is locally constrained by general linguistic theory in the same way as for example the theory of history in biology is constrained by general biological theory (i.e. evolutionary theory is a special case of non-historical biology: see the simple example in the following section). The important preliminary notion is that of the existence of a hierarchy of theories within a given domain, with a set of 'control' relations, each theory being in the 'meta-'/'object-' relation to the one below it. A metatheory in this sense defines in advance the primitive elements and operations of its object theory or theories. Therefore the outcome of a given operation within a lower-level theory – say a 'history of English' – depends for its validity immediately on the quality of the theory in a particular case, and somewhat less directly (contingently but of course importantly) on the quality of the work done within the bounds of the theory. But this quality, i.e. the 'certainty' or 'trustworthiness' of the knowledge the theory delivers if properly applied, depends on the empirical validity and coherence of the next theory up.

There is thus a hierarchy of responsibility; and if there are defects anywhere along the line, the higher up they are the more harm they do. For instance, a factual error made by a historian in interpreting a document (e.g. a misreading) is usually quite easy to remedy, and may not have a significant effect on the outcome (except in the case of a 'ghost' *hapax legomenon*, which can be handled by other principles: if a fake *hapax* fouls up a history, this is due to insufficient vigilance on the part of the scholarly community). But an error in the local theory itself (e.g. admission of a document that is not properly part of the record) can be much more damaging. And by the same token a general statement of the form 'X can be recovered from history by assuming Y' can be disastrous if the arguments for the recoverability of X or the assumption of Y are (either empirically or logically) unsound. This is one of the reasons for my concentration in this study on the structure of arguments and the claims made for the delivery of sound knowledge. But the important thing to remember is that this state of affairs demands that theories be explicit enough to be publicly evaluated, and clear enough so that given claims about the past can be accepted or rejected on principle. Since human knowledge is finite and imperfect, and since history poses special difficulties of its own, this goal may not be attainable, but our responsibility as historians is that much greater.

With this background, we can return to the basic problem, the knowability of the past. Before this digression on theory I was considering some aspects of historical knowledge which threatened to produce a hopeless paradox. If the past cannot be known directly, then if it is to be known at all it must, like any other unobservable, be known theoretically, i.e. by means of some kind of principled inference. But the nature of the material seems to make such inference impossible, and history rests on a contradiction. We can schematize this problem as follows:

(i)   Our primary evidence for the past is objects that have (apparently) survived into the present.

(ii)   But these survivors tell us nothing unless we can evaluate their reliability and interpret them, i.e. tell which are 'real' witnesses and what they mean.

(iii) But (i) and (ii) conflict, since we can't test our interpretations and judgements against the past they concern. The only way of making such interpretations and judgements is by means of principles of comparison, i.e. *a priori* criteria of reliability and meaning.

(iv)   But we cannot have such criteria; or if we do they can't mean anything, since we have established that they cannot be based on the only possible source for them, an independent knowledge of the past.

If there is any foundation for a theory of history, and for the epistemic claims of historiography, where does it come from?

3 Uniformitarianism and historical truth[7]

Let us adopt as a starting position the idealized Popperian notion that the 'strength' of a theory can partly be interpreted as its ability to 'forbid' states of affairs in nature. This will prompt us to search for a constrained and constraining theory; it may also provide a link between general methodological principles and epistemological justification, and between empirical observation and methodology.

I now suggest a preliminary answer to the question of where the foundation of a theory of history comes from: it comes from the present, by way of a pair of related axioms. The first axiom is rather simple, but I will illustrate it before stating it, by showing its use in an argument, and its particular constitutive role in a historical enquiry. The structure of the argument in any case is illuminating.

Consider the statement: '*Smilodon* (a "sabre-tooth tiger") was a cat-like carnivore of the Pleistocene'. There are two kinds of assertions here: one is a matter of historical record, of what I have called 'witnesses', i.e. there was an identifiable cat-like animal with long canine teeth that lived at a specifiable time in the geological past. The second is not a matter of record at all – that *Smilodon* was a carnivore. Yet we are pretty much as certain of this as of the other, despite the lack of reports by people who saw it eat, samples of stomach contents, etc. How do we arrive at 'moral certainties' like this? And are they valid?

I assume we would arrive at this particular certainty by way of an argumentative sequence like this:

(i)   *Smilodon* had huge pointed canines, small incisors, cheek teeth that met in a scissors-like fashion ('carnassials'), and no true grinding teeth; it had massive attachment points for its jaw muscles, and long sharp curved claws.

(ii) Among present-day mammals, the set of predicates (i) is found only in carnivores.

(iii) The 'laws of nature' are constant over time.

(iv) *Smilodon* was a carnivore. Q.E.D.

This is a characteristic form of historical argument. In addition to the witnesses (i), we invoke a present-day predicate or set of predicates (ii), and an inferential gap-filler (iii) as enabling legislation. The result is (iv).

Now observe the fruitfulness of this strategy: in addition to the

---

[7]   The material in this section is a revised and much extended version of §7 of Lass (1978).

witnesses (i), the argument has provided us with a 'new' witness (iv), which can in future be taken as part of the record. Witnesses plus a uniformitarian axiom can produce new witnesses. (Using 'uniformitarian' in the nineteenth-century sense, e.g. that of Lyell, as the opposite of 'catastrophist'.) And in further research we could bring this new information to bear, for instance, on problems of Pleistocene ecology: we might be in a position to figure out what *Smilodon* ate, etc. Aside from anything else, this illustrates the important point that we can use this kind of historical argument to produce new 'facts' that can be used to produce still more new ones.

But why should this argument be valid? What gives us the right to invoke the uniformitarian principle? Is it really the case that (ii) being true makes (iv) true? The answer of course is that strictly speaking it doesn't; it's not that because (ii) is true there is an empirical certainty that (iv) is. It is rather that the basic shape of the argument – if we assume the binding force of the uniformity principle (iii) – is one that we feel is a guarantor of validity. It is simply an instance of *modus ponens*, with the uniformity principle as a background statement of the timeless validity of the premises. That is, if we take the argument as timeless, then if p = dentition, etc., and q = 'is a carnivore', we have: $p \supset q$; p; $\therefore q$.

Not all historical arguments of course can be reduced to implications. But at least some do have (or can be made to have) this structure, enough so that if we can build this general mode of procedure into the primary framework (essentially producing history by dehistoricizing) we feel an overall confidence in the results.

For historical argumentation to have any epistemic force it must in fact be essentially synchronic, for both psychological and logical reasons. Here the primary motivation might be seen as psychological, in this sense: given certain (empirically based) presuppositions about how animals work, based on our experience of living ones, we cannot conceive that (i) should be true of any animal of which (iv) wasn't. Given (a sentence describing) some event or property p, and another (sentence describing) some event or property q; and given that in our experience it is always the case in the present that $p \supset q$; then if we have a historical record of p, q was also the case.

This may be 'irrational', in precisely the same sense as everyday induction is; it is not strictly rational (though it may be useful) to believe that constant co-occurrence in the past will be repeated in the future. And if this is so, why should we believe that the present is in some sense a 'repetition' of the past?[8] But either we believe this or we give up.[9]

The example above may have been excessively neat and rather trivial, but the principle is not. In one form or another it is the axiomatic foundation of all historiography. It can be called the 'Uniformitarian Axiom', or – clumsily but perhaps more informatively – the 'Principle of Pan-Temporal Uniformity'. In its most general form it says:

(1)   Nothing (no event, sequence of events, constellation of properties, general law) that cannot for some good reason be the case in the present was ever true in the past.

(With proper tact, as we will see, this does not rule out 'emergence', or parochial differentia: i.e. it doesn't matter that there was once a time when life didn't exist, or that *Smilodon* is not the case in the present.)

What (1) really means is that the general principles (in a sense to be made a bit more precise) that govern the world in the present hold for the past as well. Without some such control there is no way of constraining historical hypotheses, nothing to stop us from reconstructing anything at all and justifying ourselves by *ad hoc* auxiliary hypotheses ('*Smilodon* was the only herbivore that ever had all and only the anatomical characters of a carnivore'). As a corollary, then, historical inference can only take us back to the furthest-past extension of the principles that now govern the world. A time when 'everything was different' is in principle not reconstructable, i.e. not available to history.[10]

So in addition to its fruitfulness, (1) has the effect of constricting the domain of history, by expunging from it any period antedating its applicability. This means that 'prehistory' is a legitimate subject for the historian only as long as it is methodologically and theoretically

---

[8]   The *locus classicus* for the notion of induction as irrational is Hume's *Treatise of Human Nature*, I, iii. For detailed discussion of 'the problem of induction' see Popper (1973: ch. 1). For arguments for the rationality of induction see the extended treatments in Blackburn (1973), and Hesse (1974).

[9]   This may look on the face of it perilously close to a claim for a subjectivist historiography, given the emphasis on 'experience', what we can 'conceive', etc. But this is merely a shorthand for something more like 'what is true or accepted according to the consensus of competent observers', or 'what is true according to the presently accepted tenets of the discipline involved'. Thus the definition may be – ultimately – relativistic, but not subjectivist. At least not insofar as the methodological and other principles involved are 'impersonal', or intersubjectively agreed on.

[10]   The stipulation 'when everything was different' allows latitude for emergence, within (as yet to be specified) boundaries. Clearly some 'difference' must be allowed: the question is how much (cf. §§4–5).

coterminous with history proper; otherwise it is a subject for a different discipline, with a different theory and methodology. (This is in practice usually not a problem, since 'prehistory' is a relative notion: for a language discovered yesterday the day before yesterday is a 'prehistoric' period.)

Now (1) may appear too strong: after all, one of the fascinations of the past is precisely its difference from the present, its uniqueness as past. Doesn't the Uniformity Principle claim that the past was in fact no different? Yes and no: the interpretation of the principle depends on a tactful distinction between two types of properties, which once made allows the past to retain its uniqueness while still being methodologically constrained by the present. We might put it this way, as a rough preliminary formulation: History is an infinite sequence of unique, non-repeatable events, each of which is at some (theoretically significant) level a token of one of a finite set of types.

Take the case of organic evolution. Every real organism (both as individual and as member of a species) is unique, and with the passage of time it undergoes evolutionary changes which in effect transform it into other unique, non-repeatable forms (or it dies out). But the principles by which each unique organism operates, and the principles that govern the evolution of populations (the genetic code, 'natural selection', etc.) are stable and universal. Each unique (essentially contingent) organism, subject to its unique environmental, mitotic, and other contingencies, becomes another unique organism through the operation of non-unique, necessary principles.

We must therefore see evolutionary or historical processes as an interaction between what the palaeontologist G. G. Simpson has called 'immanent' and 'configurational' factors (1964: ch. vii). The operative 'laws' are immanent; they stand outside of and govern the unique individual configurations of events. There is thus a necessary non-historical background to all historical processes. And it is the immanent, not the configurational factors that the Uniformity Principle refers to (for further discussion of the implications of historical uniqueness, see §4.11 below).

We can restate (1) in a form more directly relevant to linguistic history (or historiography):

(2)   No reconstructed entity, configuration of entities, process of change, or reason for change can have been the case only in the past.

Thus if someone reconstructs a language with the vowel system **/e o a/* (cf. Lehmann 1952), we can reject it out of hand on methodological grounds, because (as far as I know) no living language has been observed with such a system. It is, in our current state of knowledge, part of the definition of natural language that one of its properties is the presence of at least one high vowel in a system. And since the only genuine observables are present observables, the properties of living languages in stasis and change define the immanent properties of the class of natural languages over time. Thus they have priority over, and constrain, the properties of all reconstructed ones.[11] Logically, if a set of properties holding (so far) universally for natural languages is a defining set, then a language or history that violates one of these properties belongs to some field other than linguistics.

There are however very few absolute universals of the kind I have been talking about: what we are usually faced with in historical inference is 'tendencies', 'widely distributed properties', and the like. But these still come under the same methodological heading, if a weaker version. Here the choice is not between the possible and the impossible, but between the probable and the improbable, or the more and less probable, where both are possible. If the strong form of the Uniformity Principle says that nothing impossible ever happened, the weaker form (which we might call the 'Principle of Uniform Probabilities') says:

(3)   The distribution of probabilities in cases where a choice is available from a set of alternatives has always been in principle the same as it is now.[12]

(Cf. Lass & Anderson 1975: ch. v; Lass 1976a: ch. 3; Lass 1978.) That is, in cases of indeterminacy, the probable happened. Probability of occurrence is thus both a constraint on reconstruction and – like the strong form of the Uniformity Principle – a source of information about the past (perhaps in a rather odd sense of 'information', but the only one we have).

---

[11] For a more delicate and detailed statement of how this ought to work, illustrated by an extended example from the history of English, see Lass (1978). For a shorter case-study along similar lines, see Lass (1976a: ch. 3).

[12] This principle is not to be taken absolutely literally, or it becomes absurd. It must allow for (although this is of course problematical) at least the possibility of contingent change in distributions (e.g. the probability of an inhabitant of Scotland being a native Celtic speaker is not the same now as it was in the ninth century). Principle (3) must obviously be refined, and used with greater precision than required by the simple example in §4 below. (Some further methodological comment follows in §5.)

4 An example and some objections

We can demonstrate this as follows. Let there be two cognate languages A and B, which are the sole attested representatives of their family, and let there be no information about A and B except the actual forms in the languages. Now let A and B, in three sets of cognates, exhibit the following correspondences:

(4)   A   B
    'VpV   'VbV
    'VtV   'VdV
    'VkV   'VgV

What happened? Under the conditions I have been proposing, specifically the Uniform Probabilities Principle (3) (which is of course what most historical linguists implicitly follow anyhow), there is no doubt that language A represents the 'primitive' situation, and that correspondences like [p]:[b] intervocalically can be turned into history by prefixing [p] with an asterisk and turning the colon into an arrow. Crudely, if C = the relation 'cognate', we can say that:

(5)   C('VpV, 'VbV) ⊃ *'Vpv → 'VbV

The point to observe here is the virtual compulsion exerted on history by the principles; in the absence of strong counter-evidence, the most probable thing happened. This is not to say that the improbable doesn't happen: take for instance the wildly improbable double strengthening (voiced > voiceless, sonorant > obstruent) in the Icelandic development of medial geminate sonorants ([nn] > [d̥n̥], [ll] > [d̥l̥], etc.).[13] This development is supported by the description of long sonorants in these positions by the medieval 'First Grammarian' (cf. Haugen 1950: 21–2), as well as by comparative evidence. The same could be said for the Germanic *Verschärfung*, the development of Latin /-i̯-/ to Italian /-dʒ-/, etc. But all 'neutral' cases, where there is no special evidence one way or the other, are settled on grounds of probability.

Thus once again we see that a principle 'produces history': our methodological principles define to a significant extent both the

---

[13] The improbability of medial double strengthening (e.g. *öllum* [œd̥lʏm] 'all, dat. pl.' < /ɔllum/) can be analyzed out of the way by taking the environment as 'syllable-final'; this then leaves word-final cases (e.g. *fínn* [fid̥n̥] 'fine, masc. nom. sg.' < /finn/) as subcases of this environment, and groups them both under a single (NOT improbable) heading (I owe this suggestion to Richard Coates). But this does not work for cases where there is no word-final change, e.g. the *Verschärfung*. The worst that could be said is that maybe Icelandic is not a good example.

possibility and the content of historical knowledge. This means then that historical knowledge contains a certain unavoidable conventionalist element.[14] If we reject the binding force of present-derived constraints on the content of history, then we are forced to reject the possibility of any interesting history, or any rational historical argument. If we do not accept that a constraint or methodological principle can be an actual source of knowledge, we reject historical knowledge. It seems that the historian must operate with a rather restricted definition of 'truth', almost in some cases a procedural one: 'true knowledge' of historical matters is to a large extent what our methodological principles tell us is (or could be) true.

Whether we like this or not, we reject it at our peril. The game simply cannot be played without some such stipulations. We must accept that there are two kinds of historical knowledge: relatively direct, gained from witnesses by the application of interpretive strategies and rules of evidence, and indirect, gained from theory in conjunction with the present state of things, and no direct witnesses. If the principles of inference we use are valid (or at least if we believe them to be), then the second type of knowledge is as useful and significant as the first. And in fact an important part (perhaps the major part) of the 'historical record' as linguists utilize it consists of second-order (purely or largely theoretical) inferential knowledge (this applies to our translations of texts in dead languages, semantic interpretations of morphological categories, interpretations of spelling, etc.). But insofar as our methodological principles and the constraints and procedural dictates arising from them have some kind of empirical substance; and insofar as some of our reconstructive techniques are in fact subject to testing, our knowledge can be said to have some claim to reliability – at the very least in the same spirit as that in which we are willing to accept 'informed guesses' made by experts.

The preceding may sound like a retreat to a fairly strong conventionalism or instrumentalism, or a plug for a 'coherence theory' of truth. And in part, of course, it is certainly the last of the three. (I don't think that admitting one's limitations or the limitations of one's discipline is

---

[14] For some similar arguments, but with specific reference to human (i.e. political, social, military) history, see Collingwood (1946: Part v). His discussion (Part v, §§2–3) of the 'constitutive' and 'self-authorizing' properties of the historical imagination is particularly relevant and has clearly influenced my own thinking. Cf. also Steinberg (1977: 113).

ever a 'retreat': not doing so is a retreat from rationality.) There is certainly no doubt that even in the natural sciences the criteria by which we judge and accept theories, and the forces that determine the tenacity with which we uphold them, are often 'esthetic' in this sense: the coherence (as well as the boldness, beauty, imaginative power, etc.) of theories will often win even in the face of disconfirmatory empirical‧ evidence (cf. Polanyi 1958: ch. 1; Feyerabend 1975; and §5.4).

But I certainly do not claim that all history (especially reconstruction) is completely conventionalist, or that it can be absolved from empirical responsibility. I simply point out that there are necessary principles which must be partly conventionalist – e.g. in the sense that Occam's Razor is a convention for well-formed descriptions or theories, not a 'fact about nature'. Even essentially positivist and anti-conventionalist epistemologies, like Popper's, are partially controlled by *a priori* (metaphysical, even esthetic) 'rules of the game': I would assert that one could even interpret the relation between deductive prediction and theoretical truth as essentially conventionalist, at least in the harmless sense in which my uniformity constraints are conventionalist. They are conventions backed by empirically motivated (if not determined) convictions too overwhelmingly self-evident for us to be able to deny them with any comfort.

It is important however not to take the uniformity principles as restrictive to the point of forbidding any novelty or emergence. For example, it was a 'law' before the appearance of man that primates do not have language. To put it perhaps more clearly, the purpose of principle (1) is not to deny that new things come into existence, even new things that may be qualitatively different from earlier ones. (Whether this is the case in the example above is of course debatable, given the evidence of Washoe and other chimpanzees.) But the principle does ensure that emergent phenomena will as suggested be allowable IN TYPE, i.e. that their differentia will not involve the transgression of other necessary principles. (The development of language, or other emergent phenomena like the vertebrate and cephalopod eyes, do not involve 'violations' of this kind, i.e. they are not 'miracles' in the theological sense, but something more like new wine in old bottles.)

The same thing clearly holds for statistical distributions. That is, it may once have been the case that all human languages were spoken in the Olduvai Gorge or wherever, and at that time were intimately related genetically, and therefore showed a much more typologically restricted inventory of processes, segments, categories, etc. than present-day languages. For example, maybe – if they were in fact natural languages in the strict sense – there happened to be none that had developed nasalized vowels at some given time. But once nasalized vowels did develop for the first time in pre-nasal environments, it was 'natural' for vowels to be nasalized in this position, and given two languages with respectively /VNC/ and /ṼC/, the same type of constraint as suggested above for the intervocalic stop-voicing case would hold. Once again, the crucial thing is the immanent/configurational distinction. (Cf. further §5 below.)

In summary, once the particular configuration in which the immanent 'laws' act is established, we can see in any given case what must (or is very likely to) have happened: this is what produces history in the absence of data. And it is here that 'natural' properties of languages, no matter how inexplicable or unintelligible they may be (not all are, but certainly some are), can serve as a basis for certain reconstructive activities.

My general impression is that outside of this use, and the related one of sharpening students' expectations by giving them a picture of the most frequent kinds of linguistic processes, the concept of naturalness is devoid of any particular interest – except of course insofar as 'naturalness' itself remains a potential explanandum (if one where the likelihood of explanation in the D-N sense is vanishingly small). Some of the reasons for this will perhaps become clearer in chapters 3 and 4, when we consider the problem of 'functional explanation' for change, and the indeterministic element introduced by the fact that language is spoken by human beings in society.

5 Two closing reflections

(a) *Time reversal*
Although I have been arguing here that historiography is in an important sense essentially a 'synchronic' discipline, particularly in terms of its methodological controls, this does not imply that it is 'timeless'. Certainly not – and this is the point of the claim of synchronicness – that the historian, in 'reversing' time, in some way suspends it. Even if the primary historiographic act is in a way an 'indwelling' in a past event, the indwelling does not involve the characteristic 'mythological' reactualization of a primordial timeless-

ness. Thus historiography is not 'mystical', it does not function like ritual, which as Eliade suggests (1963: 140) 'abolishes profane, chronological Time and recovers the sacred Time of myth. Man becomes contemporary with the exploits that the Gods performed *in illo tempore*' (though this might be the result of an extreme version of hermeneutic *Verstehen*). One of the main functions of the uniformity constraints is precisely to prevent this kind of mythologization of history, to prevent (what often seems to be the case) historical narratives becoming accounts of 'events which took place *in principio* ... in a primordial and non-temporal instant' (Eliade 1961: 57). It is, paradoxically, making history 'synchronic' that makes it genuinely and rationally 'historical'.

The important point is that the reversal of time is not its suspension, or the hypostasis of a different KIND of time, to quote Eliade again (*ibid.*), 'qualitatively different from the continuous and irreversible time of our everyday ... existence'. Time's 'arrow' always points in the same direction; the historiographer simply claims the ability to retraverse its flight path.

The assertion that historiography in this sense, i.e. its reconstructive aspect, is not 'mythological' does not however hold entirely for its explanatory (or better, 'insight-giving') function. I will argue later on (chapter 5) that there are what we might well characterize as elements of mythopoesis in historiography, which are inextricably part of the enterprise. But they are essentially shape-giving, not time-suspending.

(b) *Uniformity and emergence*
The most serious problem raised by any uniformitarianism or 'postulate of invariance' is still the matter of cut-off points: how do we square the methodological necessity for invariance with the facts of emergence (I take them as such: cf. §4.11)? One answer – not, to be sure, a very precise one – is suggested by Popper (Popper & Eccles 1977: 25); and this can serve as background speculation to whatever programme is eventually developed to deal with this matter. Popper claims that 'there can be invariant laws *and* emergence; for the system of invariant laws is not sufficiently complete and restrictive to prevent the emergence of new lawlike properties' (emphasis his). This is taken to be true of the natural world; but it can easily be extended to the social or psychological or whatever world(s) we are concerned with (for some remarks on that see §4.9).

In the case of probabilities (given a propensity interpretation) the same thing can in principle be said to hold (Popper & Eccles 1977: 30): '... the first emergence of a novelty ... may change the possibilities or propensities in the universe. We might say that the newly emergent entities, both micro and macro, change the propensities, micro and macro, in their neighborhood ... they create *new fields of propensities* ...' (emphasis Popper's).

The problem of cut-off points still remains with us, of course. Popper's solution, which in a way is similar to Simpson's, is certainly applicable to the physical (and probably the biological) world (*ibid.*; 31): '... while the invariances may continue to hold for elementary physical entities ... sufficiently distant from the newly emerged structures, new types of events may become the rule within the fields of the newly emerged structures'.

Methodologically, this suggests that historical disciplines have cut-off points (virtually interdisciplinary boundaries) after each significant emergence. Our problem in language history, then, is this: how much emergence (after the emergence of language itself, of course) do we, or can we, allow? This is the question whose answer (if it's achievable) will flesh out the rather schematic proposals I have been making.

What I have tried to do here is to provide an extremely (probably excessively) restrictive answer, at least as a first approximation. My impression – based on my own admittedly imperfect knowledge of language histories – is that over the time-span we have available to us, the global intuition that there has been little if any genuine emergence seems justified (though of course not incorrigible). If this is the case, then – again as a first approximation – a theory of constraints embodying SOME version of both uniformity principles can be taken as something more than a purely conventionalist move. Certainly the principles have to be made more precise, and in particular their ranges of tolerance have to be clarified. I have so far produced little more than programmatic assertions which, if I'm lucky, are of the general type that we will eventually need.

3 The teleology problem : can language change be 'functional'?

In nature we find not only that which is expedient, but also everything which is not *so* inexpedient as to endanger the existence of the species.

Konrad Lorenz

3.1 Introductory[1]

I have so far discussed – without making the distinction explicit – two types of explanation, both loosely 'phonetic'. The bases, that is, were phonetic, but the criteria involved were rather different. In the Austrian rounding and the Norwegian [s] > [ʃ] change, the explanation was intrinsically mechanistic: i.e. the concept of 'causality' invoked relied only on articulatory or perceptual parameters and their interactions. But in the case of homorganic nasal-assimilation or the development of canonical CV syllables, the principles were of a different order: the notions 'ease of articulation', 'optimality', and 'preference' introduced a teleological factor.

Teleology has had a chequered career as a mode of explanation; scientific and metascientific opinion have swung back and forth, pro and con, from Aristotle to the present (and the debate is not over). For Aristotle, a non-teleological universe (even with respect to inanimate matter) was inconceivable; for the positivistically inclined, from Darwin on, teleology is pretty much anathema, or at the very least weak-minded, romantic, or obscurantist (cf. Monod 1972 on Teilhard de Chardin and the comments in Lass 1974a: 346–7 on Monod). This is not the place for

---

[1] Much of the seriousness with which I take the general topic of teleology is due to the seriousness with which Nigel Vincent took an earlier paper of mine (Lass 1974a). I have been led, both by discussion with him and a paper of his (1978), to abandon some of my earlier pro-teleological views; though as will become apparent later, I disagree with him as well.

a general discussion of the issue (for a good treatment see Woodfield 1976); but I will introduce the topic in relation to language change by looking at some classic assertions of its validity (more general reflections will be relevant later).

The idea that 'function' is a significant factor in change is largely associated with the pioneering work of the Prague school. For a good programmatic assertion of a characteristic Praguian position we might take the following remarks of Roman Jakobson, in reference to phonological change (Jakobson 1961a [= Lass 1969: 8]):

The basic assumption of the neo-grammarian linguistic methodology, that of the sound law operating without exceptions in a given language at a given time, has, up till recently, repeatedly met with negative criticism, since the neo-grammarians have not been able to give a theoretical foundation for this working hypothesis. The revision of the traditional tenet leads to the recognition of the fact that language (and in particular its sound system) cannot be analyzed without taking into account the purpose which that system serves . . . The neo-grammarians did not succeed in explaining the social character of sound change (why a speech community accepts and sanctions individual slips), but this problem too finds its solution once it is posed teleologically.

More extremely (Jakobson 1961b [= Lass 1969: 7]): 'In contra-distinction to traditional historical phonetics, *historical phonology* is based on the following principles: (a) no sound change can be comprehended without reference to the system which undergoes that change; (b) each change in a phonological system is purposeful' (emphasis Jakobson's). Whatever the theoretical status of the research programme suggested here (and I will criticize it strongly below), it has certainly produced a wealth of (often interesting) literature, as well as a number of theoretical spin-offs, such as the 'centre' vs. 'periphery' dialectic (e.g. Vachek 1964), 'functional load' (cf. Martinet 1955; King 1967; §7 of the appendix to this chapter; and Vachek 1969), and the theory of the 'economy' of phonological systems (Martinet 1955).

Praguian teleology, in its beginnings at least, can be seen as an attempt to open up Saussure's famous 'game of chess' image (1959: Part 2, ch. III, §4), by extending Saussure's purely relational analysis so that the main point becomes, not the positions of the pieces, but the game (cf. Jakobson 1929: 14; Vachek 1966: 21f). This conception, which leads directly to Martinet's more elaborate theories, is essentially dialectical: changes disturb systemic 'equilibrium', and systems 'strive to re-establish' the equilibrium lost through change (cf. Lass 1976a: 60f).[2] The conception of language change that grows out of this is dramatic and 'dynamic'; and leads naturally on to the idea that change is – or can be – essentially 'therapeutic' (an idea we find, in a somewhat different connection, in writers of very different theoretical orientations, like Gilliéron: a point I will return to). There is certainly something at least superficially attractive about the resultant image of language history as a perpetual dialectic of teratogenesis and cosmetic surgery; but the attractiveness is ultimately a bit meretricious, and the apparent explanatory power specious, as I will argue below.

These Praguian notions have attracted little (explicit) attention from the generativists, by and large; though curiously, one of the pillars of 'classical' generative theory of change, e.g. as enshrined in King (1969), is the notion of optimization, which is nothing if not 'therapeutic'.[3] What I have already said about optimization in the last chapter implies that I think Shakespeare was right about roses by any other name; I will suggest in this chapter (to rape a metaphor) that the Praguian therapeutic rose is tarred with the same brush.[4]

3.2 Ground-clearing: function and the 'how else?' strategy

Even though Praguian and other writers could talk quite unself-consciously about things like 'the law of the economy of energy' (Jakobson 1961b [= Lass 1969: 8]), it is clear that these 'laws' are not like 'natural laws'. They are rather tendencies, of greater or lesser strength. What I said in chapter 2 about statistical distributions holds of course also for tendencies, trends, and the like; but here the difference is that there exist fairly explicit arguments for taking them seriously, and incorporating them into linguistic theory; as well as a claim that they are empirically based. I will look briefly at one of these attempts here, before going on to treat the issues in more detail.

Lyle Campbell (1975) makes an eloquent case for allowing genuine

---

[2] More accurately, what is established by change and counter-change is a new equilibrium (no stepping in the same river twice). The picture then is not one of homeostasis but rather 'homeorhesis' ('stabilized flow rather than stabilized state': Waddington 1968b: 12).

[3] For some comment see Lass (1974a: 337, note 1) and the references cited there.

[4] For more recent developments in teleological explanation in linguistics, see §§3.2ff and Itkonen (1978).

explanatory force to 'functional explanations' (mainly of sporadic or non-*Lautgesetzlich* changes or 'exceptions') which are based on tendencies rather than absolute rules: i.e. in something like a probabilistic explanation framework incorporating tendency-statements as explanans sentences. Here is one of his characteristic examples (1975: 389–90). In Greek, there was a 'well-known morphologically conditioned change', whereby intervocalic /s/ was deleted everywhere except in certain future and aorist verb forms. Campbell says: 'Had the *s* of the "future" been lost ..., the "future" and "present" would have become identical for most forms; removal of this *s* by regular sound change would have destroyed the form and hence the function of the "future" morpheme. Consequently, the change was prevented in order to preserve the distinction ...' He continues:

It might be asked, however, how can one be certain that this functional explanation is correct and that the preservation of *s* ... was not merely an accident? CERTAINTY IS ESTABLISHED by the fact that intervocalic *s* of the 'future' was lost freely in verbs with roots ending in a nasal or liquid, where the paradigm distinctions ... could be signalled formally by the *e* of future stems ... [Emphasis mine]

He gives as examples the familiar cases like *stel-lō/stel-e-ō* (with loss, < earlier *stel-e-s-ō), vs. *lu-ō/lū-s-ō* (with retention). His final comment is: 'The accuracy of the functional explanation IS SHOWN by the fact that *s* was lost ... whenever the paradigm distinction would be maintained (*e* taking on the function of signalling "future" in the nasal and liquid stems), but preserved when the distinction was otherwise in danger' (emphasis mine). Thus this change (and the same goes for others he cites) is not merely a case of simple 'morphological conditioning', which 'explains very little' (391). It is rather the case that 'morphologically conditioned changes are to be expected only ... where a regular sound change would create functional inefficiency, or paradigm opacity' (*ibid.*).

Whatever the merits of the particular argument and the claims made (I will go into the matter of substance below), we can of course immediately object to the apparently naïve notion of 'correctness' evidenced by expressions like 'certainty is established', or 'the accuracy ... is shown'. Campbell's arguments are (putatively) empirical, not mathematical, and there is no certainty on empirical matters. Or if one wants to claim that an answer is 'right', rather than merely slightly better than some other, this requires the setting up of an epistemology to justify that notion. (Remember that Kant thought Newton's view of the universe was *a priori* true!)[5]

Now one might take these objectionable expressions as merely figurative or sloppy usage; one might, that is, if Campbell didn't prevent us from doing so by an explicit statement. He says (403) that his argument is based on '*clincher* cases which require as the only alternatives either the recognition of the tendencies or advocacy of anarchy' (emphasis his). I will take up the implications of 'clincher cases' below. But first observe that this view ultimately reduces, as Campbell himself admits later on, to a rather more half-hearted notion of the value of non-nomic regularities, like the one I discussed above (§2.5). That is, we must pay attention to tendencies (despite the short-sighted positivist idea that they are valueless), because in the end their recognition, if we're lucky, will allow us to VINDICATE the positivist position: only this recognition will enable us to solve 'the actuation problem'. That is, there is still hope for (future) D-N explanations using as a basis Campbell's principles of 'communicative efficiency', 'maximum transparency', etc. (404). So despite his advocacy of tendencies, Campbell is really a legalist at heart; he thinks (if I read him right) that study of them will lead to the discovery of 'laws', and that this is the main justification for engaging in it.

But Campbell, like many others interested in tendencies, is not satisfied with long-term goals; and in the pursuit of short-term ones (making tendencies respectable) he short-circuits the rationality of his whole programme by an illegitimate totalitarian move. He claims, as we saw above, that we must EITHER accept his functional explanations, OR advocate anarchy.[6] Now there is no explanation whatever that is so good

---

5   I am not (necessarily) suggesting that anyone who claims validity of any kind for an assertion is bound to put his epistemology on the table: as long as he shows respect for and knowledge of the relation that his position stands in to current metascientific discussion – if that position is one that has been challenged, and is still controversial. Surely anyone who seriously claims 'certainty' as the result of a theoretical argument SHOULD be required to say what he means, and to defuse the classical arguments against this kind of claim. I am not objecting – at this point – to the set of assumptions that Campbell shares with other functionalists about what kinds of arguments are admissible; I am quarrelling with his claims about the epistemic status of the explanations themselves. My attack on the assumptions behind functionalism itself (the 'paradigm' if you will) comes later.

6   I must say that I am not convinced that 'anarchy' of a sort is necessarily a bad thing – though there are heuristic (as well as other) reasons for trying to avoid it. At the very least linguists might ultimately be allowed the same latitude of sloppiness that speakers get away with.

that the only choice is between it and nothing. This is the 'how else?' strategy, which is not a form of argument, but a confession of imaginative poverty on its proponent's part, and an imputation of that same poverty to his audience (cf. the further discussions of this strategy in Botha 1971: 125ff; and Linell 1974: §15.1). Campbell does, to be sure, produce a number of cases that CAN be explained on functional grounds, but his argument gains nothing by its exclusive disjunctiveness. There always remain at least two other possibilities: Campbell hasn't yet thought of a better explanation, or linguistic change really is anarchic. Anarchy cannot be ruled out empirically by methodological ploys.

3.3 Functional explanation, 1: preservation of contrast

But leaving aside this question of rhetoric (if all argumentative questions aren't in fact ultimately about rhetoric), there are still serious difficulties with functional explanation, which deserve close scrutiny. The main one – which I will return to in a number of connections – is that it is always irreducibly *post hoc* (in the sense of being totally non-predictive), and the functions invoked often seem rather fishy and devoid of principled support.[7]

The basic problem is null strategy. If an explanation like Campbell's of the retention of /s/ in augmentless Greek futures (however much it makes sense on the face of it) is to be accepted as explanatory, it should be the case that phenomena like this are predictable. In other words, there should not be 'dysfunctional' syncretisms brought about by sound change; or if there are, then (presumably) they should be remedied.

If one wants to argue for functional principles, then it is necessary to have at least something to say about cases where the 'dysfunction' brought about by (say) a regular sound change is not remedied (since we all know that cases like this are exceedingly common);[8] and this usually

---

[7] This is not necessarily to assert that there might not be functions of various kinds; though the objections at the moment are close to insuperable (see below, and the appendix to this chapter). In fact, the idea of functional motivation for change is distinctly attractive, in the sense that it makes the unintelligible partially intelligible, and produces order out of chaos. But even if I find the idea attractive, I don't think – at least wearing the metascientific hat I now wear – that I ought to, and this is about what one ought to do, not what one would like to do.

[8] Why for instance did the genitive singular and dative singular of $\bar{a}$-stem nouns coalesce in Latin in -*ae* but remain distinct in Greek? Why did the nominative and accusative singular of *u*-stems coalesce in -*u*, and the genitive and dative in -*a* in Old English, whereas the nom/acc remained distinct in Gothic and Old Norse, but not Old High German, but the gen/dat remained distinct in Old High German? Etc.

leads to *ad hoc* strategies (invoking new or 'competing' principles). An example is Campbell's treatment of another change, now familiar through its treatment by Kiparsky (1965) and Anttila (1972): the loss of final -*n* in Estonian. Briefly, in Southern Estonian all -*n* were lost, but in Northern Estonian the -*n* marking the first person singular in verbs was retained, while the rest dropped. The end result of this was that 'Northern Estonian was functionally more efficient for its morphologically conditioned sound change' (391).

This immediately raises the question of what it can possibly mean for a dialect to be 'more efficient' either (a) than it was before, or (b) than some other dialect. I have never seen an intelligible definition. Campbell's answer to this (not really an answer, but at least his comment) is that what was involved here was a case of two different dialects giving differential priority to different functions: 'the northern dialect gave more heed to paradigmatic factors, preserving the distinction between imperatives and 1st per sg verb forms [which would have been lost if all -*n* were dropped], while the southern dialect gave more freedom to phonotactic factors, where the loss of final -*n* produced a more optimal syllable structure' (400). This last remark is a reference to Schane's idea about the optimality of open syllables (cf. §2.6).

The trouble with arguments like this is that you can't lose. What Campbell seems to be saying is that 'paradigm conditions' are important except where something else is. To my mind the virtual invulnerability of functional arguments like this strongly militates (to put it weakly) against their acceptability. And in any case saving Southern Estonian by a principle as feeble as 'optimal syllable structure' simply won't work: consider general facts about Estonian, such as its tolerance of /VCC/ or even /VCCC/ configurations (with 'overlong' consonants). Perhaps the principle here is that open syllables are optimal in final position, but not (necessarily) elsewhere.[9]

---

[9]   Campbell suggests later (401) that one of the reasons for the optimality of CV is 'perceptual': but his example is that 'it is easier to perceive CVCV than ... CC'. But consider 'ease of perception' of final -VN vs. -V syllables: surely a vowel followed by a nasal, with the special timbre induced by nasal coupling, plus the extra segment, is (in a common-sense way) more perceptually salient than a vowel alone. Especially, as in the Estonian case, an unstressed one. Explanation on 'perceptual' grounds is in any case dubious, for the same reasons as the other types I treat in this chapter: the tradition of explanation stemming in part from the pioneering paper of Bever & Langendoen (1972) suffers from all the faults that characterize other forms, and I will refrain from going over the same ground again here. It should in any case be obvious from the arguments below how one could apply the strategy in this case.

3.4 Functional explanation, 2: minimization of allomorphy

So far, in the kinds of examples I have been looking at, it has turned out to be impossible to predict particular implementations of a function out of a set of choices, to predict priorities among competing functions, or even to predict any implementation at all. The 'theory of functional change' (if there is any such thing) is apparently so constructed that almost anything can be a supporting example, and nothing can be a counter-example. In this section and the following I will explore the consequences of this a bit further, with an eye toward suggesting that 'function' itself – in reference to language – is an incoherent concept.

Let us start off with two famous eponymous principles: 'Sturtevant's Paradox' and 'Humboldt's Universal'. The first (Sturtevant 1947: 109) says that phonetic change is regular but produces irregularity (e.g. variant allomorphy), while analogical change is irregular but produces regularity (by ironing out the results of phonetic change). The second (christened by Vennemann) is the principle of 'one-meaning-one-form' (Anttila 1972: 92, 98, 100–1) or 'form-meaning biuniqueness' (Ohlander 1976) or minimization of allomorphy within a paradigm (Kiparsky 1971: 588; Campbell 1975: 399–400). The 'function' of analogical change, apparently, is to arrange things in accordance with this principle. Now there is no doubt that the principle serves as a possible explanation for the cases discussed by Anttila, Campbell, etc. But let us look at a fairly typical problem that arises if we try to apply the principle to developments over a long period of time.

Consider this portion of the paradigm of a typical liquid-stem class I weak verb in Pre-OE, here the ancestor of OE *tellan* 'tell':

(1)   PRESENT   PRETERITE
    Infinitive: taljan ⎫
       1 sg: talja ⎬ talda
       3 sg: taliθ ⎭

(For details see Campbell 1959: §750.) Here we have one stem allomorph throughout the paradigm, as shown in these characteristic forms (the -*j*- is a 'thematic' element: cf. Lass & Anderson 1975: appendix 2). In the subsequent development, however, a number of changes take place, which have a drastic effect on the paradigm: I present them below in a somewhat simplified form.

(i) West Germanic Gemination: consonants are geminated after a short vowel and before a following -*j*-. This gives **talljan*, **tallja*, but leaves **taliθ*, **talda* unchanged. We now have two stem allomorphs, **tall-* and **tal-*.

(ii) Anglo-Frisian Brightening: **a* > **æ* in certain contexts (cf. Lass & Anderson 1975: ch. II and refs.). So we now have **tælljan*, **tælljæ*, **tæliθ* and **tældæ*. The stem allomorphs are now **tæll-*, **tæl-*.

(iii) Breaking: **æ* > **æu* before -*ld*.[10] The only form affected is **tældæ*, which becomes **tæulde*. We now have three stem allomorphs, **tæll-*, **tæ-*, **tæul-*.

(iv) *i*-umlaut: **æ* > **e* before *i*, *j*. We now have **telljan*, **teliθ*, but **tæuldæ*. The stem allomorphs are thus **tell-*, **tel-*, **tæul-*.

(v) Deletion of -*j*- and reduction of unstressed vowels. Up to now, despite the proliferation of alternants, the paradigm has been 'transparent': the environments for gemination, umlaut and breaking remain on the surface. But now, except for breaking, the paradigm is opaque. A further rule (tentatively called 'diphthong height harmony' in Lass & Anderson 1975: ch. III) adjusts the -*u* in the *æu* diphthong to *a*, giving a sequence spelled in the later orthography as *ea*. The forms are now (historical) *tellan*, *telle*, *teleþ*, *tealde*: still three allomorphs, but an opaque paradigm.

(vi) Loss of the effects of Anglo-Frisian Brightening and breaking. Toward the end of the OE period *ea* and *æ* disappear and merge (in the dialects ancestral to the modern 'standard' ones) with *a*. The paradigm is now *tellan*, *teleþ*, *talde*.

(vii) Lengthening of vowels before sonorant + homorganic voiced stop (cf. Lass 1974a and refs.): thus *talde* > *tālde*. The stem allomorphs are now *tell-*, *tel-*, *tāl-*.

(viii) Loss of long consonants: in early ME (cf. Kurath 1956) the C/CC opposition seems to have been lost, through simplification of the geminates. The ME paradigm at this point is thus *telen*, *teleþ*, *tālde* (unstressed -*a* > -*e*). One stem allomorph goes, and we now have *tel-*, *tāl-*.

(ix) Rounding of *ā*: in the early fourteenth century (Jordan 1934: §44) *ā* > *ǭ* in the non-northern dialects. This gives *telen*, *tǫlde*, and with later loss of unstressed -*e* and of the infinitive ending, *tel*, *tǫld*.

---

[10] The famous ordering problem (why does breaking occur only before original -*ll* as in *eall* 'all' but not before -*ll* from gemination, even though breaking follows gemination historically?) is not germane to the simple historical chronicle here. (Cf. Hogg 1971, and Lass & Anderson 1975: appendix 2.)

(x) Great Vowel Shift and later changes: ME *tǭld* > ENE /toːld/; later developments give /tould/. The present stem is still /tɛl–/.

There has, in most dialects of English, been no paradigmatic levelling: the verb still has two stem allomorphs, /tɛl–/ and /toul–/. In many Scots dialects, however (whose developments do not include (vii) and (ix), so that we expect *tell*, **tauld* /tɔld/ – or **taud* /tɔd/ because of special developments connected with post-vocalic *l*), there has been levelling: we get *tell, tellt*. (A /t/-allomorph of the regular past is quite common in many forms of British English after stems in /-l/, e.g. *spelt, smelt*, alongside *spelled, smelled*; and of course there is the 'sub-regularity' involving /t/ in sonorant-final stems with a shortened vowel in the past, e.g. *felt, dreamt*. So there is something of a gesture in the direction of 'levelling' here.)

Looking at the overall (non-Scots) history, we find that out of ten changes affecting this paradigm, the score is as follows:

(2)   (a) 'Pro-Humboldt' (decreasing the number of allomorphs): (viii) = 1.
      (b) 'Anti-Humboldt' (increasing the number of allomorphs): (i), (iii) = 2.
      (c) 'Humboldt-Neutral' or 'Structure-Preserving' (keeping the number of allomorphs constant): (ii), (iv), (v), (vi), (vii), (ix), (x) = 7.

Of the seven changes under (2c), however, we observe that five – (iii), (iv), (vii), (ix), (ix) – serve to increase the phonetic difference between the allomorphs. And one of them, (vii), effects a rather important change (in reference to paradigmatic phonology) by establishing a /V/ ~ /Vː/ alternation. Further, only changes (vi) and (viii) decrease this difference. Note also that the essential present/preterite distinction is maintained ('redundantly') in both stem and endings at all times from (iii) on.

Let me add another example before commenting. Consider the histories of OE class I weak verbs with historical velar-final stems, the ancestors of e.g. *bring, think, teach, seek, buy* (OE *bringan, þencan, tǣcan, sēcan, bycgan* < **braŋgjan, *θaŋkjan, *taikjan, *sōkjan, *bugjan*), preterites respectively *brōhte, þōhte, tǣhte, sōhte, bohte*. These verbs have also had a history in which the two stem allomorphs have become increasingly dissimilar. Look for instance at the gradual dissociation of allomorphs in *bring*:

(3)

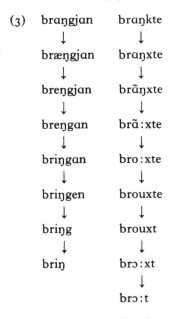

braŋgjan	braŋkte
↓	↓
bræŋgjan	braŋxte
↓	↓
breŋgjan	brãŋxte
↓	↓
breŋgan	brã:xte
↓	↓
briŋgan	bro:xte
↓	↓
briŋgen	brouxte
↓	↓
briŋg	brouxt
↓	↓
briŋ	brɔ:xt
	↓
	brɔ:t

(Forms opposite each other are not necessarily chronologically parallel.) Note also that when 'analogical' reformations occur, e.g. in children's speech, it is I think the experience of most English speakers that the analogies are not always the type that produce forms like **bringed*; we get **brang* or **brung* at least as often, i.e. analogy to another 'non-biunique' paradigm.

Considering all this, we can now say confidently that Humboldt's Universal 'explains' what happened in Scots; but that it simply 'failed to apply' in *tell/told, bring/brought*, etc. Back to square one. Since non-applications are both possible and common, and there seem to be no well-defined principles governing them, how can we argue that any particular case of APPLICATION genuinely involves the principle, and isn't just a random event? What is the status of 'tendencies' when they are also invoked as 'causes'? If they are causes, then they are neither necessary nor sufficient. What kind are they, then, and what kind of causal argument (for that is surely what its proponents see it as) is one invoking Humboldt's Universal? Is it in fact possible to argue against it? If not, if it can simply be implemented or not at will, what good is it as an explanation of what happened in any particular instance?[11]

---

[11] Cf. my arguments against the possibility of assigning genuine 'etymologies' to proper names, on more or less the same grounds (Lass 1973).

Some other questions come to mind. Why do natural languages exhibit so much allomorphy (making life interesting for generative phonologists), if minimizing it is such an important principle? Why are changes that violate the principle so common and so apparently tolerable, and why do 'instantiations' of the principle virtually always show up as rather inefficient *post facto* mopping-up operations? And even more important, why do languages tolerate 'bad' situations long enough to let them get into the historical record? Or do we have to add some kind of time-factor, e.g. that 'excessive allomorphy' is tolerable for *n* time-units, and then the principle takes over?

I would maintain that in this area, at least, we have no respectable notion either of 'causality' or 'explanation'; we haven't a clue as to what (if anything) causes or constrains linguistic change.

3.5 Functional explanation, 3: avoidance of homophony

It has frequently been asserted that there is a kind of pragmatically oriented 'therapeutic' motivation of certain (usually sporadic) changes or exceptions to changes, namely 'avoidance of (excessive/harmful) homophony'. This view has a reasonably long history, going back at least to Gilliéron (1921); it has been taken up again recently by M. L. Samuels (1965, 1972) and Lyle Campbell (1975), among others. Let me add another example to the already long list beginning with cats in Gallo-Romance – one which has not as far as I know been discussed in detail before (for obvious reasons, as will become apparent).[12]

Consider the vocalism of English *shut*. This comes from a Germanic **skutjan* (cf. OFris. *sketta*, MLG *schütten*, G. *schützen*), and its immediate etymon is OE *scyttan*. Now the usual development of OE /y/ is NE /ɪ/: *bridge, din, dint, dip, shippen* 'byre', *stilt*, etc. (OE *brycg, dynn, dynte, dyppan, scyppen, stylte*). NE /ɪ/ represents OE /i/ as well (*sit, bit,* etc.), so that overall we have a merger via a simple unrounding rule – at least in the North and East of England:

(4)   OE   ME   NE

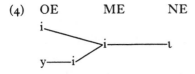

But OE /y/ had a threefold ME development (cf. Jordan 1934: §§39ff): it unrounded in (roughly) the North and East, came down as

---

[12] There are hints, however, in Samuels (1972: 143). See below.

ME /e/ in Kent (actually the /y/ > /e/ change here goes back to OE), and remained /y/ in the South-West and South-West Midland dialects, normally spelled *u*. But this *u* did not rhyme with *u* that represented OE /u/ (*but*, *cup*, etc.): i.e. it was ME /y/ in those areas, not ME /u/. This last point is important, because of the number of modern forms with *u*-spellings that go back to OE /y/, but have NE /ʌ/, i.e. ME /u/.

This three-way split is supposed, in the traditional Anglicist mythology, to account for spelling/pronunciation disparities in forms like *busy* < OE *bysig* ('SW spelling' but 'N/E pronunciation'), and the like. That is, these forms represent a peculiarly complex kind of borrowing. But this can't be true for historical /y/ forms with NE /ʌ/: since the ME *u*-spellings represent a graphic merger only, not a phonetic one. When *u*-forms were lost in ME in the *u*-areas, they were replaced by *i*-forms (Wyld 1927: §§158-9). This means that any (etymological) OE /y/ forms with NE /ʌ/ cannot be 'borrowings'; they must go back to ME /u/ < OE /y/, not ME /y/.

That is, they are the result of a sporadic rule, which applied even in the *i*-areas, whereby some OE /y/ went to /u/, not /i/, in ME. This rule is in fact the norm for the ME interpretation of Anglo-Norman short /y/ (*just*, *judge*, *study*, *rush*, v.). But it also applies to a good number of native forms, e.g. *crutch*, *cudgel*, *rush* 'sedge' < OE *crycc*, *cycgel*, *rysc*. (I will return to the two *rush* forms below.)

But back to *shut*. It is clear that if the 'normal' development had taken place, the result would be *shit*. This is because OE /y/ falls together with OE /i/, and *shit* is from an /i/-grade (IE zero-grade) (preterite plural or supine) stem of a class I strong verb (*scītan*, supine *-sciten*: cf. NEng/Scots *shite*, G. *scheißen*). This particular homophony would be, I should think, about as 'pernicious' as any.

But the argument that the /y/ > /u/ change in *shut* is DUE TO the need to avoid homophony with *shit* falls down on a number of grounds, the first weak but at least entertaining, and the others stronger and rather duller.

(i) There is at least one record of a dialect in which this very merger seems to have occurred; in, of all places, an Elizabethan Scriptural Dictionary (William Patton's *The Calendar of Scripture*, 1575), where on f. 183 we read: 'Conclusus: ... Thrust bak. Shit vp' (I owe this example to Ken Miner). It COULD be a typographical error, of course.

(ii) There are cases where the very same sporadic change has PRODUCED homophones, e.g. *rush* 'sedge' < OE *rysc*, *rush* 'hasten' < OF *re(h)usser, ruser* (where $u = $ /y/).[13]

But, the proponent of 'therapeutic' change might counter, (ii) is not at all the same thing as the *shut*/*shit* case. The latter involves 'taboo', but this doesn't. All right, I reply, then what about U.S. *ass* 'arse' < OE *ears* and *ass* 'donkey' < OE *assa*? Both are /æs/ (cf. Southern English /ɑːs/ vs. /æs/, or Scots /ars/ ~ /ers/ vs. /as/). Is it a matter of 'degree of taboo'? And worse, notice that in the *ass* case, the change that PRODUCED the homophony is a sporadic and relatively rare one: the usual reflex of OE *earC* in these dialects is /ɑːrC/ (*sharp, harp*), not /æC/.[14]

In this instance, however, my adversary might counter by pointing out that the NON-homophony of *arse* and *ass* in British English is due to the failure of a regular sound change. In the seventeenth century the two forms would have been /ærs/ and /æs/; lengthening before /r/ and before /fθs/ would have given /æːrs/ and /æːs/; loss of /r/ would have left both forms /æːs/, and later changes would have produced /ɑːs/ for both. This then means that avoidance of indelicate homophony must be culture-specific: we have a case of sporadic failure among the polite British, while the grosser colonials were able to tolerate, even welcome, the homophony.[15] This would at least parochialize the principle.

(iii) This brings me to my next point, which is that all such explanations seem to be *ad hoc*. Samuels, for instance (1972: 143) goes through the whole catalogue of unexpected /ʌ/ and /ɛ/ forms for OE /y/ (the latter of which could be borrowing from the SE, since they are normally spelled with *e*), and comes up with the following motivations: (a) 'conditioned phonetic variants': forms with following palatals or /r/ (he doesn't state how palatals can 'condition' the retraction of a high front vowel); (b), getting rather more desperate, 'avoidance of homonymy': here we have *left* < OE *lyfte* (because of *lift*), 'and perhaps *dull* (cf. *dill, dell*)', as well as *hemlock* (why not **humlock*?) – '(cf. *him*: apart from *hymn* there are no common words commencing with /hɪm/)'; (c) taboo: here we have *shut, shuttle*; (d) 'phonaesthetic reasons: *knell* (cf. *bell*)'. He adds (143: note 1) that the 'residue' of forms, including

---

[13] Phonological change is of course constantly producing homophones through merger. Campbell replies (incomprehensibly) to this objection by claiming that 'it begs the actuation question' (1975: 403). I suspect however that it is Campbell who is fudging the issue by refusing to give a straight answer.

[14] For some discussion of the history of *ass* and related forms see Eustace (1972).

[15] In this general vein, it seems curious that the 'avoidance' principle fails to extend (to any massive degree) to 'harmful polysemy' as well: e.g. *prick, ball, snatch, screw, plough, lay, Dick, pussy* etc. Or is it just that no one has worked on it yet?

cudgel, fledge, shed, might, by 'phonaesthetic research', be shown to belong under (d).

But what determines whether homophony in any given case is either 'harmful' or 'excessive'? How much of it, and where (in what grammatical classes, lexical fields, etc.) can a language tolerate? Surely until there are some principles that can be stated in advance, any such 'explanation' is suspect, if not vacuous.

In an attempt to salvage homophony as a factor, especially in the light of Wang's claim (1969: 10) that it is 'ancillary and particularistic', Samuels (1972: 67–8) attempts to show that there are factors that militate against 'harmfulness', such as meanings different enough to prevent ambiguity, membership in different word classes or in different specialized fields of the same class, so that their 'ranges of collocation' will not overlap, etc. But homophones do persist; and Samuels finally comes up with an argument that with the greatest charity can only be called absurd:

However, the mere fact of the survival today of homophones that are not obviously safeguarded ... does not prove that they are no disadvantage. For example, the verbs *lie* 'recline' and 'tell lies' are both intransitive, and *lie* 'recline' need not ... be followed by an adverb of place. Here, the fact that *he lies/is lying* is often replaced by *he tells lies/is telling a lie* (or by *he's a liar*) shows that interference exists.

If an argument like this can 'show' something, then no wonder survival is such a 'mere fact'. Can the existence of periphrases really be taken as evidence for 'interference' when the pattern of periphrasis is a productive one (*he's napping/taking a nap, bathing/taking a bath, shaving/ taking a shave*)? What evidence is there, anyhow, that the use of *telling lies* or *liar* is a 'replacement', and not just a free stylistic choice?

(iv) A more general, in this case logical, objection. This holds for nearly all functional explanations, whatever the function involved, but I bring it in here since the homophony cases furnish a particularly transparent example. In every instance I know of, from Gilliéron on, the strategy seems to be the same:

(a) Here is a 'function' X;
(b) Implementation of X would cause Y;
(c) Y happened;
(d) Therefore there has been an implementation of X.

Logically this seems to be of the form:

(a) p ⊃ q

(b) q

(c) ∴ p

That is, it is an instance of the fallacy of affirming the consequent.

(v) Finally, even if speakers do avoid homophones, how do they do it? If we take most avoidance arguments (even good ones, relatively speaking, like some of those in Samuels 1965 or Campbell 1975) at face value, it seems that speakers avoid homophones by prolepsis, i.e. by taking avoiding action in advance. That is, since the homophones, in these cases, don't materialize, we must credit speakers with the ability to compute the potential effects of sound change in advance, and shunt (potentially) offending items into the requisite minor rule ('If I let /y/ unround, 'shut' will come out *shit*; better retract to /u/').

But this is surely absurd. And in any case, since there seems to be no real evidence that sound change ever takes place by 'categorial' rule addition, but rather that it does so by allophonic drift (cf. Lass 1976b, 1978), such a procedure would be impossible.

So the only mechanism left is for speakers actually to produce the offending articles, and then, having discovered what they've done, to remove them ('My God, I've just said "please *shit* the door"'; better change it to *shut*'). But in this case, how does the speaker know that his /i/ is in fact a ME /i/ from OE /y/, and therefore that the etymologically appropriate vowel is /u/? This difficulty would seem to make even relatively persuasive cases for *post facto* implementation of function like those in Vincent (1978) problematical: Vincent says (416) that 'sound change can only proceed remorselessly on, leaving the speaker to do the best he can to mend any pieces of language that get broken in the process'. Any possibility of giving this claim an interpretation will depend on it being actually possible to recognize a broken piece of language; I assert that it isn't, and will supply the requisite arguments in §§3.7–3.8.

I submit that anyone who wants to argue seriously for the avoidance of homophony as an explanation for irregular changes must find a way of neutralizing the objections I have been setting out.[16] Merely on the

---

[16] One functionally oriented linguist, Chen (1974: 63) admits that because of mergers that do occur, 'the teleologic argument based on semantic distinctiveness or avoidance of homophony' is undercut; and that 'the inability to define what would constitute crucial counter-evidence renders the functionalist explanation rather weak' (!). But, he says, current debate on rule-ordering has turned up cases where 'a functional explanation seems to be the only viable one' – e.g. where in some Austrian dialects two counter-feeding rules are needed (at least according to one particular analysis) to prevent *Wahn*/*Waden* from collapsing in [vã:]. The old problem crops up again: when it works, we have 'function'; but the mergers are still unaccounted for. See below.

evidence provided so far, if my arguments are sound, the proponents of any functional motivation whatever for linguistic change have to do one of two things:

(i)   Admit that the concept of function is *ad hoc* and particularistic, and give up;

or

(ii)   Develop a reasonably rigorous, non-particularistic theory with at least some predictive power; not a theory based merely on *post hoc* identification plus a modicum of strategies for weaseling out of attempted disconfirmations.

This is the picture as I see it: (i) is of course the easy way out, and (ii) seems to be the minimum required if (i) is not acceptable. I am myself not entirely happy with (i), and it should probably not be taken up – though failing a satisfactory response to (ii) it seems inevitable. But at least the responsibilities of a properly explanatory theory are fairly clear; though it will have in addition to cope with the objections I am about to produce.

These objections are less linguistic and more generally philosophical, though questions about the nature of language are involved; there are serious problems involved in any attempt (not necessarily a narrowly 'functionalist' one) at arguing for any teleological motivation for language change, and special ones which I haven't yet touched on involved in the idea of function. I will now turn to these general issues.

3.6 'Teleology of function' and 'teleology of purpose'

I think we can characterize the type of explanation based on 'tendencies', 'naturalness' and the like rather simply. As Andrew Woodfield has suggested (1976: 7), 'appeals to natural tendencies are non-explanatory unless there is or could be evidence for them which is independent of their alleged manifestations'. The problem is that in the cases we have been looking at – especially the ones in this chapter – there is no evidence for the goalhood of any particular goal other than the fact that a sequence of actions seems to move toward it. This makes 'goal' an empty notion: a goal is simply something that stands at the end of a sequence that (apparently) leads to it. This confuses, as Woodfield argues (1976: 85) the concepts 'goal' and '*de facto* terminus'. The invalidating fallacy is *post hoc, ergo propter hoc*.

Thus given, say, a 'law' of the form 'languages tend to avoid harmful homophony', it is analytic that anything that could count as an 'avoidance' is an instantiation of the law, and no counter-example refutes it, since 'tend' functions as a 'blocking device' (Botha 1971) to prevent disconfirmation. A blocking device is simply a clause that weakens a theory so as to prevent disconfirmation by negative evidence; thus all claims about the existence of 'developmental laws' which are not nomically binding are empty, and no invocation of such a law is an explanation.

So one invalidating factor in many teleological arguments is the failure to distinguish between goals and termini. This confusion probably invalidates the rather elaborate case I made (Lass 1974a) for the existence of a 'conspiracy' to lose phonemic vowel length in English. In that paper I adduced a long sequence of changes in the history of English, each of which resulted in an increase in the redundancy of vowel quantity. That is, each change (like shortening before CC, lengthening in open syllables, etc.) produced a neutralization of the original free vowel length in some environment. All the changes, while formally unrelated to each other for the most part, nonetheless conduced, in a 'conspiratorial' fashion, toward the increase of complementary distribution between long and short vowels. I claimed that this sequence over time was 'orthogenetic', i.e. an example of 'straight-line' (directed, finalistic) development.

My basic justification for this claim was a form of argument that I now regard as invalid: an attempt to elevate the 'how else?' strategy (cf. §3.2) to a principle. I suppose that if nothing else the paper is now interesting as an example of an explicit formulation of this (mistaken) principle, the only one I know of. The methodological justification was (Lass 1974a: 312):

I would claim that there are cases where events precede (in time) their 'final' causes. The classic instance will be where a given synchronic state will be insightfully interpretable (or interpretable at all) only as either the aimed-at result of a series of past events, or as a stage in the implementation of that result. And the past events themselves – i.e. without reference to their ultimate goal – will be 'irrational', that is unconnected, inexplicable. They must be viewed, in order to make sense, as steps in the implementation of the synchronic state to be explained, and that state itself serves as *their* explanation. [Emphasis in original]

One 'metajustification' for this is that arguments of this kind are 'coincidence-avoiders' (1974a: 314): '... given some phenomenon, and a choice between a null hypothesis and *some* principled explanation, the explanation (if it's not idiotic) is preferable, at least as an interim attempt' (emphasis in original). Such attempts also have heuristic value (*ibid.*): 'a good guess is better than nothing... If we do away with such guessing, we lose a valuable heuristic, and fail even to identify certain interesting questions.' There may indeed be some justification for such strategies in one's private (pre-publication) work, or under the conditions of a different metascientific outlook from the one I am adopting here. But in this context they are invalid.[17]

Nigel Vincent (1968) has come up with a very nice essentially methodological argument against my (1974a) analysis. He claims that it is an example of (inadmissible) 'teleology of purpose', i.e. Aristotelian teleology involving backwards causation. What is allowed is 'teleology of function', which does not involve this apparent temporal paradox.

But whether teleology of purpose is allowed or not must surely depend on the nature of the domain involved: I don't think anyone but the blindest behaviourist would deny that it is possible for human beings to take action with respect to future goals, i.e. to intend to reach some goal. In this sense we do not have 'backwards causation', but 'motivation', presumably based on knowledge of the world and one's own capabilities, inductive expectation, etc. In language history, on the other hand, if change does not involve (conscious) human purpose (which I think can be accepted without argument), then teleology of purpose is of course not admissible (unless one personifies 'language' itself as an agent, posits an intervening agent with a purpose, like God, or, like Itkonen (1978), allows for the possibility of 'unconscious rationality').

But the problem cannot be solved so easily; even the admission of teleology of function ends up raising the possibility of purpose (as the earlier discussions of 'avoidance' or 'minimization', etc. suggest). In fact, my argument in what follows will be that Vincent did not go far enough: that even teleology of function raises so many epistemological

---

[17] For a spirited defence of the position I took in Lass (1974a), and of teleological explanation in general, cf. Itkonen (1978; especially §8). Itkonen's paper arrived too late to be incorporated into the body of this book, but his defence does raise some interesting issues: particularly the notion that 'functional' change can be seen as the operation of 'unconscious rationality' (45), and that this leads to a lack of predictability since 'rational behaviour is unpredictable ... and irreducibly so' (*ibid.*). But Itkonen also takes the view that 'explanation equals systematization' (36), which I do not accept (cf. §5.5 below); though I do accept the importance of systematization, of course (chapter 5 below, *passim*).

and methodological difficulties that it too is inadmissable in the explanation of language change.

3.7 How do we define a function? 'Survival' and 'fitness'

Let me now try and generalize the preceding arguments by discussing the question of 'teleology of function' in broader terms. We seem to have reached the conclusion that any teleological argument in which a goal is not identifiable independently of the behavioural manifestations leading to it is not explanatory. For instance, the only evidence for the principle of homophone avoidance in natural languages is the fact that events occur in language histories whose non-occurrence would have led to homophony (or events fail to occur whose occurrence would have led to it). But in the absence of a quantification of 'tolerable' homophony, 'harmful' becomes synonymous with 'having been avoided' (or in less theoretically objectionable language, 'not in fact having been produced'), and 'tolerable' becomes synonymous with simply being there (*pace* Samuels' claim that even the ones that are there are bad).

So how would we go about defining a piece of behaviour as actually having a function? In his detailed and useful discussion, Woodfield (1976: 128) argues that in order for us to be able to identify something as a function of a particular behaviour, we must at least be able to say that the behaviour 'characteristically and normally' contributes to the achievement of a particular goal. This has certainly not been shown for linguistic change as related to the achievement of ease of articulation, optimization of syllable structure, paradigm simplification, avoidance of homophony, etc.

One possible definition of a function is that it is something whose implementation can be seen as 'contributing to the survival and maintenance of an organism' (Woodfield, 115). But, this gets us into the familiar circularity that bedevils ('classical') evolutionary functionalism in biology as well:

(i) The fact that an organism is alive at a given time shows that it is 'fit to survive'; i.e. 'this (living) organism is fit' is analytic.

(ii) In the case of an organism that has failed to survive, the only ones where we actually know the precise cause of extinction usually do not give evidence of maladaptation in the usual sense: i.e. for the immanent 'unfitness' of the organism itself. I will return to this below.

Let us consider how this looks if we substitute languages for organisms. The fact that a language is used by a speech community is, I take it, *eo ipso* evidence that it is functionally appropriate to be so used. The fact that a language is no longer spoken can be due to a number of different causes; but no one has seriously argued – or provided good evidence – that maladaptation to speakers' needs is one of them. There are three basic reasons why a language can die, I think, and only two of them lead to genuine 'death':

(i)   Through externally conditioned replacement (conquest, political pressure, shift of prestige norms in a bilingual community, etc.). This would account for the extinction of Germanic in France, Celtic in Lowland Scotland, various American Indian languages, etc.

(ii)   Trivially, through extinction of all its speakers.

(iii)   Through normal (internal) processes of change, by which it 'becomes another language'.

Cases (i) and (ii) are 'accidental' or contingent in the same way that most extinctions of biological species in historical times seem to be. The passenger pigeon, dodo, and great auk did not become extinct because they were 'maladapted' (except in the odd sense that being edible and non-bullet-proof is maladaptive; and this doesn't count because edibility is not an inherent character, and it is not available to birds to become bullet-proof by normal evolutionary processes). If for instance the passenger pigeon had been maladapted, it would not have been as common as it was; by all criteria except edibility and vulnerability to shot it was a superbly adapted and successful organism. It is rather the case that human technology and greed were such that nothing could have survived under those precise conditions. (One could perhaps argue here that the predator was maladapted to the function of maintaining its prey population.) I would therefore count such an extinction as of no evolutionary significance – i.e. as not constituting relevant evidence for any adaptiveness arguments. It comes under the actuarial heading of 'natural disaster' or 'act of God'.[18]

The same is clearly true of 'language death' (cf. Dressler 1972;

---

[18] One could think of many parallel examples. Say an atom bomb was dropped on the small area in SW China that constitutes the whole range of the giant panda. This would wipe out the population at one blow, but would not be the basis for a (biological) argument against the panda's 'fitness'. By most everyday criteria, in fact, the panda is strikingly 'unfit': it breeds slowly, takes a long time to mature, is limited to a highly

Dorian 1973). It is not any immanent properties of Breton or East Sutherland Gaelic that have led to their present state of decline, but a combination of contingent factors like the size and influence of the Breton and Sutherland Gaelic speaking communities, the political situation in France and Scotland, the history of these minority groups, etc.

In case (iii) the vacuity of survival arguments is clearest: if it were true that language change in general is functional, then it would be true that (as some Prague scholars think) the history of language is 'adaptive' history. And this would mean – since as far as we know languages all change continuously – that no language is ever 'adapted' or 'fit', but is continuously attempting to become so (and never quite making it). This could of course be maintained on purely metaphysical (*a priori*) grounds, e.g. on the basis of a belief that the only thing that produces change is striving after the fulfilment of goals (a position that seems to be approached in Itkonen 1978). But no one has yet produced any rational basis for such a theory: no one has ever identified independently the stigmata of 'unfit' languages, except of course *post* (and *ad*) *hoc*: 'They wouldn't have changed if they'd been fit.' This is surely unacceptable. The implication would be, for instance, that Old High German 'evolved into' Middle High German because it was no longer adapted to the needs of its speakers, and the same for Vulgar Latin and the Romance vernaculars, etc.

But this view has a further, and undesirable, implication. Unless we attribute all adaptive change to precognition ('If we lose our case endings and don't stabilize our word order, we won't be able to tell subjects from objects'), we must admit, even insist on, the possibility of massive 'communicative failure', gross enough to require action ('We've lost the subject/object distinction; better fix the word order and get it back'). No one, to my knowledge, has ever demonstrated an actual case of this, though it has been suggested as a possibility (cf. the brief discussion of this problem in Weinreich, Labov & Herzog 1968: 100–1). Certainly some such view underlies Jespersen's notion of 'progress' in language (e.g. 1964: chs. XVII–XVIII), but his criteria are purely esthetic

---

specialized diet but has a digestive system quite unsuited to cope with it, etc. But it has survived. This suggests that even the usual criteria of 'efficiency' etc. are not really relevant, and that 'fitness' is indeed analytic (and empty). I will return to criteria of fitness below (and cf. the epigraph to this chapter).

(avoidance of ambiguity is 'good', etc.), and can't be taken seriously from a communicational point of view. If there are such things as (structurally induced) 'failures', then by the pan-temporal uniformity principle (cf. appendix to chapter 2) they can't belong to the domain of linguistics proper, since they have never been observed in the present and are only true historically; thus functional explanation in this sense would belong to some other discipline, like 'palaeolinguistics'.

3.8 'Paradigmatic natural goods' and the problem of 'dysfunction'

If the only general criterion of function is implementation, then we could argue that all changes are (analytically) functional: otherwise they wouldn't have occurred. Even 'musical chairs' phenomena like cyclic shifts, tone circles, etc. must occur 'for a reason'.[19] Thus the identification of functions is limited only by the cleverness of the people looking for them, and lack of obvious motivation becomes evidence merely of the linguist's dullness and/or lack of insight, or 'the state of our understanding'. (If we had spectacles of the right shade of green we could see leprechauns.) They are not *de facto* evidence for lack of function. The reason I state this position in detail is that, given our current inability to produce an independent identification of a function, this kind of absurdity is inseparable from the assertion that ANY change whatever has a function.

That is: unless it can be shown that a particular change does in fact contribute to the 'survival and maintenance' of a language, we cannot ascribe a function to it. And since there seem, as far as I know, to be no causes of language death that can be shown to have been CAUSED by failure to implement a function, half the argument is missing. We can't show that non-implementation of a function is either a necessary or a sufficient condition for maladaptation, since there are no unequivocal cases of maladaptation (except circularly, if we define change as evidence for it). And, as I have argued, the concept of function is in any case so feeble that if we recognize it in one case, we must perforce do it everywhere, unless we simply single out some functions as 'real' ones by intuition (which is I suspect what most functionalists really do). All functional arguments reduce in the end to counter-factual conditionals –

---

[19] For some arguments to this effect for Grimm's Law see Lass (1974b).

with the interesting property that neither the contrary-to-fact situation nor the condition can ever be known to be realized. They are an instance of what I have called elsewhere the 'If my aunt had wheels she'd be a bicycle' strategy (cf. Lass 1976a: 28).

We cannot in fact distinguish linguistic functions from epiphenomena. To illustrate this, let me take an example of Woodfield's (after Hempel): 'Why . . . is it incorrect to say: "the function of the heart is to make beating noises, relative to the end of making the world noisier"?' (1976: 120). It is intuitively clear (whatever that means) that the 'true function' of the heart is to circulate the blood, while the noise is epiphenomenal; but arguing for it is another matter. According to Woodfield (121), the argument is to be put this way: 'Circulating the blood is a function because it contributes to survival, and survival is, for a living being, a paradigmatic natural good.' Contrariwise (*ibid.*), 'Producing heart sounds is not a function, because it does not contribute to anything good' for the organism.

In linguistics, then, our problem is that we cannot define anything like a 'paradigmatic natural good' for a language, since our record consists only of successful languages: no corpses whose death can be ascribed to immanent properties, no abortions, no monsters.[20] We might sum up by saying that insofar as languages have immanent ends (e.g. to serve as means of communication for speech communities), and insofar as no language has ever been observed (except under conditions of an essentially 'political' nature) that did not fulfil these ends, it makes no sense to consider any synchronic language state or aspect of such a state as 'pathological' or 'maladaptive'. Since all languages are by definition

---

[20] I am referring only to natural languages in the strict sense. If Esperanto were to collapse suddenly this would not prove anything relevant. (The restriction to 'natural languages' *sensu stricto* also excludes changes like Pidgin > Creole, which MAY involve 'function'. My concern, like that of the literature in general, is with native languages of the usual type.) In any case we need a fully developed (or even rudimentary) theory of language teratology before we can spot things that have to be 'remedied'.

One step toward laying the groundwork for a definition of 'functional adequacy' however has been taken by Trudgill (1978), who adduces some evidence suggesting that native languages (here Arvanitika or Greek Albanian) can BECOME, through what he calls 'reverse creolization', in some sense 'inadequate'. But interestingly, the end-result in such cases is not 'functionally motivated change' or 'repair', but replacement by another language. Trudgill's example is in any case one of possible incipient language death in a bilingual community, where the 'causal' factors would seem to lie outside the language itself, in the social context. But this work deserves consideration even in the light of functionalism of the usual type.

'normal', it follows that abnormality is an incoherent notion, and hence that no linguistic change can have a function[21] (cf. §4.10).

3.9 A note on teleology and the system concept

Observe finally that scepticism about teleology or function as an explanatory device in linguistics does not entail any denial whatever of the existence of teleology in general, or any claim that at least some forms of it are beyond rational – even deductive – description and explanation: e.g. mathematical modelling, etc.[22] The advances that have been made in certain aspects of 'general system theory', for instance in the modelling of self-regulating open systems, have shown clearly that this is possible, and even insightful. But my concern here has been more with a 'local' issue, i.e. the structure of particular explanation types in linguistics, and the models they imply. It is obvious that if in fact one can develop a predictive mathematical model for the development, say, of an open system over time, the equations in the model would satisfy the deducibility requirement for D-N explanations (cf. the mathematical treatments of self-equilibrating biological systems in von Bertalanffy 1968: ch. 5). Even 'adaptations' of certain kinds within systems are amenable to mathematical treatment (von Bertalanffy 1968: 45). But the important characteristic of proposals of this kind is

[21] Cf. the definition of function (specifically in the social sciences) in Parsons (1965: 59–60): 'If one has the conception of a homeostatically controlled boundary-maintaining system ... then all one means by functional analysis is a set of classifications of the problems of such a system – either the conditions under which the stability will be maintained or the conditions under which it will be sufficiently disturbed so that it will go into some other state of organization, or one of disorganization.' These two sets of conditions are precisely what cannot be established for natural languages.

[22] These arguments do not apply for instance to functional teleological arguments in biology, which can be shown to be coherent (if not empirical: cf. Woodfield 1976: ch. 8). It is precisely because notions like 'normality' and 'survival' have a fairly consistent empirical interpretation in biology that functional explanation can at least make sense; i.e. because the concept of 'paradigmatic natural good' is definable for an organism, as it is not for a language. But even Woodfield admits (137) that no teleological explanation in biology achieves D-N status: they all remain 'explanation sketches'. Cf. also the comments on biological (especially evolutionary) explanation in Beckner (1967: 157) and Popper (1973: 276). Beckner remarks that 'no defender of the deductive model has succeeded in producing a single plausible example of a historical explanation, expanded with the help of laws, that fully meets the deducibility requirement'. (I will suggest in chapter 4 why this is in fact the case.) Popper's summation is that 'all that has been shown is that such explanations might exist'.

that they stipulate that the behaviour of the system involved be expressible in terms of algorithms, i.e. that it be in principle a deterministic system: thus von Bertalanffy says of teleology that 'it is a form of behaviour which can well be defined in scientific terms and for which the necessary conditions and possible mechanisms can be indicated' (1968: 76).[23] This is pretty obviously not the case with language change.

In fact, even though 'system' is used very loosely in describing various aspects of language, it seems doubtful that the term, in the mathematical sense, is appropriate; its use in linguistics can never be anything more than a false – if sometimes useful – metaphorical extension. I do not think that languages are 'systems' in the technical (systems-theoretical) sense, or that they can be profitably viewed diachronically as if they were. The most this would be likely to do is to give us pseudo-precision, i.e. create a false sense that there are algorithms at the bottom of the garden – when we get there. Von Bertalanffy himself is very much aware of this possibility (1968: 21):

Concepts and models of equilibrium, homeostasis, adjustment, etc., are suitable for the maintenance of systems, but inadequate for phenomena of change, differentiation, evolution, ... production of improbable states, building-up of tensions, self-realization, emergence. ... The theory of open systems applies to a wide range of phenomena ... but a warning is necessary against its expansion to fields for which its concepts are not made.... In the last resort, disappointment results from making what is a useful model in certain respects into some metaphysical reality and 'nothing-but' philosophy ...

We know this already in linguistics from the fate of all 'nothing-but' metaphysics (e.g. Bloomfieldian reductionism).

3.10 Some preliminary conclusions

Within the framework in which I have been arguing (which is essentially a version of the 'unified science' view of explanation: cf. §1.1), I have reached a set of negative conclusions. These concern the nature of the yield – in terms of 'knowledge' – of various fairly standard explanatory

[23] Some philosophers of science (and biologists) have suggested making a distinction between genuine teleology (if it exists), where the goal is externally fixed, and is in some way operative in steering the trajectory toward itself and 'teleonomy' or 'quasi-finalism', which has no such implications (cf. Waddington 1968b).

strategies applied to problems of language change. They can be summed up as follows:

(i)   There are no D-N explanations in historical linguistics, because 'laws' of the appropriate kind do not exist.

(ii)   There are no probabilistic explanations, because these are not explanations in any reasonable sense. They are merely *post hoc* recognitions of sets of conditions that fit certain generalizations, but fail to account in any principled way for the cases that don't fit; they have no 'empirical' status in the strict sense of this term. (If it is the case that (i) is really correct, then probabilistic explanations can't even be salvaged as 'pragmatically defective' D-N explanations, or as 'explanation sketches'.)

(iii) There are no functional explanations, because (a) we have no principled definition of 'dysfunction'; because (b) we therefore cannot define what constitutes a 'function'; and (c) because (derivatively) of (i)–(ii).

As far as any 'straight-line' explanations of linguistic change, we are faced with a total vacuum.[24] This is in fact to be expected, I think, considering the nature of our subject matter. It is also, of course, bound to be a source of intellectual discomfort to many linguists: which means that either they must come up with convincing counter-arguments, or learn to live with things as they are (cf. chapter 5).

---

[24] For somewhat similar conclusions, including sketches for arguments like some of those I have been using, cf. Saussure (1959: Part 3, ch. II, §4).

Four problems related to the question of function

1 Functional load

I will deal in this appendix with four problems related in one way or another to the issue of 'function' in the explanation of linguistic change. I put them in an appendix, not because they are of marginal concern, but because I am not sure how well I understand them, and what their systematic import is – especially with relation to the fairly direct line of argument I have been trying to pursue. But they do all relate, and can be read as discursive footnotes to the main argument.

The first of these concerns function in a fairly elementary way. 'Functional load' can be said to be 'in its simplest expression . . . a measure of the number of minimal pairs which can be found for a given phoneme. More generally . . . it is a measure of the work which two phonemes (or a distinctive feature) do in keeping utterances apart' (King 1967: 831). The relation of this concept to functionalism in the usual sense is fairly straightforward. Consider an extreme view like that of Martinet, who claims (1955: 49) that 'les changements phonétiques ne se produisent pas sans égards aux besoins de la communication', and that 'un des facteurs qui peut déterminer leur direction, et même leur apparition, est la nécessité foncière d'assurer la compréhension mutuelle en conservant les oppositions phonologiques utiles'. If we accept this, we can go further; Martinet argues (54; cf. the discussion in King 1967: 833f) that, all things being equal, 'une opposition . . . qui sert à maintenir distincts des centaines de mots parmi les plus fréquents et les plus utiles n'opposera-t-elle une résistance plus efficace à l'élimination que celle qui ne rend de service que dans un très petit nombre de cas?' This argument rests on the rather dubious assumption that language is solely or merely a maximally efficient tool for communication (cf. below and §4.10). But if we accept it provisionally, we can (as Martinet did not) make it explicit and derive some test implications.[1] I will take up the question of explanatory relevance later: for now let us consider prediction.

In a useful study, King (1967) has derived a set of predictions from Martinet's impressionistic and rather inchoate theory, and confronted them with a fair-sized corpus of data. King derives three subhypotheses from the general one of functional load, as follows (834f):

(i)   'The Weak Point Hypothesis': *ceteris paribus*, 'sound change is more likely to start within oppositions bearing low functional loads', or 'a phoneme of low frequency of occurrence is more likely to be affected by some change than is a high-frequency phoneme'.

(ii) 'The Least Resistance Hypothesis': *ceteris paribus*, if 'there is a tendency for a phoneme x to merge with either ... y or z, then that merger will occur for which the functional load of the merged oppositions is smaller'.

(iii) 'The Frequency Hypothesis': 'if an opposition x ≠ y is destroyed by merger, then that phoneme will disappear ... for which the relative frequency of occurrence is smaller'.[2]

I will not go into the mathematics of King's functional load measure, or his data and computations; the first seems reasonable, and I have no reason to doubt the accuracy of the latter. In a series of phonological changes in Germanic dialects which illustrate the cases (i)–(iii) above, he found the following degrees of support for the three subhypotheses (848): (i), 8 cases for, 13 against; (ii), 4 cases for, 5 against; (iii), 7 cases for, 6 against.

Assuming the correctness of King's measure, and the relevance of the cases treated, the test-implications show the functional load hypothesis to have no predictive value (7:6 in favour is not a 'success'). I conclude that within a D-N framework functional load is not an explanatory concept. Indeed, since its proponents, like those of markedness, have merely adduced certain examples that COULD be taken as explained by it, there is no occasion for surprise at its failures. (In this connection cf. the league-tables for success of markedness predictions in Lass (1975: 478–83). It is important to remember that in the D-N framework the

---

[1] The fact that Martinet did not formalize his theory or attempt to derive test-implications from it is not very surprising, considering his avowed distaste for hypothetico-deductive methods: cf. Martinet (1975), and the discussion in Lass (1976c: 347f).

[2] As Richard Coates has pointed out to me, (iii) must be taken to refer only to a case where the product of the merger is identical to one of x, y.

successes don't count, since it is not in essence 'verificationist': it is the counter-predictions that refute, not the successes – especially when the maximum success-rate is not much over 50 per cent – that confirm.)

Note in addition that the criterion of explanatory relevance has generally not been invoked in functional load theory. The notion is based on a simple and rather sloppy metaphor, with no empirical support that I know of. And this is that in some way it takes 'work' to 'maintain' an opposition, and therefore that it's not worth the effort if it doesn't really pay off. It seems curious, considering what is actually known about changes that do and do not take place, that anyone can take such a simple-mindedly 'economic' view of how language works at all seriously. Certainly any further theory of functional load will have to develop some empirically based theory of 'effort' – as well as adducing genuine reasons for believing that it tends to be minimized.

2 Variation and function

Another difficulty for functionalist theories is the empirical evidence available from studies of change in progress concerning the manner in which it seems to proceed. That is, leaving aside other problems, a functionalist approach might be shown to be plausible if it could be demonstrated that language change (in particular, phonological, since this is the most commonly studied kind) is categorical and abrupt, but not otherwise. But if change in general proceeds by small increments (cf. Labov 1963; Labov, Yaeger & Steiner 1972, etc. and Lass 1976b, 1978), and by means of gradual selection over often fairly long periods of time of particular members of a co-existing set of variants (cf. Labov, etc.), then there is a serious conceptual problem.

Consider: if a change $x > y$ implements some function F, this makes sense if in fact $x > y$ is really the shape of the change. That is, if there is a clear causal nexus between F and not-x, and the development of y. But what if, as is usually the case, $x > y$ is an artefact of a theory that eschews graduality, i.e. that the correspondence $x:y$ is simply turned into a change $x > y$ by the techniques of reconstruction and their controlling theory? And what if the theory, as is also usual, has no place for variation, but assumes only two possible states for each variable, x and not-x, not-y and y? Most often of course, the correspondence $x:y$ is the end-product of a long series of gradual favourings of particular variants, often with many intermediate stages: e.g. $x \sim x' \sim x''$ for some time, then $x' \sim x'' \sim y$, $x'' \sim y$, and finally y to the exclusion of any other derivative of x.

In this case, the first thing that has to be demonstrated (and this is not usually too hard) is that the gradient $x > x' > x''$ is as much an instantiation of F as is the (putative) change $x > y$. But even if this can be shown, we still have to account for the variation, and this is difficult if we see functions simply as 'given'. Take a simplified case, where we have a variation $x \sim y$, with y finally selected and x suppressed. The implication of the fact of variation itself must be that the driving force, causal power, 'motivation' or whatever of F IS NOT A CONSTANT. When the speaker says y, F is operative, but when he says x it isn't. If the variation is directional, as it would have to be to yield the x:y correspondence, then this means that the motivating strength of F must be increasing as the 'goal' of all-y, no-x is approached. That is, at the beginning of the change $x > y$ of which F is the 'agent', F has minimal causal force or effective power, and this is also periodic; it is only as the chain that F was supposed to have started in the first place becomes more like an implementation of F that F has the strongest effect. This almost looks more like $x > y$ bringing F into being by way of the variation $x \sim y$. This is surely not what a 'functional explanation' is supposed to mean.

I conclude that the available empirical information on how change proceeds makes functional explanation of the classical type conceptually dubious; unless we introduce the idea of variable and increasing functions, which take on causal power as the actual needs they are supposed to represent decrease. This is not in the spirit of the fairly straightforward causal relation usually assumed; and is also, as far as I can see, quite unintelligible.

3 Locating functions: the unobservability paradox

This is a general methodological problem, which has more of a bearing on the whole enterprise of deductive explanation of change than on functionalism in particular, though there are some relations. But in any case it's an interesting problem, and might as well be discussed here.

It is well known that one of the putative contributions of 'variation study' (cf. Lass 1976b) to historical linguistics is its (apparent) resolution of the famous 'unobservability' problem. Bloomfield (1933: 347ff) claimed that sound change was in principle unobservable, because it is too gradual, and the steps by which it proceeds are too small to be measured. Hockett (1958 : 444) went rather further, and developed the following paradox: phonetic change is unobservable, for Bloomfield's reasons; but phonemic change is unobservable for the opposite reason, i.e. because it is too abrupt. For example, we can't observe the drifting of the allophones of /x/ in the direction of those of /y/, because the stages in the shifting of 'local frequency maxima' are too small: but as soon as an allophone of /x/ has become identical to one of /y/, the system is immediately restructured, and this too is unobservable. Therefore neither of the two central phenomena of interest to the historian can ever be precisely localized or observed.

It might seem that studies of 'change in progress' (e.g. those of Labov and his school) have neutralized this problem (indeed, I said something to this effect in Lass 1976b). But this is not entirely true. The Labovian techniques do not allow us to observe what we are really after, which is the point of 'actuation': it is this which must be spatiotemporally located, and which still cannot be. All the studies of change in progress allow us to see is the working out of a chain of effects at some unspecifiable point after actuation.

The irreducible fact seems to be that we can never observe the 'exact moment' when a change begins (except by accident – and even then we would still have no way of knowing what we were actually observing). Theories may help; but the help that they can give us makes the problem irresolvable, if it is taken as an empirical one. This can be illustrated with a simple hypothetical case.

Say that my informant said [e] in a word of etymological category X when I transcribed him yesterday, and today he says [i], in the same word. Unless I know that today's [i] was the first one (at 5.32 p.m. on 17 November 1978, [e] > [i]), I would still have only a diachronic correspondence [e] : [i]. And it gets worse if you take it further.

Suppose I knew that the [i] UTTERED at 5.32 p.m. on 17 November was in fact the first utterance of any item of category X since 5.32 p.m. on 16 November, and that at that time the speaker said [e]. Would I be any better off? The answer here depends on the kind of linguistic theory I happen to believe in. For instance, if I held a 'mentalist' theory, in which the phonetic actualization of a change is simply a contingent matter of when the 'deeper' grammatical change (of rules or whatever) happens to give rise to an output, I would have a period of 24 hours in which the 'real change', of which the first uttered [i] is only a situationally determined exponent, could have occurred. In this case [e]:[i] would still only be a correspondence, and I would not have observed the change. All I would have is a *terminus ante quem* and a *terminus post quem*. If however I believed in a non-representational, purely behaviouristic linguistic theory (which seems dubious on many grounds), then I would be better off, and the observability problem would be solved. This is because first utterance = *df* moment of change within such a theory. Thus what I observe is conditioned by my beliefs: the unobservability problem is built into all theories that do not insist that change takes place only at the periphery, but allow 'mental' representations.

This relates to the problem of function as follows: if the change [e] > [i] was the implementation of F, when did F operate? Does a function continue to be a function after the change has occurred? If I hold a representational theory, when does F become inactivated: after the underlying rule change, or at the moment of utterance? (What in fact is the ontological status of a function when it has caused something?) It seems as if since changes cannot be spatiotemporally located with any exactness, functions are even less localizeable: we have causal agents whose spatiotemporal boundaries are indeterminate. I merely raise this problem here, but I think it needs some work, conceptual clarification if not actual empirical 'discovery', which may be impossible in principle.

4 Are functions individual or collective?

Finally, I turn briefly to another problem that concerns both the locus of change and the means of its transmission. Do functions reside in individual persons, or are they in some occult (essentially Saussurean: cf. §4.5) way properties of the community? This is not as absurd a question as it seems at first, as the argument below will indicate.

There is no problem at all in this regard if language change is immediate throughout the community; indeed, the ideal argument for functionalism would be a situation where a change hit all members of the community at once. Now as far as we know there is no evidence that this ever happens or ever has: changes start SOMEWHERE, and they travel through communities, at varying rates of speed, etc. We don't know how they do, but this is perhaps a problem for empirical investigation, not a conceptual difficulty.

The problem is this: if a change starts in one individual (or simultaneously, in a small group) and is transmitted to other members of the community, this must mean that even in the same social group, speaking the same language, there are at a given time some people for whom some function F is a motivating force for change, and some for whom it is not; and in order for the change (which is functionally motivated *ex hypothesi*) to be propagated, the function F must be propagated along with it (or before it). This is the only way in which functionalism could be incorporated into a reasonable, empirically based picture of how change is propagated in speech communities.

Aside from the multiplication of entities this involves (functional motivations have to be transmitted, then the changes they motivate develop), it raises the problem of naturalness: if the functions have some 'natural' basis, how is it that they have to be transmitted? Since as far as we know change often travels along gradients of prestige, power, and the like, this would mean that speakers could adopt functional motivations as a matter of class-consciousness, imitation of prestige models, and so on. Is this really in keeping with any naturalistic theory of functionalism?

4 Causality and 'the nature of language'

> ... in civilizations we often find something that hardly ever occurs in species: so-called luxury forms, i.e. structures whose form is not caused by the selection pressure of a system-preserving function, not even by one that was active in the past. Man can afford to carry around more useless ballast than any wild animal.
>
> Konrad Lorenz

4.1 Where do we go from here?

This enquiry has so far been conducted pretty much within the limits of what Geoffrey Sampson (1976: 963) has called 'the philosophy which dominates the intellectual life of the English-speaking world', which he characterizes this way:

According to this view there is only one method of adding to ... human knowledge ... 'explaining' observations by postulating systems of laws and specific 'initial conditions', which on the one hand entails the observations (via the ordinary rules of deductive logic), and on the other hand lays itself open to refutation by being incompatible with specifiable, logically-possible, future observations. The paradigm for scholarly research is natural science, particularly physics.

Further, any discipline that claims to deliver 'knowledge' but fails to share this methodology is 'mere charlatanry'. Thus in any discipline not oriented toward the natural sciences 'there is no question of "knowledge"; e.g. literary criticism is concerned with taste and emotion rather than knowledge' (*ibid.*). This suggests a rather limited view of what literary criticism is supposed to be about (it confuses 'appreciation' and 'interpretation'); but this aside, it is a good illustration of a kind of radical positivist idealism.

I have quoted Sampson at length because his position is, in the current climate of opinion, a respectable one, and he has given a particularly clear (if extreme) account of it. But it is, on a number of grounds, debatable. Purely descriptively, it may simply be wrong (i.e. not a correct account of the way the natural sciences, the paradigm instances of this philosophical tradition, are actually conducted). If the scenarios for the conduct and development of science proposed (in their different ways) by Kuhn, Lakatos, and Feyerbend are right, then Sampson's characterization is simply a projection onto history of a rather simplistic version of Popperian idealism (even if, taken as a *desideratum*, it might be all right). But this is not the place to deal with this issue (cf. chapter 5).

Methodologically, empirically, and philosophically, however, there may be more things wrong with it. For example, the determinism it entails may be untenable outside macrophysics; it may involve an unwarrantable extension of a methodology only suitable for the sciences dealing with inanimate matter onto planes where it is entirely inappropriate; and it may involve a constricted and in many cases counter-productive epistemology, which unjustifiably devalues many important kinds of human knowledge: indeed, one might argue, that it devalues even the central achievements of the physical sciences themselves (again, cf. chapter 5 below).

At any rate, we can now proceed, on the basis of the discussion in chapters 1–3, to come to grips with the fundamental problem. After examining current modes of explanation in historical linguistics I have concluded that there exists at present nothing that looks remotely like the positivist ideal. As far as I can see, there seem to be no 'laws' of the requisite type, and the causality (if that's the right term) of change is either too sloppy or too complex for 'straight-line' D-N explanations to be possible. The burden of this chapter will be that this 'failure' is in fact to be expected, and indeed that only a particularly blinkered kind of reductionist metaphysics would allow one to be surprised at it. This will not of course be of any comfort to functionalists, nor indeed, I suspect, to anyone else.

But let us assume for the moment that there is a way out (following my earlier criticism of Lyle Campbell for claiming exclusivity, I can't deny this in any case). If this were true, there would still be two research directions worth pursuing:

(i)   Really get down to the detailed business of overcoming the ignorance that makes all our explanations at least 'pragmatically defective', and discover the laws that must be there (I will take up the implications of this direction in §4.2).

(ii)   Admit defeat in the deductive arena, and develop an epistemology that will make non-deductive explanation respectable; or substitute, as the desired output of the historical linguist's labours, some kind of structure other than explanation. (This will be the substance of chapter 5.)

Direction (i) is a necessity (on heuristic grounds at least: cf. §2.5) even if we believe it's a lost hope; and for some scholars (of Sampson's persuasion) it is a necessity on metaphysical grounds as well. Direction (ii), for all its problems, is worth following, for three reasons. First, because since we can't tell when – or if – we will get any joy out of (i), we ought to have a reserve strategy, i.e. something to do in the meantime, until the laws turn up; or for the future, in case they fail to, or it becomes apparent that there are good reasons why they won't. (We might call this the argument from occupational prudence.) Second, (ii) is worthwhile in principle for those whose metaphysics allow them to live with (i) as a lost hope. And third, because in an anti-totalitarian spirit I take it as *a priori* right and good that intellectual disciplines should be reasonably pluralist; no one has the right to say 'there is only one method' of doing anything (at least in the current state of our ignorance of the fundamentals of almost everything interesting). Some (Sampson for one, I think) would call this an argument from intellectual sloppiness; I prefer to see it simply as a neutral alternative, or 'retreat from commitment'. (For further comment on 'commitment' see §5.6.)

Let us remind ourselves of one point before going on: if Sampson is right in saying that deductive explanation is the only source of genuine knowledge, and if I am right in saying that deductive explanation of language is in principle impossible, then we cannot have any genuine knowledge of why language changes. I might add – in advance of the arguments to come later on – that I think there is a sense in which both positions are correct, and that there is a certain type of knowledge which is in principle unavailable in linguistics. I will argue in chapter 5 that there are other kinds which in their own way have something (if something less) to offer.

4.2 Some implications of the positivist view

It is obvious that what lies at the centre of the whole D-N idea (and perhaps, in a rather flabby way, at the centre of probabilistic explanation) is the notion of causation: as early as Popper's 1934 discussion (now Popper 1968a: §12) explanation, prediction and causation form a single complex. Thus (1968a: 67): 'The "principle of causality" is the assertion that any event whatever *can* be causally explained – that it *can* be deductively predicted' (emphasis Popper's). The principle, however, is ambiguous in this form (*ibid.*):

According to the way in which one interprets the word 'can' in this assertion, it will be either tautological (analytic) or an assertion about reality (synthetic). For if 'can' means that it is always logically possible to construct a causal explanation, then the assertion is tautological, since for any prediction ... we can always find universal statements and initial conditions from which the prediction is derivable ... If, however, 'can' is meant to signify that the world is governed by strict laws ... then the assertion is admittedly synthetic ...

But the synthetic version (for Popper at that point) is too 'metaphysical'; he claims that it can be replaced by a 'methodological rule' of which the 'principle of causality' can be regarded as a 'metaphysical version'. This is 'the simple rule that we are not to abandon the search for universal laws and for a coherent theoretical system, nor ever give up our attempts to explain causally any kind of event we can describe' (*ibid.*). This is of course direction (i) in the previous section. It is an attractive notion, since it enables us to be optimistic about all current failures, at least in the synthetic version. Whether or not the programme can (a) actually be carried out, and (b) will lead to anything but dead ends (either in general or in specific domains) is an open question. But it is certainly a reasonable frame of mind in which to approach a domain like physics.

What I question, however, is its appropriateness to other domains, like linguistics, for example. The real problem is the implications of the notion 'cause'. All the forms of explanation for linguistic change that we have been looking at have been essentially causal, at least in intent: the idea has been to find situations in which a given change can be seen as in some sense the (expected) result of some set of empirically relevant interlocking conditions and laws.

One question that arises in this connection is how we are to interpret a notion like the deductive explicability of 'any event whatever' (in Popper's terms): does a language change constitute such an event? (Cf. the discussion in the appendix to chapter 3, §3, which may cast some doubt on this.) And is language change 'in the world', insofar as by that we mean macrophysical nature? Assuming deductive causal explanations to be valid in that world (as opposed to the microphysical world,

which is not in question here), how far are we willing to extend its
boundaries? If we extend it as far as Sampson (judging from the passage
I quoted) would like us to, then we must end up as behaviourists, and
reduce man to a *bête-machine* (going even further than Descartes, of
course, because this kind of determinism would surely not allow for the
independence of 'mind'). At least I don't see how, if we hold this radical
a view, we can exempt individual psychology, and avoid asking
manifestly absurd questions like 'What is the D-N explanation for
Sampson's holding his particular views?' If this is the case, then we
must assume, I suppose, that language may be one of those areas about
which 'knowledge' is simply unavailable. Which is not a view that
Sampson holds.

We will see in the next section that there is considerable doubt that
simple causal explanations are possible even in some of the natural
sciences, e.g. biology. But I will preface this discussion by raising a
question which suggests that the notion 'cause' in general may be
fundamentally inappropriate for any discipline whose main interest is in
the behaviour of sentient beings.

Two cats, A and B, are sitting on the lawn after a good meal, and a
mouse runs in front of them, crossing both their visual fields. Cat A
stiffens, goes into a hunting posture; cat B follows the mouse for a
second with its eyes, then turns away and washes its face. What
happened? If we want to talk of 'causes', then obviously the movement
of the mouse across A's visual field is the 'stimulus' that 'released its
hunting instinct': we have a purely mechanical activation of a classical
S-R chain. But what about B? Did his instinct 'fail to function'? Or was
he just not interested at the moment? We could then explain B's
behaviour as the result of a conjunction of 'instinct' and (say) 'desire': if
the latter isn't present, the instinct will not be released. But if this is the
case, A and B are qualitatively distinct individuals, no longer *bêtes-
machines*, and their actions can no longer be said to be nomically
'caused'.

Unless of course we make the assumption that 'desire' etc. are
themselves merely physico-chemical phenomena, i.e. that the 'mental-
istic' terms are just names, growing out of cultural habit and contingent
ignorance, for lawfully caused internal states, independent of individuality, 'mind', etc. (Cf. Bloomfield's behaviourist fable of Jack and
Jill, 1933: 22ff, and the critical discussion in Wunderlich 1974: §9.25.
For further comment on the illegitimate shifting of mental terms into

the pseudo-domain of 'pure' behaviourist explanation, cf. Polanyi & Prosch 1975: 47f.) In the end (even if it should be 'true' in some way), such an assumption is probably to be taken as morally inadmissible, because of its power to conduce to Skinnerian Utopias (cf. Lewis 1947); but in any case it is only one possible belief out of many, and has no particular empirical evidence in its favour that I am aware of. The metaphysical notion of 'necessity' involved may be attractive to some, but it is no more intellectually respectable than non-reductionist views, and in the case of living beings, probably less so (cf. §§4.9ff).

These issues converge on the question of language change in a number of ways. For example, if we assume that change is 'psychological' or even 'psychosocial', is it then law-governed? If we assume that it is mechanical, proceeding *mit blinder Notwendigkeit*, how do we account for its 'failures' and irregularities, and for the vast spread of individual differences, non-implementation of natural changes, and the like? Can we in fact say that language change is 'caused', or do we have to invoke some other concept?

4.3 Causality in living systems

Let us turn to the problem of applying the general notion of causality to enormously complex systems, such as we might expect to be involved in linguistic change. Could it be the case that we require here a much more subtle notion of 'cause'? There is an excellent discussion of the problems involved, specifically in biology, by Ernst Mayr (1968), which may be a good introduction to the concerns of this chapter.

Mayr points out that in biology, unlike more restricted domains like classical mechanics, a single event may not have a single cause, but rather a set of causes. For instance (Mayr 1968: 45), why did a particular warbler begin its southward migration from New Hampshire on 25 August? There are, says Mayr, four 'equally legitimate causes':
(i)   'Ecological'. There are no insects around in the winter, hence no food for the warbler.
(ii) 'Historical'. The (historical) genotype induces the warbler to respond in a particular way to environmental stimuli of certain kinds; this is closely connected with
(iii) 'Intrinsic Physiological'. Migration is tied up with photo-periodicity, and on 25 August the day-length has dropped below a certain minimum.

(iv)   'Extrinsic Physiological'. A cold air mass passed over the area on
       25 August, and the sudden temperature drop affected the bird,
       which was already in a state of 'physiological readiness' (due to the
       interaction of (ii), (iii), where presumably (ii) is in part an effect of
       selective pressures (i) on the genotype, etc.).

Causes (i)–(ii) are 'ultimate', and (iii)–(iv) 'proximate'; and the
ultimate causes are historically incorporated into the system. Both sets
are equally necessary for an explanation.

Mayr thinks that this example is too complex to be handled by
'classical' causality theory (i.e., though he doesn't call it that, D-N
explanation). He invokes instead a definition of cause from an
unpublished paper by Scriven, which is 'a nonsufficient condition
without which an event would not have happened', or 'a member of a set
of jointly sufficient reasons without which the event would not happen'
(46). But, he says, even though definitions like this are applicable to
complex phenomena, 'they seem to have little operational value in those
branches of biology that deal with complex systems' (like organisms,
communities, ecosystems, etc.). He concludes (*ibid.*):

I doubt whether there is a scientist who would question the ultimate causality of
all biological phenomena – that is, that a causal explanation can be given for past
biological events. Yet such an explanation will often have to be so unspecific and
so purely formal that its explanatory value can certainly be challenged. In
dealing with a complex system an explanation can hardly be considered very
illuminating that states: 'Phenomenon *A* is caused by a complex set of
interacting factors, one of which is *b*.' Yet often this is about all one can say.

Unfortunately, this is not true of the warbler example. This one can
be reconstructed in D-N form (without the 'ultimate'/'proximate'
dichotomy). The resultant schema would be exceedingly complex (since
it deals with more complex phenomena than the usual, rather trivial,
textbook examples of pendulums and breaking wires), but I see no
reason in principle why points (i)–(iv) in Mayr's exposition can't
deductively imply the sentence 'the warbler migrated on 25 August'. (I
will spare the reader the formalization, since the point seems clear.)

This, however, as it turns out, is merely a matter of Mayr's having
chosen an initial example illustrating only complexity, and not genuine
qualitative failure of causal explanation, or the need for some non-
classical concept. He later shows precisely the areas where this turns up,
i.e. when we extend our interest to much more complex phenomena, and
try to maintain the deducibility (predictability) requirement. There is in

fact a gradient of predictability in biological domains, from nearly 100 per cent to zero.

Thus there is what he calls (50) 'prediction in classification': given a binomial (genus/species) classification of an organism, one can 'predict numerous structural and behavioural characteristics'. Even given only a generic classification, one can still predict a good deal (e.g. if I know that x is a specimen of *Drosophila melanogaster* I can tell you how it mates, how many wing-veins and bristles it has, what colour its eyes are, etc.; if I only know it's a *Drosophila*, I can still tell you what it eats, etc.). There is also prediction on the molecular level: we can predict 'with very high accuracy' with respect to 'most biochemical unit processes ... such as metabolic pathways', as well as 'biophysical phenomena in simple systems, such as the action of light, heat and electricity in physiology' (51).[1]

But in more complex systems (e.g. ecological interactions) the success rate of predictions in much lower, and interesting patterns of indeterminacy arise. A classic example is this (Mayr, 51): 'When two species of flour beetles (*Tribolium confusum* and *T. castaneum*) are brought together in a uniform environment ... one of the two species will always displace the other. At high temperatures and humidities *T. castaneum* will win out; at low temperatures and humidities *T. confusum* ... Under intermediate conditions the outcome is indeterminate ...'[2]

And at the low end of the gradient, prediction of evolutionary outcomes is virtually impossible. 'Looking at the Permian reptiles, who would have predicted that one of the most undistinguished branches would give rise to the mammals?' (*ibid.*). Similarly, it is well known to students of natural and artificial selection that 'independent parallel lines exposed to the same selection pressure will respond at different

---

[1] I question whether we have 'explanation' or 'prediction' in both cases. The second involves biophysical 'laws' in the D-N sense, but the first seems purely definitional (an explanation in terms of 'natural kinds': Nagel 1965: 21–2). Suppose I know (not Mayr's example) that some plant x is a member of the genus *Laburnum*, and that this genus is included in the family *Leguminosae*. I can then 'predict' that it will have nitrogen-fixing bacteria living in nodules on its roots. But is this a 'prediction' in any substantive sense? Or merely a consequence of the fact that 'having nodules ...' is a predicate of the class *Leguminosae*? If N = 'having nodules', and L = 'being a legume', it is not the case that $L(x) \supset N(x)$, but rather that $L(x) = df\ N(x)$, i.e. this is a stipulated definition, not an entailment, and should not be called a 'prediction'.

[2] Assuming of course complete control for all variables, i.e. an ideal 'closure' (on this concept see Bhaskar 1975). The assertion that if all variables are known all systems will ultimately be reduced to closures is metaphysical.

rates and with different correlated effects, none of them predictable' (52). Whatever predictability there is is purely statistical (with all the problems this raises in assessing causality: cf. §§1.6, 2.2–4).

Mayr suggests some reasons for this kind of indeterminacy, and these may be relevant to the problem of predicting linguistic change as well. I will outline his explanation here, and attempt in the following sections to tie some of these things in with language change.

(i) 'Randomness of an event with respect to the significance of the event' (52). For example, spontaneous mutation, which is not controlled BY selection pressures, but whose results are responsive TO them. Change in the genotype is (supposedly) random, but affects the phenotype, which responds to selection pressures, which in turn have (positive or negative) effects on the perpetuation of the genotype.[3] In any case, 'the precise results of a given selection pressure are unpredictable because mutation, recombination, and developmental homeostasis are making indeterminate contributions to the response to the pressure' (*ibid.*).

(ii) 'Uniqueness of all entities at ... higher levels of biological organization' (*ibid.*). Organic entities are unique individuals, not merely members of classes (like lumps of iron, volumes of gas). This is true of all individuals, life-cycles, populations, species and higher taxa, interindividual contacts, natural associations, and evolutionary events. This is not to say that all organic entities are tokens, and that there are no types; but 'predictions' about biological individuals (and one would think, *a fortiori*, about conscious individuals) will probably have at most 'purely statistical validity'; Mayr insists that it 'is quite impossible to have for unique phenomena general laws like those ... in classical mechanics' (53).

(iii) 'Extreme complexity' (*ibid.*). This is nearly self-evident: 'Every organic system is so rich in feedbacks, homeostatic devices, and potential multiple pathways that a complete description is quite impossible.'

(iv) 'Emergence'. This is a complex notion, but an important one. Mayr gives (53) a 'dogmatic statement', which is: 'when two entities are combined at a higher level of integration, not all the properties of the new entity are necessarily a logical or predictable consequence of the properties of the components'. If there is such a thing, and if biological

---

[3]   This is of course an oversimplification; cf. the theory developed in Waddington (1957).

systems can show emergent properties, it follows that at least these properties are in principle immune to prediction, and that there can be no causal (D-N) explanations for them[4] (cf. §4.12).

Mayr emerges from his study with two conclusions that seem particularly relevant. One is as it were logical, and the other partly descriptive and partly metaphysical (54):

(i) 'In view of the high number of multiple pathways available for most biological processes ... and ... the randomness of many of [them], particularly on the molecular level ... causality in biological systems is not predictive, or at best is only statistically predictive.'

(ii) Explanations of all complex biological phenomena, especially those that can only be understood (at least in part) in terms of their evolutionary history, are 'sets of causes'. Further, 'Each set is like a pair of brackets that contains much that is unanalyzed and much that can presumably never be analyzed.'

The metaphysical component of (ii) is the assumption that complete analysis of the conditions for biological prediction is unachievable; this ultimately pessimistic notion co-exists uneasily with another metaphysical assumption, akin to the synthetic version (I think) of Popper's 'principle of causality' – cf. Mayr's remark quoted earlier that causal explanations are possible in principle for all past biological events. Mayr's position could probably be fairly described as metaphysical optimism coupled with methodological pessimism: belief in an ultimately causal universe, and a conviction that it is too complex ever to be encompassed by any causal theory that human beings can produce; as well as a conviction that progress can be made, in bits, and will only be made by holding to a belief in a causal universe.

It is important however to note that both the conviction that the universe is causal, and the conviction that it can never be shown to be so, are neither of them 'empirical' or 'scientific' positions, but reflexes of metaphysical world-views, involving a strong component of essentially 'religious' commitment. Let us not forget that all such positions are

---

[4] It is a truism in any case that wholes are often 'greater than the sum of their parts' ('holism' vs. 'reductionism'). This is a bit of ancient non-reductionist wisdom one of whose vestiges is the notion 'quintessence', the 'fifth essence' of the alchemists which transcends the four elements out of which anything is made. For some historical background and exegesis cf. Lass (1966); for biological holism see the pioneering effort of Smuts (1961) and the more recent developments reported in the papers in Koestler & Smythies (1969). I will return to this and some related matters in §4.11.

matters of faith (even if there is some empirical input to the faith): the only sort of position that may not be is a frank confession of ignorance. (Atheism is a religious faith.)

4.4 Preliminary implications of Mayr's analysis

I have considered Mayr's views in such detail because of his special qualifications for dealing with problems of this kind in biology: he is not only a 'metabiologist' reflecting on the practice of the discipline, but a distinguished practitioner as well, whose special field is evolutionary theory. I also chose a biologist's problems as my illustration because the phenomena he has to deal with are more like the linguist's than the physicist's are (and it is generally the physicist who has been the paradigm example for philosophers of science).[5] That is, linguistics involves biological systems (men), as well as mental activities and capacities (whatever domain they belong to); though note that among the complicating factors Mayr adduces he does not include the existence of mind and/or free will. And these systems are of interest to the linguist precisely in terms of their characteristic behaviour and local properties, not their physico-chemical structure. It seems on the face of it that if we accept Mayr's assessment of the possibility of D-N explanations for interesting (i.e. complex) phenomena in the infrapsychological domains of biology,[6] we might expect the situation in linguistics (which is both biological and historical, whatever else it may be) to be several orders of magnitude worse.

---

[5] This is one of the sources, I assume, of Sampson's oversimplifying equation of 'the natural sciences' with physics. It is a hangover from the 'unified science' ideal, and as such only one metaphysical stance possible for even an English-speaking philosopher of science or scientist. For a sharply opposed view cf. Feyerabend (1975), and the discussions of reductionism in Koestler & Smythies (1969); Grene (1974); Polanyi & Prosch (1975); Lorenz (1977); Popper & Eccles (1977). For some instructive examples of what the philosophy of biology looks like, and how different it can be from physics-based metascience, see the essays in Grene & Mendelsohn (1976).

[6] Calling biology 'infrapsychological' does not imply that linguistics is 'psychological' – certainly not that it is in any sense coterminous with or included in psychology of any sort (*pace* Chomsky and Derwing, for different reasons). At best there is an interaction between 'language and mind', not an identity. Cf. §4.9 and the elaborate theory of interaction developed in Popper & Eccles (1977). (I assume that the hierarchical ranking of physical and mental phenomena implied by 'infra-' is reasonably uncontentious; it can if necessary be taken as historical, i.e. ontogenetic. I make no commitment to a position on the 'mind–body' problem though my sympathies are obviously with some kind of (dualist) 'interactionism'.)

The reason for the failure of deductive explanation may simply be that the perfectly laudable and not idiosyncratic attempt to treat languages as 'natural objects' or closed systems has miscarried: these alone (and only up to the pre-biological level of complexity) are the object-domain for D-N explanation, and whatever languages are they are not subliving natural objects. If this failure is a real one, which I shall argue below in more detail is the case, then we may be forced into one of the two positions below, in place of (i) and (ii) in §4.1:

(i') Regard language change as incomprehensible in principle, and revert to bug-collecting.

(ii') Develop and justify a mode of explanation or 'rendering intelligible' that is satisfactory without being either empirical (in the Popperian sense) or predictive.

If purely naturalistic explanation (which is epistemologically 'field-independent' in the sense of Toulmin 1958, i.e. meta-empirical) is inappropriate, do other strategies exist? If so, do they deliver any non-subjective knowledge (is historical linguistics any different from literary criticism or the study of angels on pinheads? I return to this in chapter 5).

4.5 Excursus: Scriven on non-predictive explanation

I have argued at some length that explanations without 'laws' are essentially useless – however superficially attractive they may seem. But at least one philosopher, Michael Scriven, has attempted to grapple squarely with this problem, and to transcend it. What he comes out with is a putative rescue strategy, which seeks to make explanations without laws respectable by means of something like a new schematic logic for them. He attacks this problem in two major papers (1959, 1963), and I think he fails; but his attempt is worth looking at. If his programme were to succeed, it might end up by allowing us to salvage probabilistic explanations and similar types whose future looked so bleak after chapters 2–3. But the failure has interesting implications, and can serve to sharpen our perception of some major problems.

Scriven's attempt is partially vitiated at the outset by his initially assuming what his programme is designed to demonstrate. He claims that neo-Darwinian ('synthetic') evolutionary theory is genuinely explanatory, even though it is non-predictive and doesn't contain laws, and that therefore we can have genuine explanations without laws. He begins (1959: 477) with this assertion:

The most important lesson to be learned from evolutionary theory ... is a negative one: the theory shows us what scientific explanation need not do. In particular it shows us that one cannot regard explanations as unsatisfactory when they do not contain laws, or ... are not such as to enable the event in question to have been predicted. This conclusion, which is contrary to the usual view of scientific explanation ... has important consequences for research in those subjects in which serious errors are known to arise in the application of the available regularities to individual cases.[7]

These are the 'irregular subjects', e.g. anthropology, history, much of biology, and quantum physics. Since the 'irregular' domain includes at least two of the 'human sciences' (anthropology and history), it can be taken to include linguistics as well (plus, I assume, psychology, sociology, economics, and so on).

Scriven's basic claim is that we have genuine non-predictive explanations in these fields; that Darwin, for example, is 'the paradigm of the explanatory but non-predictive scientist' (477). In the irregular subjects (*ibid.*) there are 'two key types of proposition ... associated with explanations'; one is 'a weaker relative of predictions, and the other ... is a weaker relative of laws'. What we get is 'hypothetical probability predictions': these are of the form 'if X occurs, then Y would be *likely*' (478). This allows us to '*explain why* certain animals and plants survived even when we could not have *predicted that* they would survive' (emphasis his). But I don't think it does; nor do I think that what

---

[7] It is quite easy to argue against Scriven's assumptions about the status of Darwinian theory; at least against the idea that is either very explanatory or very profound. For an overall view, see Macbeth (1974). For an interesting (technical) discussion see the Maynard Smith–Bohm–Waddington–Grene exchanges in Waddington (1969: 82–105): especially Marjorie Grene's comments on the current failure of neo-Darwinism to recognize problems that Darwin was aware of (97). Her summary of Maynard Smith's pro-Darwinian argument is especially pertinent (98):

'He wants to show that the theory is not tautological: that it is not just a device for measuring the survival of what survives. To do this he has to distinguish the "fittest" as the "harmonious" or the "adaptively complex" from the genetically "fit," i.e. those most likely to leave descendants. But either ... such "complexities" are again to be assessed as superior in adaptivity ... and so the theory collapses into tautology. Or "complexity" is not reducible to survival value, and then ... Darwinism or neo-Darwinism has no theory of increasing complexity at all. But increasing complexity is an essential feature of evolution. So neo-Darwinism provides an excellent and ingenious set of analytical instruments for measuring selective phenomena, plus either a vacuous theory of evolution or none at all.'

Scriven proposes here is really different from, or better than, a probabilistic explanation of the Hempel type. He fails to show how our mere knowledge that something would be likely serves as an 'explanation'; as far as I can see we are still no further forward than being able to say (cf. the quotation from Polanyi 1958 in §2.3 above) that if the likely happens, this simply confirms our knowledge that it was likely.

But what makes us want to try and justify such explanations is the following (and here Scriven is right) (478): '... it is a feature of the irregular subjects that, unlike classical atomic physics, the irregularity-producing factors lie outside their range of observation and are not predictable by reference to any factors within this range'. (I will return to the possible relevance of this observation to language change below.)

But he goes astray by invoking an exceedingly misleading analogy: he says that given 'partially random processes' (like genetic mutation), we can nonetheless predict likely outcomes: 'we are not hard put to explain that a man's death was due to his being struck by an automobile, even when we could not have predicted the event' (479). There is a confusion here: he lumps two separate things under the single heading of 'the event'. One is the car striking the man, and the other is his death after being struck. Granted, the accident itself is (or may be) a random event; but we could easily enough predict the death, given a full enough statement of the local initial conditions (the kind of damage the car did) plus a set of general laws ('fractured ribs penetrating the heart cause death', etc.). The 'randomness' of the accident is a red herring; we still can have a D-N explanation for the death. (As long, that is, as we are not seeking an 'ultimate' explanation, but merely a reasonable 'local' one.)

The same objections hold for his justification of what he calls causal explanations without predictions: there are cases where statements of the form 'the only cause of X is A' are compatible with statements of the form 'A is often not followed by X'. His example (480) is 'The only cause of general paresis is syphilis', but most cases of syphilis don't lead to paresis. He sums it up as follows (480; emphasis his): 'Hence, when A is observed, we can predict that X is *more* likely to occur than without A, but still extremely unlikely. So we must, on the evidence, still predict that it will *not* occur.' If however it does occur, we can appeal to the causal statement 'to provide and guarantee our explanation'.

But this is surely wrong: Scriven fails to distinguish between necessary and sufficient conditions. Granted that the presence of an infection by *Treponema pallidum* is a necessary condition for paresis, there are still a whole set of sufficient conditions that have to be met for paresis to occur (the infection having gone on long enough to reach the tertiary stage, presence of the organisms in the central nervous system, etc.: cf. the discussion of Achinstein's penicillin-allergy example in §1.3). By conflating two kinds of causes Scriven makes it look as if the kind of explanation involved here is NECESSARILY non-nomic, whereas it is merely (in this case perhaps deliberately) only 'pragmatically defective'. The correct causal statement here is that syphilis causes paresis just in case some further set of conditions (C_1, ...) is met, not just 'syphilis causes paresis'. The apparent paradox of effects not following their causes evaporates when the causal statement is not tendentiously oversimplified (for some similar examples cf. Blanshard 1962: 452). I conclude that Scriven's examples do not show that there is some special type of non-predictive explanation which must be accepted because we already accept the explanation anyhow, and must continue to even if it proves non-predictive. There is nothing in the argument, as far as I can see, that neutralizes any of the objections I raised in chapters 2–3.

In his later paper (1963), Scriven makes another attempt to validate non-predictive explanation. Here he invokes two governing ideas:

(i)   '... subsumption under an empirical regularity is not, as such, explanatory' (344).

(ii) 'The strength that a general law has by comparison with a possibility statement is logically redundant for explanatory purposes' (354).

Both of these are assertions, which are not defended by any very strong argument. The essential point of (i) seems to be that merely invoking a law does not provide any 'understanding': it simply shows that some event E is an instance of the law L. And merely knowing that E is an instance of L is a taxonomic, not an explanatory generalization. This is of course true (perhaps even in the presence of knowledge of empirical relevance); and it brings to the fore a fact about D-N explanations that I will return to (§5.2): they are not, strictly speaking, NEW understanding or knowledge, but rather special confirmations and restructurings of previous knowledge. Since the aim of a D-N explanation is that the explanandum sentence be analytic, it is clear that the D-N schema is 'non-ampliative' (Botha & Winckler 1973), i.e. it does not furnish any knowledge that wasn't in the premises anyhow. But there is still no doubt that a D-N explanation has at least whatever force or 'strength' something like the *modus ponens* has – and this is no small virtue.

Which brings us to Scriven's second point. It is not correct to say that the strength of a 'law' is logically redundant. Consider these two statements:

(i) $p \supset q$

(ii) $P(p \supset q)$

(where 'P' is the modal operator 'it is possible that'). Surely there IS precisely a logical difference, in that only the nomic statement can be expressed in simple propositional calculus. But I'm not sure if this is what Scriven means (i.e. this notational matter). From any other point of view, however, he is even less right: there is certainly an immense psychological difference, for one contemplating (i) and (ii), with respect to expectation of q in case p, or one's interpretation of the efficacy of p in producing q. This makes Scriven's following statement (1963: 354) hard to accept:

... we can have good historical explanations without having good predictive laws: from (1) 'Y is a possible explanation of X, and was present' and (2) 'No other plausible explanation of X appears to have been present', it follows that Y is *the* (most plausible) explanation of X, subject to the usual assumption that there is an explanation for everything. [Emphasis Scriven's]

First of all, this is an instance of the 'how else?' strategy (cf. § 3.2), and therefore probably inadmissible. Further, if we are to accept the notion 'most plausible explanation', it must be from a totally different standpoint from the one we adopt when accepting a D-N explanation. It requires a kind of mental *volte face* whose force Scriven underestimates (since he doesn't mention it), and a different notion of what an explanation is, what 'it follows' means, and what interpretation we can give to the concept of 'knowing that Y explains X'.

In the earlier paper (1959: 478), Scriven makes a remark which seems useful, in that it points up at least a fruitful direction in which to look for an account of what our participation in such an explanation must be, and what its epistemic value is. He defines Darwin's particular contribution this way (emphasis his): 'He did not discover *an exact universal law*, but the utility of *a particular indicator* in looking for explanations.' (The 'particular indicator' here is the association of 'fitness' with survival, which as we have seen (§3.7 and p. 110, fn. 7) is not really very impressive.)

But one would have to be hard-headed to the point of priggishness to deny that Scriven has explicated, in a fashion, the colloquial notion of 'explanation', and has attempted to give substance to our everyday notion of 'understanding'. It is certainly true that many people are happy with Darwinian 'explanations', that these and similar objects give them a feeling of understanding, that they tend to render their explananda 'intelligible'. In this sense at least non-predictive explanations can be considered (if they work) to be something like happy illocutionary acts, or better, speech-acts with happy perlocutionary effects.

But it is a very different thing to give this felicity an epistemic status. It involves a retreat from the position of 'third worldism' which I suggested was the proper approach to the matter of explanation. I will examine the consequences of such a retreat in more detail in chapter 5, after I have produced more justification for engaging in it.

Let us note in closing that Scriven's attempt to salvage non-nomic explanations appears to fall between two stools. Insofar as he fails to distinguish (or refrains from distinguishing) necessary from sufficient conditions, he produces nothing more than defective D-N explanations, or schemata with all the failings of Hempelian probabilistic explanations. And insofar as he insists that these are nonetheless genuinely explanatory, he simply makes an assertion, without giving any criteria for explanatory goodness. Assuming that a given explanation is 'good' (which is undefined),[8] and which in any case we have to take his word for, and that it is non-predictive, he 'demonstrates' that non-predictive explanations are good. This is merely circular.

In essence what Scriven appears to be doing is trying to stick to the old deductivist framework by talking about 'causes' – but without the logical rigour required by that framework. We should keep this in mind as we consider the nature of our own 'irregular subject' in more detail.

4.6 Some reasons why language change ought to be indeterministic (Saussure)

If, as Mayr suggests, we find considerable apparent indeterminacy even in biological systems at fairly high levels of organization, we shouldn't

---

[8] For an indication of some of the kinds of criteria by which explanations (as instances of argumentative schemata justifying or leading to assertions of knowledge) can be evaluated for 'goodness', see Hamblin (1970: 224–52), and the discussion in Wunderlich (1974: §2.2). These are of course criteria transcending the merely formal ones I have assumed (in the D-N model) to be defining ones, and this is relevant to Scriven's non-deductive approach.

be surprised to find the same – or worse – in systems involving far more complex and less well-understood properties: e.g. mentation (conscious or unconscious), and its various offshoots such as symbolic behaviour, socialization, etc. We might expect language – and especially its history – to be a paradigmatically non-nomic domain.

This is the conclusion that Saussure, for example, was forced into (reluctantly) by a consideration of the facts of change. I think it will be instructive for our purposes here to examine Saussure's treatment of this problem in some detail, and then try to recast his conclusions. Let us begin from a somewhat neo-Saussurean point of view, that of Hjelmslev. One way of handling linguistic phenomena which might seem at first to open the way to a genuinely 'lawful' treatment is to adopt what I will call the 'autonomy thesis' – that language can be taken as a completely 'autonomous' object (perhaps in something like the 'naturalistic' sense that I suggested above (§4.2) might be inappropriate). Hjelmslev asserts this programmatically as the *conditio sine qua non* for doing serious linguistics. Thus he says (1963: 5–6): 'Linguistics must attempt to grasp language, not as a conglomerate of non-linguistic (*e.g.* physical, physiological, psychological, logical, sociological) phenomena, but as a self-sufficient totality, a structure *sui generis*. Only in this way can language itself be subject to scientific treatment ...' Any connection of 'linguistic' reality with other kinds is a secondary 'projection': what linguistics must seek (8) is 'a *constancy*, which is not anchored in some "reality" outside language' (emphasis Hjelmslev's). It is only after this has been grasped that it can (if necessary) be projected onto some external (social, psychological, etc.) reality; this projection must be done in such a way 'that, even in the consideration of that "reality", language ... remains the chief object ... as an organized totality with linguistic structure as the dominating principle'. I will return to the implications of this in (§§4.7–4.8).

We might see Hjelmslev's rigorous autonomy as descending in part from the legacy of confusion left by Saussure. The interaction of language and individual minds was for Saussure a *locus desperatus*, which became most troublesome when he tried to deal with historical phenomena. This aspect of Saussure's thought has not received the attention it deserves; and I think that in the context of a search for an ontology it is worth looking at.

Saussure's theory of change rests on his theory of synchronic structure; but this is not as clear as it seems at first. He appears to begin by arguing (at least half-heartedly) against what he saw as an excessively 'naturalistic' position characterizing the generation of linguists before the advent of the 'new linguistics' (the latter being represented by Whitney and the Neo-grammarians). He sums up their achievement (1959: 5, n. 2), by saying that 'One no longer dared to say, "Language does this or that," or "life of language," etc., since language is not an entity and exists only within speakers.' But he adds a significant rider, which becomes more important – even theoretically dominant – in the later parts of the *Cours*: 'One must not go too far, however ... certain metaphors are indispensable.' In fact the metaphors take over, as we will see.

It seems at first, anyhow, that language is not an autonomous entity; indeed, Saussure claims (6) that his theory is totally projectionist (in the sense of 'projection' defined above in the quotation from Hjelmslev). 'Everything in language is basically psychological.' But on the other hand (9), 'Language ... is a self-contained whole and a principle of classification.' One is tempted to ask 'which?' Or better, what does 'psychological' mean? Saussure is not very helpful. He tells us (14) that language is essentially collective, that 'it is not complete in any speaker; it exists perfectly only within a collectivity'. And further, that it 'is not a function of the speaker; it is a product that is passively assimilated by the individual'. And finally: 'It can be localized in the limited segment of the speaking-circuit where an auditory image becomes associated with a concept. It is the social side of speech, outside the individual who can never create nor modify it by himself; it exists only by virtue of a sort of contract signed by the members of a community.' (In this sense language is like the 'systems of social rules' of post-Wittgensteinian use-theorists and hermeneuticists like Itkonen.)

The 'psychology' here is problematical, since individual minds seem to be excluded in principle. Indeed, Saussure effectively gets rid of the individual speaker by his hypostasis of the collective, which makes linguistic 'psychology' radically trans-individual (cf. Fischer-Jørgensen 1975: 13–14). It is the (non-linguistic) psychologist who 'studies the sign-mechanism in the individual; this is the easiest method, but it does not lead beyond individual execution and does not reach the sign, which is social' (17). But even this social character of the sign is a problem; Saussure remarks that the 'distinguishing characteristic' of the sign is 'that in some way it always eludes the individual or social will' (*ibid.*).

In fact the question of the 'localization' of language leads to a paradox

(19): 'Language exists in the form of a sum of impressions deposited in the brain of each member of the community, almost like a dictionary of which identical copies have been distributed . . . Language exists in each individual, yet is common to all. Nor is it affected by the will of the depositories.' Despite his surface psychologism, it seems clear that Saussure holds an essentially 'naturalistic' view of language, and takes it to be at least in large part autonomous. The presence of dictionaries in speakers' brains seems to have little to do with language 'itself', as he makes clearer when he comes to talk about change. And this leads him to a number of contradictory conclusions.

First of all, since *langue* must be rigorously separated from *parole*, it would seem that any aspects of the 'depositaries' concerned with substantial manifestation of the contents of the dictionaries must be excluded. 'The vocal organs', he says (18), 'are as external to language as are the electrical devices used in transmitting the Morse code to the code itself.' And this means that 'phonation', i.e. the execution of 'sound images', in no way affects the system itself. This is of course the lead-in to the famous analogy of language to a symphony – 'what the symphony actually is stands completely apart from how it is performed' (*ibid.*).

But here a contradiction arises, and what Saussure has given with one hand he takes away with the other. It seems that change in *parole* can and does modify *langue*: 'speaking is what causes language to evolve: impressions gathered from listening to others modify our linguistic habits' (19). This is strange, because it would seem that whatever else *langue* is, it's not a 'habit'. Saussure apparently has a problem in coping with the 'elusive' quality of language, and the fact that it is constantly being used, or manifested in speech. There is a real conceptual crux, then: how do we account for change? Since *langue* and *parole* belong to different orders of being, it is inconceivable that the latter should affect the former. What we get in fact is this paradox (74):

Time, which insures the continuity of language, wields another influence apparently contradictory to the first: the . . . change of linguistic signs. In a certain sense, therefore, we can speak of both the immutability and the mutability of the sign.

In the last analysis, the two facts are interdependent: the sign is exposed to alteration because it perpetuates itself.

Despite all the previous psychologizing, it looks as if we are on our way to a hypostasis of language. And indeed, in a rather desperate scholium to this passage, Saussure's editors remark that what he is really saying is that 'language changes in spite of the inability of speakers to change it' (74, n. 3). It would seem that the complete autonomy position has been reached by the scholiasts, if not by Saussure himself. But Saussure too approaches more closely a bit further on (75): 'Language is radically powerless to defend itself against the forces which from one moment to the next are shifting the relationships between the signified and the signifier. This is one of the consequences of the arbitrary nature of the sign.'

The approach to a theory of change here involves a third hypostasis, that of time. Note that Saussure said that time has two contradictory influences – ensuring continuity and producing change. This is made more explicit shortly after the passage quoted immediately above, where Saussure finally objectifies time (77): 'Time changes all things: there is no reason why language should escape this universal law.'

This hypostasis of time acting on a hypostasized language system which is somehow both immune to and subject to speakers at once, leads to another problem – and another contradiction. At the beginning of the *Cours*, Saussure announces a classical positivist programme: one of the main tasks of linguistics (6) is 'to determine the forces that are permanently and universally at work in all languages, and to deduce the general laws to which all specific historical phenomena can be reduced'.

But this programme unfortunately conflicts both with Saussure's own knowledge of language change, and his (theory-defined) view of how it changes. He is thus ultimately driven to exclude all diachronic phenomena from the domain of the 'reducible' (i.e. nomic). The way time works on language is by giving 'social forces' (77–8) the chance to act on signified/signifier relations. And the result of this is that (87) 'everything comes about through sheer accident. Language is a mechanism that continues to function in spite of the deterioration to which it is subject'. In the end (93) 'diachronic events are always accidental and particular.' Thus he comes out with a theory (or at least a metaphysics) in which synchronic language states are lawful and structured, and language, however it's 'deposited', is really an abstract semiotic system, with an equivocal relation to its users. In this view history must always be anarchic, since the metaphysics allows no genuinely intelligible way for language to change. Part of the problem, as we will see later, is the insistence that language is *sui generis*, and not simply one cultural artefact among many.

Saussure's position can probably be summed up as follows: language is autonomous, but not insulated. Without positing any explicit mechanism – and indeed within a framework where such mechanisms are nearly inconceivable – he allows 'deterioration' in use to alter the signifier/signified nexus, through the intermediation of occult 'social forces'. But he nonetheless makes it clear that what some of us would now call (phonetic) 'performance effects' are in principle irrelevant.

Hjelmslev gives us a hard-edged theory of autonomy, but without a theory of change; Saussure gives us a fuzzy autonomy theory, but at least makes an attempt to account for change. The question now is whether autonomy theories of any kind (as opposed to projectionist ones) are coherent, and whether they can form the basis of any kind of explanatory theory of change.

I think that despite all the unclarities, Saussure was really on the right track; that he managed to focus some of the most striking and important properties of language in its relation to man and time, and that his contradictions really ought to inspire less desperation than they might seem to. In anticipation I will assert that the essential point – which vitiates any positivist attempts at explanation, and suggests that we need to revise our evaluation of proper goals – is this: while synchronic states are (within limits) 'lawful', history is by and large contingent.

4.7 A radical autonomy thesis

The discussion in chapters 1–3 implicitly assumed an ontology (if a rather inchoate one). It is now time to look at this in some greater detail, against the background of the question of the 'appropriateness' of an explanatory strategy for a particular type of explanandum domain. In other words, to consider where 'language' is to be located in the world, its relation to the speaker (which was brought into prominence as a problem by Saussure's difficulties), and whether consideration of these matters has any bearing on the explanation of change.

The inchoate ontology I referred to simply involves the apparently traditional and rather common-sensical notion that language is a 'possession' of speakers, as well as one of their (rule-governed) 'activities'. But in addition, that it is crucially bound up with the needs as well as the capabilities and (in an odd sense) 'preferences' of its speakers. This view, however sensible (and even inescapable) it seems at first, is neither very traditional within linguistics, nor entirely uncontroversial. I will return to this below.

It is clear at least that any further discussion of change must rest on more precise foundations than we have so far laid, especially with reference to the questions that the above characterization rather begs. I want to explore the problem of what kind of thing language is, or perhaps more accurately, as we will see, the problem of whether the question 'what is language?' should be asked in that form, and the implications of the answer for the central issue of how to explain change. If we are going to get any further we need a clearer idea of just what sort(s) of thing(s), engaged in and subject to what kinds of processes, we are in fact trying to explain. We have tended simply to assume it. (I take it that this is not a Wittgensteinian 'puzzle' that can be made to go away by conceptual explication, ordinary language analysis, etc., but a serious metaphysical – and perhaps partly empirical – issue.)

We can approach this by means of the appropriateness problem already raised: should language be treated as an object? And if so, what kind? That is, what are the merits of a conception of 'language' (in the sense of 'the subject matter of linguistics') very different from the one that tacitly underlies the positions and arguments of chapters 2 and 3? Those positions and strategies (excluding the statistical interpretation of naturalness) were implicitly based on the notions suggested above: language as a 'possession' of speakers, something that they 'know', 'do', and 'participate in', in such a way that the speakers are obviously our central topic of concern, because it is their transactions with it that in some way are responsible for change.

But, curiously, this view has been more honoured in the breach than the observance. Indeed, even though there exist many arguments that presuppose it, the overall orientations of most schools of linguistics (even avowedly functionalist ones) have in fact generally denied its importance: though usually only in practice, not in theory (or not in programme). Linguists have, I would maintain, normally treated language as if it were in fact an autonomous natural object (or an autonomous formal system): 'language changes' – it is not (necessarily) speakers that change it (cf. the remark of Saussure's editors cited in the previous section). This is essentially true even of the majority of those linguists who claim to be interested in one way or another in 'psychology': we saw a particularly nice example in Saussure.

This is due to a number of factors. One is the legacy of the nineteenth-century attempt (continued by Bloomfield, and in a different way by Chomsky and his *Nachfolge*) to treat language as if it were either a non-human organism or a physical or mathematical system (to make linguistics a 'science'). Another factor may be the apparently hypnotic spell cast by the fact that some aspects of language can be formally represented in such a way that it LOOKS LIKE an autonomous object (whether it 'really is' or not). There are in addition purely institutional factors (demarcation disputes, etc.), e.g. the need felt by many to keep linguistics an autonomous discipline, to prevent it from slopping over into psychology, sociology, neurophysiology, etc.[9]

Various post-Saussurean attempts to introduce the speaker, as it were, into linguistic theory have generally been both superficial and otiose. This is true for instance of much (if not all) Praguian theory, where the 'dynamic' element is ontologically centred in the 'system' – not its 'possessor' or 'user'. Martinet's theory of 'economy', for instance, can easily be interpreted as referring to self-existent systems, with the speaker peripheral, or for all practical purposes non-existent.[10]

I do not think there is any very strong evidence that existing speakers are a necessary assumption (much less a central concern) for any important school of general linguistic theory. (Chomsky has certainly argued that speech itself isn't: cf. the anti-Gricean arguments in Chomsky 1976: ch. 2; on the incompatibility of the Chomskyan notion of 'competence' with the existence of real speakers see Wunderlich 1974: ch. 11.) It has been suggested (by Labov and his school) that the 'community' is necessary: but even this is a very tenuous abstraction, and does not presuppose that language has to any significant degree a (personal) psychological substrate. All it assumes is the 'weak mentalist' position (Ringen 1975) that language is a 'cultural object' known in some way to and (perhaps) represented by its speakers; in this view so is the community. But neither is necessarily 'intrapsychic', and neither seriously presupposes the existence of individual speakers.

One might therefore ask whether, considering what looks like a fair

[9] Chomskyan 'mentalism', it should be noted, is not – despite Chomsky's assertion that linguistics is 'a branch of cognitive psychology' (1972: 1) really a move away from this. In orthodox TG at least the 'psychology' is little more than programmatic window-dressing (cf. Derwing 1973; Ringen 1975). TG itself, of course, has in fact slopped over into something else: probably pure axiomatics or analytical philosophy (Ringen 1975).

[10] Actually Martinet is somewhat ambiguous on this point. Cf. his remark (1955: 156) that languages 'ou mieux leurs usagers, ne sont jamais guidés par une aversion ou une préférence pour tel ou tel type articulatoire, mais ... tel ou tel type articulatoire représente de préjudiciable ou d'avantageux pour l'économie de la langue à un moment précis de son histoire'. Clearly 'language' here is independent of the speaker – though he may apparently 'do things for it'.

consensus, there is really any need to invoke human beings (messy, complicated things) at all, even as 'intermediaries' between the *Ding an Sich* and the linguist. That is, can language be said to change, for instance, only in relation to itself, and not to speakers' needs, etc.? This would present the possibility of a linguistic 'World 3': parallel to Popper's 'epistemology without a knowing subject' (1973: ch. 3) we could have 'language without a using/knowing speaker'.

This is not merely an eccentricity, if my reading of the history of linguistics is fair. Certainly this idea has been explicitly proposed by Hjelmslev (cf. §4.6), and it is implicit in the work of many who do not specifically espouse it, as I suggested above. It seems reasonably clear to me (and cf. Kac 1978: ch. 6) that most if not all of the more striking and fruitful developments in linguistic theory, from the Neo-grammarians on, are in principle quite independent of any theory whatever about speakers or their relation to language. Linguistic theory has in this sense always been a paradigmatically 'structural' discipline, in which speakers are peripheral or a mild embarrassment. I think one could possibly say that all the no doubt solid progress in the understanding of linguistic structure achieved in the past century or so is independent of any psychological assumptions (or lack of them) that have gone along with any major research paradigm. These assumptions may have been useful heuristics (e.g. the Jakobsonian idea that perception is based on either/or choices), but they have nothing to do with the success or failure of the actual proposals that have been made. In general, linguistic theory, where it has been fruitful, has been the study of formal objects and their mutations over time, not the study of their inventors or users. (For further discussion of this view of the history of linguistics, cf. Eliasson 1977: 60–7.)

The possibility of a 'speaker-free' as against a 'speaker-centred' linguistics provokes the following considerations:

(i)   If it is legitimate to exclude the speaker, then functional explanation (based on any human need, faculty, limitation, etc.) is beside the point.

(ii) If the speaker is implicated, then this brings language directly into the non-nomic domains of psychology and culture, ruling out all D-N explanations except of the trivially (and peripherally) physical.

Since the tradition seems overall to have been that linguistic research is conducted under the assumption (i) – at least the base assumption, without its corollary of the impossibility of functional explanation – it might be worth pursuing this view somewhat further. That is, let us see what a non-projectionist theory really looks like, and what its epistemological nature and explanatory force might be.

The implications of this view have not been fully drawn out for linguistics, as this is not the kind of question linguists have typically been interested in (though there are suggestive remarks in the work of Harris – see below – and others). But something of the consequences can be seen in some proposals about the physical sciences made by Eddington (1958) in his speculations on the boundaries between meta-physics (not necessarily the same thing as 'metaphysics') and physics. This is typified by his view of the nature of 'structure' in the physical universe, and thus the nature and relation to its investigators of that universe itself. Consider the following remarks (Eddington 1958: 141–2):

Properly to realize the conception of group-structure, we must think of the pattern ... as abstracted altogether from the particular entities and relations that furnish the pattern. In particular, we can give an exact mathematical description of the pattern, though mathematics may be quite inappropriate to describe what we know of the nature of the entities and operations concerned in it. In this way mathematics gets a footing in knowledge which intrinsically is not of the kind suggesting mathematical conceptions. Its function is to elucidate the group structures of the elements of that knowledge. It dismisses the individual elements by assigning to them symbols, leaving it to non-mathematical thought to express the knowledge, if any, that we may have of what the symbols stand for.

This conception grows out of Eddington's essentially 'epistemological' view of what knowledge of external (i.e. extrapsychic) domains consists of. Briefly, he suggests that the study of a (putatively) 'empirical' domain is not to be viewed as a 'direct' study of the domain itself, but rather a study of our knowledge of it. This knowledge is largely determined by the nature of the equipment we use to obtain it (our minds, our senses and their extensions). He thus distinguishes what he calls 'epistemological physics' from earlier forms, which were based on a naïve ontology. Epistemological physics 'directly investigates *knowledge*, whereas classical physics investigated or endeavoured to investigate an *entity* (the external world) which the knowledge is said to describe' (1958: 49; emphasis Eddington's).

This leads eventually to an emphasis, in any investigation, on 'the nature of the frame of thought' (116), and this allows us to 'be forwarned of its impress on the knowledge that will be forced into it. We may foresee *a priori* certain characteristics which any knowledge contained in the frame will have ... These ... will be discovered *a posteriori* by physicists who employ that frame of thought, when they come to examine the knowledge they have forced into it.'

This does not make Eddington an 'idealist' in the strict sense; rather it simply displays an acute consciousness of the power of an epistemological framework to dictate the shape of its own contents – as well as the fact that it always stands as an insuperable barrier to 'direct experience' of anything (there are no theory-free observation languages). But the relativism this produces is liberating, not harmful. Eddington's 'moral' judgement (121) is that in part at least 'we emancipate ourselves from a frame of thought when we realize it is only a frame of thought and not an objective truth we are accepting. Any power for mischief it may have is sterilized so long as it is kept exposed.' This is surely a reasonable point of view; it is in fact what I will return to in chapter 5 as a partial definition of the aims of intellectual enquiry.

Now where would this kind of view leave us with respect to the 'objectivity' of a World 3 artefact? In part, with an infinite regress: not only is language a World 3 artefact, but so (of course) is any theory we use to characterize it. Any theory of theories of World 3 artefacts is itself a World 3 artefact, and so on. So any starting point is arbitrary, and all we have to do is relegate higher-order theories to 'unproblematical background knowledge' (Lakatos 1970); in any case we have no choice about this kind of relegation, because of the limits of our abilities for 'focal' comprehension (Polanyi 1958).

If we were to adopt an autonomy thesis for language, and follow (roughly) Eddingtonian precepts, we should probably have to accept a view like this: our theories do not in any sense map *realia* directly, but are analogues to them, based on structures we discover in (or impose on) certain aspects of the sensible world (in this case languages, their histories, and our transactions with them). Our theories and descriptions then become theories and descriptions of STRUCTURE only (in the mathematical sense), with no attribution of the structure to anything but our 'knowledge' (such as it is) of the particular *sensibilia* we happen to be investigating, attempting to model, etc. This leads us eventually to an 'ideal' formalized theory, virtually an uninterpreted calculus. We reach a point where, in Eddington's terms, we confine all our assertions strictly to structural knowledge, and where 'every path to knowledge of what lies beneath the structure is ... blocked by an impenetrable mathematical symbol' (142).

We are then left with an ontology of 'pure structure'. To quote Eddington once more (151):

The physical universe is a structure. Of the X of which it is the structure, we only know that X includes sensations in consciousness. To the question: what is X when it is not a sensation in any consciousness ...? the right answer is probably that the question is a meaningless one – that a structure does not necessarily imply an X of which it is the structure.

In its essentials this is certainly Hjelmslev's view, and the one that Saussure would like to have held for all domains (and probably did synchronically); with the addition of an instrumentalist metaphysics it is Harris' view, and, with added explanatory pretensions and a rather vague and naïve psychologistic projection, it is Chomsky's. Thus for instance Harris (1960: 18) claims to operate with no ontology at all: the constructs of linguistic theory are not 'realities', but 'purely logical symbols, upon which the ... operations of mathematical logic can be performed'. But this is of course an ontology of a sort, as much as any theory that attributes reality to a projection of theoretical entities: only the world in which the entities live is World 3, not any of the 'lower' ones. A theory of 'structures of X' is as much a theory of something as a 'theory of X' with an empirical interpretation: only its explanatory (as opposed to modelling) force is bound to be different.

In this connection, one might ask whether it is possible for a position like this to lead to an explanatory theory. Since it is an uninterpreted calculus, the answer would appear to be negative: if explanation demands the fulfilment of criteria of relevance, it is difficult to see where they would come from in a theory whose primitives have no empirical interpretation. But this is not as great a problem as it might seem, given the larger perspective of the history of linguistics, and a willingness to abandon some popular slogans. Up to now, linguistics has never been (regardless of what some people have claimed or wished at times) an explanatory discipline. (For some, its greatness has been the fact that it wasn't: cf. Joos 1957: 96.) If we define explanation in terms of the D-N paradigm, it is doubtful if any well-formed explanation for an interesting linguistic phenomenon has been adduced in the entire history of the subject.

But this is not necessarily a condemnation; there is nothing wrong with good descriptions, good taxonomies, or thought-provoking and imaginative models. Linguistics up to now has been the descriptive human science *par excellence*, and the steady increase of its descriptive and systematizing power has been one of its glories – as well as the envy of other disciplines, and one of the sources of its influence on anthropology, sociology, and other fields.

I will return to the question of non-explanatory excellences in chapter 5. But considering the prevalence of the autonomy model, and our central concern with explanation, we ought to pursue this matter further in a historical context.

4.8 Explaining change in an autonomous theory

What would a theory of change look like under a radical autonomy interpretation? Would it be either intelligible or explanatory? I suggest below that such a theory would produce a conceptual mess, but a very illuminating one that will help to clarify some basic principles.

Assuming that language is a formally structured World 3 artefact, it is possible to construct a purely mathematical theory of its 'structure' (in Eddington's sense). And this has, as I have suggested, been the fundamental aim of linguistics, at least in the Harris-Chomsky line of succession. The fact that in post-1957 Chomskyan interpretation, these structures are supposed to be 'known' to speakers (as such, or in terms of some as yet unspecifiable isomorphy) is beside the point: mathematizations of language are neutral with respect to locus, means of representation, etc. (see the discussion in Miller 1975). I think we can take it that as far as synchronic linguistics goes, this goal is intelligible and coherent, and may even be achievable.

Now it is clear that in principle the mutations over time of a mathematically specifiable system can be modelled; we have the tools for doing this (cf. §3.9). But this is the case only if the changes in the system are either truly nomic, or governed by formulable stochastic laws, so that we can compute probability distributions of particular states of the system. My previous arguments have suggested that historical change is an area in which we cannot make either of these types of prediction, and that therefore we cannot have independent functions mapping between successive synchronic grammars. (The fact that we can formalize such relations particularistically after the fact is not to the point, if we are interested in explaining: this is merely a matter of our having good taxonomic machinery.) In this respect at least the goal of prediction and hence D-N explanation is not significantly furthered by formalization, and in particular, neither an autonomous theory nor a projectionist one will make any difference in the degree of predictive success. (Especially since even in an avowedly projectionist theory the bases for statistical prediction, such as naturalness, are still empirically uninterpreted.)

But an uninterpreted 'structural' characterization can bring one important problem into focus: assuming such a characterization, how do we explain, not particular changes, but the fact of change itself? Consider an 'ideal' situation, in which we constructed a locally omniscient Laplacean Demon, who could predict some limited set of future changes on the basis of a single ('complete') state-description. Would this help? Descriptively, perhaps. Explanatorily, not at all, because in a purely formal autonomous description there can be no criterion of explanatory relevance – since such criteria are empirical, and demand that the calculus be interpreted. In this case (and cf. the discussion of non-explanatory prediction in §1.7) we would understand as little as we did before, even though we might be able to predict.

That is, any such system could predict change ONLY IN RESPONSE TO PREVIOUS CHANGES. Every known language state has presumably been brought about by previous changes, and change is arrested only by the limitations of our ability to reconstruct. So even given a self-equilibrating system, we would still have to get change into it somehow. In the kind of autonomous model we have been considering, the only way to do this would be to introduce change as an axiom. In such an ideal system, one change might be deducible from a previous (change-induced) state, say as 'compensation': but change itself, which is what we want to understand in the first place, must be introduced as a primitive term.

Thus we could introduce 'optimization', for example, as some kind of homeostatic device that would, given a particular state-description, predict certain changes; and we could (which is what the generativists and Praguians do, regardless of what they say) do this within a mathematical system that presupposed no particular nexus with speakers. But in order to get a system where non-optimal conditions could arise in the first place, if optimality is interpreted as a transcendent global condition on languages, we would have to introduce an unpredictable (and counter-optimizing) 'mutability factor' in the first place.

This is the central conceptual difficulty in an autonomy theory, at least one that wants to be explanatory. Why should such a randomly mutable system exist? (This is not of course a compelling counter-argument: the world is full of apparently purposeless complexity. But it does make one wonder.) It is clear at any rate that a pure autonomy metaphysics is likely to raise a number of deep problems, and even if it removes the messiness engendered by speakers, it fails to explain anything. The most obvious way to introduce mutability (though this isn't without its problems, as the arguments in chapter 3 suggest) would be to take language as a self-regulating OPEN system, i.e. to introduce an extralinguistic world, and make change a function of something like the relationship between an organism and its ecological surround (Saussure is I think hinting at something like this.)

A similar problem arises in evolutionary biology. It is possible to imagine an axiomatic theory of evolution, where 'selection', etc. are mathematically characterizeable, and the life histories of natural populations are provable theorems (cf. Ruse 1973). But this too would operate only on contingently evolved populations as inputs, and would be non-explanatory, even if it furnished some correct predictions. And again, the theory would have to introduce variability as an axiom, or develop an interpretation in terms of contingent extrinsic factors, because the substrate of the variability is extratheoretical (empirical), and its controlling factors are unpredictable.

Given these considerations, it looks as if the demands of explanatory relevance would require the abandonment of a totally World 3 conception of language. We need a more complex model, where we introduce both the World 3 object (which language in some sense undoubtedly is) plus speakers and their transactions with it. That is, a theory in which the World 3 object is mathematizeable, but only as long as it does not come in contact with World 1 or World 2 or time (whether time is 'in' any of these worlds is a separate issue). In this view, time and Worlds 1 and 2 are essentially 'destructive' (in Saussure's sense). I think we can make a case for the position that Saussure (apparently *non sponte sua*) ends up advocating as being the only realistic one: but if we do this, we must clarify the speaker/abstract object nexus, and develop some reasonable and satisfying way of dealing with this interface. Whether this will in the end yield anything like 'explanation' is dubious – it may be the one thing that really makes it impossible. We can conclude by noting that if languages are autonomous systems, there is no conceivable reason for them to change; if they are not, it is still debatable whether there are such reasons.

4.9 What really bothered Saussure

Perhaps the chief source of difficulty for Saussure was the notion (which I think many linguists share) that the question 'what is language?' has a single answer. We might perhaps clear the air by repudiating any such simple-minded ontologies, i.e. that language 'is' some particular thing, like a 'formal object', a 'system of rules', a 'system of conventions', a 'form of behaviour', a 'set of habits', etc. To hold such a view is to put ourselves in the position of the blind men and the elephant. We ought instead, I suggest, to view language as a complex human activity-and-product (as well as all the other possibilities, and more). As an activity, it rests on two kinds of substrates: let us call them 'biophysical' and 'psychosocial'. In Popperian terms, these may be interpreted roughly as World 1 and World 2 respectively (linked with World 3 in a complex relation whose properties are virtually unknown). As product, it is a World 3 artefact, self-existent in that world, but manifested by an infinitely complex and delicate World 1–World 2 interaction.[11]

To be more precise, I assume that when we talk of a child 'acquiring his language' we are not reifying illegitimately when we assert that there is SOMETHING – independent of 'representations' in his parents' brains – that he is acquiring. It probably makes sense to assume (thus avoiding Berkeleyan paradoxes) that language 'exists' even when no one is

---

[11] I am thinking here of Popper's distinction (1973: 112 ff) between the way things are produced and the things themselves. These are of course related, but in principle separate: e.g. we can study an animal's nest (with a certain degree of insight) without presupposing anything beyond the fact that an animal made it. In this way we grant 'objectivity' to World 3 objects; we subsume them under the class-label 'artefact' and turn the study of artefacts into an independent 'structural' discipline – more or less as I suggested in §4.7. Popper thinks that knowledge and language are both objects that ought to be studied this way (1973: 113). In particular, the study of the structure of mental products is independent of psychology (if he developed a linguistic theory it would be non-projectionist, like Hjelmslev's); though of course these things have a bearing on psychology. I have already shown that an extreme form of this view cannot cope with language change, and in principle probably excludes all explanation. I will explore some consequences of the 'bearing' of products on producers (or better, of their mutual implicatedness) in this section.

speaking or knowing it. The problem arises in the World 1/World 3 nexus.[12]

At one level, language (even if it is a World 3 object, mediated by a *faculté de langage*, or whatever) has a neurophysiological substrate; but the *faculté* itself is only one aspect of a total psychology, which also encompasses will and intention; and the individual participant in a language, who already carries about and is carried about in this complex structure is in turn a member of a society, where social considerations (World 3 rules, conventions, etc., also represented in World 2 psychologies, and often associated with World 1 sanctions) can thwart, direct or otherwise influence the individual will.[13]

Now the extent to which the neurophysiological domain (which may, since it is subject to physico-chemical 'law', be in a sense deterministic) is SOLELY involved in anything interesting is, as we have seen, negligible. At most it can be said to 'contribute' in a minor way (see below). Language 'itself', both in synchrony and change, is subject to a hierarchy of controls, increasing in power as they decrease in lawfulness. Thus the properties of the vocal tract, insofar as they are neuro-physiologically defined, establish a set of boundary-conditions within which such things as the possible phonetic forms of human utterances are defined ('boring universals': cf. §2.1).[14] But the possibilities within the area defined by the boundary-conditions are to a large degree under

[12] I am using Popper's three 'Worlds' as an expository metaphor, without asserting either that World 3 is completely coherent and problem-free, or that I have a fully articulated idea of its ontological status. But I certainly find nothing *prima facie* absurd or disturbing (quite the opposite) in Popper's assertion that a World 3 object 'is a real ideal object which exists, but exists nowhere, and whose existence is somehow the potentiality of its being reinterpreted by human minds' (Popper & Eccles 1977: Dialogue III, 450). While World 3 has its problems, certainly World 1 is self-evident, and the philosophical and neurophysiological arguments for World 2, as an independent, non-physical 'self-conscious mind' (Popper & Eccles 1977: especially Part II) seem to me quite convincing. I will continue to subscribe to the three-Worlds doctrine in what follows, even if with some reservations. I will assume at least that it is clear which objects belong in which worlds.

[13] That this sociobiological complexity ('dual setting') constrains the human sciences is an insight going back at least to Comte: on this and the general problem of 'a purely naturalistic theory of the social and cultural world' see the discussion in Cassirer (1944: 64ff).

[14] Even this is probably trivial in the end. It is true that a neurophysiological system is in principle 'subject to law'; but there are many different kinds of lawful systems, and in living ones there is always the problem of 'multiple pathways' (Mayr). There is also the further problem of whether the properties of higher-level systems are ever truly 'reducible' to those of their component lower-level systems: cf. §4.11.

individual or social control, and hence in principle unpredictable, and therefore in a D-N sense inexplicable. (Note that 'unpredictable' here does not mean 'subject to stochastic laws': cf. §2.4.) Here I assert, I hope not too contentiously, something like freedom of the will as a metaphysical principle – though not in the sense of suggesting that linguistic changes are 'human actions' (which they may or may not be).

Thus it is a function of the defining neurophysiological boundary-conditions that it is 'easier' to produce a homorganic NC cluster than a heterorganic one; but it is a matter (loosely) of 'choice' whether or not to capitalize on this. In general: it is a physical (universal) or perhaps definitional fact that an assimilation will lead to a 'reduction of energy expenditure' on some level. But it is a contingent, undetermined matter whether a given individual or speech community will value this 'saving' highly enough to implement it. (Or better, perhaps, to BOTHER to implement it; note that if an 'unnatural' or 'difficult' articulation is a long-standing habit, it could be argued that it requires some effort to undo it and return to the more 'optimal' way of doing things: *pace* Stampean speculations on the effort involved in 'suppressing' natural tendencies.)

I would claim then that linguistic change is entirely a domain of options, including the zero option. NO CHANGE IS EVER NECESSARY. If it were, it would already have happened everywhere, and we wouldn't know about it, since by definition its input conditions could never be realized. (One could fudge this by invoking a 'time-factor': cf. §3.4.) This is what I meant by saying above (§2.1) that the 'universally necessary change' is a fake.

This would all follow more or less from the ontology I have been sketching so far, as a kind of extension of the Saussurean picture. As linguists then our concerns will cover (complementarily) at least the following:

(i) The structure of the object ('language') itself, in general terms (divorced from consideration of any parochial variants) – i.e. 'universal grammar'.

(ii) The structures of particular parochial variants, divorced from contingent physical or substantial realizations – i.e. 'particular grammar'.

Domains (i) and (ii) may be taken as essentially studies of 'form', in the sense that biological morphology as a theoretical study can be (e.g. D'Arcy Thompson 1942).

(iii) The interaction between the 'representational' faculties of individuals and 'forms' of types (i) and/or (ii), i.e. the modes of representation in World 2 of World 3 entities.

(iv) The interaction between the 'mental representations' of (iii) and the peripheral systems (World 1) involved in their manifestations, as well as the study of these systems themselves.

(v) The interaction between the interactions of (iii) and (iv) and the social contexts of use.

Domain (iii) is roughly 'psycholinguistics', (iv) includes 'neuro-linguistics', experimental phonetics, etc., and (v) is broadly speaking 'sociolinguistics', 'pragmatics', and the like.

Overall we are dealing basically with human (individual, social, cultural) interactions with FORM, as well as with form itself.[15] These interactions may be said in any given case to be controlled by the set of boundary-conditions on the relevant systems, but not determined (this is the point of the notion 'boundary-condition'). Language is not a 'thing', but a congeries of structures and processes in interaction; and since all of the systems involved are to a greater or lesser degree non-deterministic (in the sense of 'free' rather than 'stochastic'), neither the fact of any particular change nor its character can be predicted. If the ontology I have been proposing is plausible, the notion 'cause' in the deductive sense is wholly inappropriate: our explanandum domain is a set of interactions between non-deterministic open systems ('clouds' rather than 'clocks': cf. Popper 1973: ch. 6; Moore 1976). In other words, we are dealing with cultural phenomena, and these are not 'caused'. Language is essentially cultural, and only derivatively biological (and thus even more derivatively – and distantly – physico-chemical). Linguistic change should thus in principle be no more predictable than change in art styles. This does not make it, as I will argue, unintelligible (though it does make it inexplicable, which is not

---

[15] In an interesting study, Berger & Luckmann (1967) suggest that there is a special sort of 'dialectical' interaction between man and his 'social world'. Man, they argue, 'is capable of producing a world that he then experiences as something other than a human product'; put another way, 'the product acts back on its producer'. They claim that human institutions, partly because of their historicity (i.e. the fact that the participants in general were not present at the inception of the institution, but 'receive' it) become OBJECTIVE (in something like Popper's World 3 sense), and thus gain a kind of ontological independence that allows for – even predicts – the kind of interaction I have been suggesting.

the same thing): but it does make its study qualitatively different from that of a deterministic, sub-living domain.

4.10 Functionalism in a cultural perspective

We can now return to the problem of function. If we accept that language – whatever else it may be – is a 'cultural institution', then we can see some further reasons why change should not be naturalistically explicable, and why functionalism should be vacuous. One of the origins of functionalism seems to be an attempt (if an inexplicit or even unconscious one) to view the history of language in an 'evolutionary' way. (Note that neo-Darwinian theory, even if not teleological in the sense of ascribing 'purpose' to evolutionary developments, is functionalist in that it is the fulfilment of particular functions that constitutes the material for selection.) That is, an attempt to superimpose the metaphor of 'adaptation' on what would otherwise be viewed as 'straight' (i.e. directionless) history. A particularly gross example is Jespersen's naïve 'progressivism' (1894): this would probably invoke smiles even from present-day functionalists. What we might call a 'sophisticated' functionalist view lies somewhere between the two metaphorical poles of aimless non-directionality and 'historicist' progressivism.

Now this metaphor is borrowed from a discipline that deals essentially with events in the natural world; and we have already seen that there is some reason to question the transference of strategies from this realm to that of human behaviour. Certainly the metaphor fails here: the notion that languages have to 'adapt' to anything, except in the rather trivial sense of acquiring new lexis for new concepts, has never really been argued for, but simply taken by its proponents (like Martinet) as self-evident. At least I have seen no strongly argued cases for the existence of 'speakers' needs' and the like. I question whether (a) the kinds of things that normally happen in language change can ever be interpreted as 'responses to needs' (as should be obvious from the arguments in chapters 2–3) and (b) whether in any case an adaptational model is appropriate to describe the kinds of things people do with their cultural artefacts.

Granted, language is in part utilitarian: we use it for things. But since no one seems ever to have bothered to refute the claim that all languages are by definition equifunctional (cf. §§3.7–8) I take it that is reasonable to claim that nothing a speaker does with the structure of his language can possibly make it any better (or any worse) than it is for its immanent purposes.[16] The boundary-conditions – at all levels – in fact take care of this. As long as language stays within these (rather loose) confines, i.e. as long as it remains within the defining limits of 'possible natural language', there can in principle be no significant 'qualitative' differences between successive states of the same language, or between different languages, with respect to any possible function.

Ideologically speaking, I find it rather odd that such essentially mechanistic notions as generative optimization theory or (neo-)Praguian functionalist theory should arise in what are – ostensibly – 'humanistic' world-views (cf. Chomsky's stress on 'creativity' and 'freedom', Anttila's on 'culture', etc.). It is precisely in the domain of culture that we should expect the kind of utilitarian concerns that these theories embody to have the minimal possible force. It is merely a truism that the cultural (= symbolic) behaviour of human beings is in some sense defined and limited by purely biological capability; it is a category error to extrapolate directly from the biological to the cultural.

There is an essential difference between the natural and the cultural universes (World 1 vs. Worlds 2 and 3, the biosphere vs. the noösphere). This difference is nicely summed up by von Bertalanffy (a biologist) as follows (1968: 208):

Natural science has to do with physical entities in time and space ... social science has to do with human beings in their self-created universe of culture. The cultural universe is essentially a symbolic universe. Animals are surrounded by a *physical* universe with which they have to cope ... Man, in contrast, is surrounded by a universe of *symbols*. Starting from language, which is the prerequisite of culture, to symbolic relationships with his fellows, social status, laws, science, art, morals, religion ... human behaviour, except for the basic ... biological needs of hunger and sex, is governed by symbolic entities. [Emphasis his]

---

[16] Note that I am talking here about 'structural change' in the usual (historical) sense, not about an individual speaker's use of the resources of his language to accomplish particular tasks. Of course topicalization, etc., as activities that speakers can engage in (even if topicalization is a 'rule' in a language, an instance of it represents a speaker's act) are 'functional' in the sense of being directed toward (local) goals, definable within a particular speech-act. But this kind of functional behaviour merely involves the use of possibilities already present (perhaps by definition) in any natural language. This must not be confused with change 'for the sake of' fulfilling functions not catered for (or catered 'badly' for) in a given language state.

It seems difficult to imagine anyone who is seriously 'humanistic' – whatever his particular views about natural science – holding an essentially naturalistic and mechanistic view of what is perhaps the chief of man's cultural artefacts; and any functionalist position is just that. If carried far enough, it reduces all of culture (including linguistics) to a drearily utilitarian role; and aside from the ideological (moral) arguments that could be brought against this, it simply does not seem to bear much relation to the facts. Even if, as the Marxists think, language evolved out of the necessities of division of labour, or had some such utilitarian origin, this does not mean that these factors are still operative. The important point is that most of culture – including language – is from a biological point of view quite useless.

If language is, as I think there is good reason to believe, both 'free' (in the sense of being, beyond its boundary-conditions, biologically undetermined) and creative, then in fact it comes rather more under the heading of 'play' than anything else. Here I mean 'play' in the sense of Huizinga's study (1944) of what he calls the 'Spielelement der Kultur'. For Huizinga (12), play is 'zunächst und vor allem *ein freies Handeln*' (emphasis his). 'Free' in the sense especially that freedom defines it ('befohlenes Speil ist kein Spiel mehr').

Many of the characteristics that Huizinga proposes as definitive for play seem to fit language equally well: it is, for instance (14–15) 'uninteressiertes Handeln'. This does not mean it cannot be used for things (one can for instance play football or chess for money), but rather that in its essentials it is (13) 'nicht das "gewohnliche" oder das "eigentliche" Leben'. It belongs to its own world, it is a 'zeitweilige Sphäre von Aktivität mit einer eigenen Tendenz' (*ibid.*).

Play, further, imposes order, and may be virtually defined as order itself, or at least an ordering principle; it has an 'innige Verknüpfung mit dem Bergriff der Ordnung' (17). And the rules are critically definitive: 'die geringste Abweichung von ihr verdirbt das Spiel, nimmt ihr seinen Charakter' (*ibid.*).

The rules are both arbitrary and definitive; they determine, within the world of the game, 'was ... gelten soll' (18). Huizinga's defining summary is I think particularly suggestive (21–2):

Der Form nach betrachtet kann man das Spiel also zusammenfassend eine freie Handlung nennen, die ... außerhalb des gewöhnlichen Lebens stehen empfunden wird und trotzdem den Spieler völlig in Beschlag nehmen kann, an die kein materielles Interesse geknüpft ist und mit der kein Nutzen erworben

wird ... die nach bestimmten Regeln ordnungsgemäß verläuft und Gemein-
schaftsverbände ins Leben ruft ...

These represent the points where language, ritual, art, science, and
other forms of what Huizinga considers activities possessing the play
characteristic to a large degree tend to fall together.

This is not to claim that language 'is play' – rather that it (just like
science) shares some of its characteristics. In particular its freedom, its
arbitrary rule-governedness, its essential separateness from considerations of material interest (whatever its particular uses can be), and its
socializing power (institution-formation, creation of in-groups, foster-
ing of exclusiveness and xenophobia).

It is interesting to note that one of the most important contributors to
the development of the theory of optimization in generative phonology,
Morris Halle, has recently espoused a similar view (1975: 527–8). He
quotes with approval a passage from Novalis, who says that language is
'ein blosses Wortspiel'; that language and mathematical formulas are
similar in that they create 'eine Welt fuer sich aus – Sie Spielen nur mit
sich selbst, druecken nichts als ihre wunderbare Natur aus'. And he
adds (528) that because 'language is not, in essence, a means for
transmitting information' (a metaphysical claim, to be sure, but
certainly one as tenable as Martinet's) 'it is hardly surprising to find in
languages much ambiguity and redundancy, as well as other properties
that are obviously undesirable in a good communication code'.

Halle, to his credit (especially considering my strictures against him
for being a monist in Lass 1976a: ch. 7) considers this view to be
complementary to the view of language as a means of communication,
and neither 'correct' nor 'incorrect'.

I have been trying in this section and the last to stress the importance
of a complementation of approaches. The methodological point may be
expressed this way: if many different kinds of systems, all communica-
tionally deficient in one way or another from an ideal information-
theoretic point of view, seem to serve human communities perfectly
well; and if language is many things other than a communication
system, including a form of play; then change can occur, presumably,
for reasons totally unconnected with communicative 'function', and
connected solely with the play element. If this is so, it is a further reason
why we should not expect lawfulness or predictability. And therefore a
further reason why we should not expect language change to be
naturalistically explicable.

4.11 Historical uniqueness, emergence, and 'reducibility'

I now return to the relevance to the explanation of language change of two phenomena alluded to earlier: the uniqueness of historically evolved entities (§3, and briefly in §4.3) and the existence of emergent properties (§4.3). We have already seen the problems they pose even in infrahuman biology.

Uniqueness is of particular importance in the context of a search for D-N explanations, because of the essential contradiction between the concepts 'instance of a law' and 'unique event/object'. G. G. Simpson (1964: ch. vii) in a detailed study of the problems caused by the entry of history into a science, has put this as follows. Recall the distinction between 'immanent' and 'configurational' properties discussed in the appendix to chapter 2: the immanent properties are 'laws of nature' in the usual sense, and the 'configurational' ones the particular (historically induced and at least partly contingent) constellations of properties that the immanent ones affect. The immanent ones are 'nonhistorical, even though they ... act in the course of history'; but the 'actual state of the universe ... at a given time ... is not immanent and is constantly changing' (Simpson, 122). This leads Simpson to a definition of history as 'configurational change through time, a sequence of real, individual but interrelated events' (*ibid.*).

This distinction becomes particularly important in the light of the hierarchy of complexity manifested in objects in the universe. This leads in turn to a hierarchy of uniqueness or individuality, from physics upwards to biology (and beyond, to the human sciences): an organism is more complex and more individual than a molecule, a man than an insect, etc. This can be expressed (Simpson, 124–5) in terms of the number of 'taxonomically discrete objects in any field of study'.

The property of uniqueness bears on the applicability of the concept 'law'. Laws (126) 'are complete abstractions from the individual case', i.e. from the contingent configurations on which they act.[17] Because of their immanence, they are defined (rather obviously) in terms of their REPEATABILITY. Simpson claims (128) that for this reason 'the search for historical laws is ... mistaken in principle. Laws apply ... "other things being equal." But in history, a sequence of real, individual events, other things never are equal.'

---

[17] This has led some philosophers to insist that even D-N explanations of singular instances have no scientific value; they are only significant when they cover classes of events (Salmon 1975: 119).

This may be glossed as follows: the utility of the concept of law decreases with decrease in the repeatability of the event, i.e. with increase in its individuality. Of course this necessitates a certain amount of tact in determining what is meant by a 'real, individual event'; a point I have so far skirted. I am not sure that a non-intuitive definition is really possible, but I do think that we can establish fairly uncontroversial limits of tolerance.

Let us say that 'history' proper is a term applicable only to domains consisting of 'individuals', and let us draw the following preliminary demarcation: atoms, molecules (even macromolecules) are not individuals in the relevant sense, but organisms are (forget about the grey area in between, consisting *inter alia* of viruses and unicellular organisms, the members of colonial organisms like *Volvox* or sponges, and so on). If we can agree that organisms are individuals, whereas the molecules (and organs?) that compose them are not, we can say that 'individuality' in this sense depends on complexity (above some unspecified but fairly obvious point). And the more complex an object is, the more likely it is (a) to be a recognizable individual, and (b) to have a history in which its interactions with surrounding contingencies will be in part a function of its individuality. In other words, we will not deny that human beings (and *a fortiori* their social aggregations) and their cultural artefacts are 'taxonomically distinct' individuals, and that they therefore have individual histories.[18]

Now it follows from this that the more complex an individual is, the more factors we have to know about if we want to predict how it is going to respond to contingencies.[19] And of course the problem with language is not merely a matter of complex individuals (whether speakers, communities, or languages themselves, or the confluence posited in §4.10) facing simple (and known) contingencies; we really have no idea of what the contingencies themselves are, and whether they are even

[18] It is complexity, not sentience, that produces individuality; thus our galaxy is an individual with its own history, distinct from that of any other galaxy, and the same holds for our solar system, our earth, and so on. The more complex an individual is (according to whatever measure) the more it interacts with contingencies – or perhaps better, the more different kinds of interactions it is capable of.

[19] Of course prediction will fail for quite simple entities, e.g. at the microphysical level. But this is a rather different kind of failure. In such cases the number of possible states to be predicted will usually be very small (e.g. a photon will either go through a hole in a screen, not go through it, or the outcome will be indeterminate). Whereas the number of different state-changes for a language (even if not for an individual item in it) is indefinitely large.

implicated in language change. (We do know about some rather gross ones, like contact phenomena; but even here we can't predict the behaviour of languages. For example, whether a language will prefer calquing to borrowing a lexical item: Old English religious writings calque L. *patriarchus* as *hēah-fæder*, but Middle English is happy with *patriarch*, and so on.) The subject matter of historical linguistics is thus – at present anyhow – a set of unimaginably complex individuals, whose immanent 'lawfulness' (if there is any, except at the most trivial level) is ill-understood, and which operates in a universe of unspecified contingencies. The most important limiting factor in our ability to explain change is thus the opacity of the extent to which nomic factors operate not only in language and its speakers, but in the whole socio-cultural-historical 'ecosystem' of which it is part (something like this is largely the case even in organic evolution).[20] My own feeling, as is no doubt clear, is that this is a matter of principle, not of linguists' own (contingent and remediable) limitations. But this is arguable, and should be argued; I am attempting to provoke argument, not prevent it.

The individuality problem raises another conceptual difficulty: the old problem of 'comparability' of systems. That is, we do not as yet have any way of deciding which events in linguistic history can count as 'repetitions' – though we often talk as if we can do this without difficulty. If languages (in whatever sense) are individuals (which no one would deny absolutely, I should think), then we need some way of establishing the limiting conditions on individuality. If every language is radically unique, then of course there is no linguistics; the *reductio* of this is the kind of 'idiolectology' that some forms of linguistics have threatened to collapse into, where no generalizations are possible (cf. Weinreich, Labov & Herzog 1968).

But if we allow any individuality, the problem of demarcation remains, and we need some criteria for solving it. If all events in language history are irreducibly unique, then there are of course no generalizations; but if we want to limit uniqueness (establish types, and decide which items are tokens of which types), we need some better way of doing it than the purely intuitive way we usually proceed. Let us consider a simple example. Say two languages both show a change which can be described (roughly) this way: velar stops become palatal

---

[20] Cf. the discussion of historical uniqueness in Lorenz (1977: ch. 13). Lorenz argues that like natural species 'culture develops independently, at its own risk and by its own means, in a historically unique, unprecedented process' (233).

before non-low front vowels. Surely, in anyone's estimation, a 'natural' change, even close to (but only close to) 'predictable'. But this could be begging a question, and we do not yet know how important this question is. Say that the two languages in question are Swedish and English, and that they both 'have a phoneme /k/', which is a velar before back vowels, etc. Phonetically, however, it is not the case that a Swedish '/k/' is the same as an English '/k/'; it is (as far as I have observed) invariably much fronter in all environments than an English one. For example, the 'palatal' in Sw. *kan* is much fronter than what a dialect of English (say a Standard Scottish or Northern English) with the same vowel quality ([a]) has in *can*. So are we justified in calling both cases 'palatalization of velars'? That is, to what extent does the whole system, even down to microphonetic detail, prejudice identification? I do not think we have any theoretical criteria that permit us to make judgements even as elementary as this with any confidence; and yet without them we could not even begin to have 'laws' covering classes of events, since we would have no criteria for grouping events into classes.

The problem of individuality (at whatever level) is closely related to that of emergence. 'Emergence' is rather a simple (though in some circles still controversial) notion, with two main aspects, a diachronic and a synchronic. Diachronically, emergence is 'invention', the appearance of genuine novelty, or what Lorenz (1977: ch. 2) has called a *fulguratio* or 'creative flash'. Synchronically, it is what might be called holistic transcendence, or the difference between the 'specific character of things' (Waddington 1977: 140) and the properties of the things they are made of. That is, the properties of 'new' things in history are not necessarily deducible from those of their predecessors (plus 'natural laws'), and the organizational (structural, systemic) properties of complex wholes are not necessarily deducible in any straightforward way – or at all – from the (pre-systemic) properties of their components.

Both the diachronic and synchronic aspects of emergence in organic evolution, to take one example, are characterized by Lorenz (1977: 35) as follows:

... no system on a higher level of integration can be deduced from a lower system, however fully one may understand this lower system. We know ... that higher systems have arisen from lower ones ... We also know ... the earlier stages in development from which higher living beings emerged. But each step forward has consisted of a *fulguratio*, a historically unique event in phylogeny which has always had a chance quality about it – the quality, one might say, of something invented.

(The kind of emergences Lorenz is referring to may be seen against a wider cosmological background as well: cf. Popper's list of major emergences, which includes those of the heavier elements, of macro-molecules, of life, of consciousness, and of language: Popper & Eccles 1977: 27.)

Even for purely material (i.e. non-living) systems, this general position can be argued to hold: that structure and organization (higher-level properties) are not derivable only from the physico-chemical laws that control component entities: they stem from higher-order prin-ciples, which at the moment at least are irreducibly emergent (and therefore, if you will, occult). Lorenz (1977: 29ff) gives a striking example where the result of coupling together two electrical circuits gives rise to a new entity with properties not predictable from the properties of the two component circuits; and, to take another more familiar example, Ayala (1976: 18) points out that 'water is formed by the union of two atoms of hydrogen with an atom of oxygen, but ... exhibits properties which are not the immediately apparent consequence of the properties of the two gases'. And Polanyi (Polanyi & Prosch 1975: 164–73) presents a powerful argument to the same effect concerning the relation between DNA and the genetic code. The simple point is that principles of order do not – and cannot – derive simply from properties of the entities that are ordered: phonologies do not derive merely from phonetic properties, syntax does not derive from morphology, the structure of a sonata-form movement does not derive from the properties of its notes or harmonies, but from abstract principles like key-relations and the return of particular melodic shapes, etc.

If emergence is something that must be accepted, then it poses serious difficulties for any programme of reductionism. It may conceivably be possible in future to effect a complete set of reductions: e.g. of linguistics to biology, biology to chemistry, chemistry to physics, and so on. And thus to reduce to lower-level laws the properties of complex, historically derived, and transcendently structured objects. But it is to be remembered that this is merely (for some) a hope, not an empirically based possibility; considering the kinds of arguments available against even the possibility in principle of such a reduction (e.g. Polanyi & Prosch 1975: ch. 11; Popper & Eccles 1977: Part I, §§8–9, 16–27, 56), it is a pretty remote one.

Perhaps the best image of the relation between levels of organization in any complex domain is not one where each level can be REDUCED to the one below, but rather where each higher level represents an ENRICHMENT of the one(s) below. Thus linguistics would not be 'reduced to' biology, but its domain would, like that of any 'social science' represent an enriched biology, as biology is an enriched chemistry and chemistry an enriched physics (cf. Popper & Eccles 1977: 20f).

Given a view like this, Popper argues (*ibid.*) that even though some (or even most) higher-level principles may in the end be reducible to lower-level ones, and even though of course 'lower levels remain ... valid within the higher levels', this still disallows complete determinism, and allows emergence: the retained validity of the lower levels merely blocks 'miraculous' emergence (enrichment does not entail suspension of law). Since on this interpretation even the macrophysical world is not fully deterministic (much less the specifically biological and human worlds), the hope of any 'deep' D-N explanation is vanishingly small, because the ways to it are always being cut off by new emergences.[21] Given the current situation, we might argue with Ayala (1976: 318) that because of the present impossibility of any real reduction, and because we have no idea how a full reduction might eventually be accomplished, 'whether the reduction will be possible in the future is an empirically meaningless question'. While local reductions to law are possible in some cases, it seems doubtful that very far-reaching ones will ever be accomplished. As I said above (§§2.3, 4.3), claims for ultimate reducibility to law (in any domain) are confessions of faith; as well of course as stimuli to greater efforts. But they require at least the specification of a research programme before they can be taken seriously.

---

[21] On emergence in general see further Harré (1972: 145f), and from a rather different point of view, Polanyi (1967: ch. 2). On the general issue in biology, especially in relation to the problem of 'reduction', see Grene (1974: ch. IV). On the concept of emergence in the social sciences, see Wisdom (1970).

5 Conclusions and prospects : the limits of deductivism and some alternatives

Well this is I think all very crude analogical talking, but, if we can't talk better, we have to talk the way we can.

Sir John Eccles

5.1 Prospective summary

The arguments of the last four chapters have, I think, made a good case for the following propositions:

(i) That 'naturalness' is not an explanatory notion; because it is in most cases merely statistical and empirically uninterpreted; and even when it is (physiologically, perceptually) interpreted it is non-predictive.

(ii) That 'function' as a motivation for language change is not an explanatory notion, because: (a) it has no coherent definition; (b) there is no strong evidence in any case that there is such a thing, however defined; (c) because it is non-predictive; and (d) because (a)–(b) lead to logical fallacies in attempted functional explanations of change.

(iii) That there are (as yet) no D-N explanations for any linguistic change.

The arguments in chapter 4, while weaker than those in 2–3, seem to give support anyhow to the propositions:

(iv) That given the complexity and mysteriousness of the phenomena subsumed under 'language', and the likelihood that many of its (necessarily complementary) aspects are non-deterministic, it is not surprising that (iii).

(v) That given this complementarity, and the fact that language is many things besides a 'means of communication' (formal system, plaything, set of interactions between partially open systems, etc.), it is not surprising that (ii).

These conclusions may be taken either as grounds for pessimism, or as a spur to conceptual clarification and further empirical work (both certainly needed in any case); the latter with a view toward partial or complete refutation of any or all of (i)–(v). Now I have, as is obvious, no particular hope of this myself, since I have argued for (i)–(iii), and I believe (on fairly good grounds, I think) that (iv)–(v). But this is not important here; my purpose is to present a critical interim report, not an exhaustive final statement. I have merely portrayed, as clearly as I can, a situation where it seems clear that something has to be done.

From one point of view it would be very nice if all my arguments and assertions could be shown to be wrong, since in that case the future would look (for those of certain persuasions) a lot rosier, and the discipline a lot healthier. But if nothing else, the suggestion that there is work to do – even on absolute fundamentals – represents a note of mild optimism: the field still looks at least marginally viable, and maybe just beginning. (Not that I know, except in a rather vague way, what to do, or precisely where to begin: except that getting rid of error is always a good beginning, and maybe the best thing of all to do: cf. §5.6. But, as I said in §1.2, making positive suggestions is not the critic's business.)

I did however claim (§4.1) that there were two possible starting points for further work: developing our empirical base to the point where we can posit laws, or developing and justifying a non-deductivist epistemology. The first direction seems fairly straightforward: it is I presume largely in the hands of experimental phoneticians, psycholinguists, even psychologists, neurologists, and other workers in fields outside linguistics. The second however is not straightforward at all, and deserves some comment. I don't think it's possible at this point (if ever) to 'solve' a major problem like this, but I think it is possible to clarify some of the difficulties involved. Certainly it might be worthwhile to bring into focus some of the criticisms that have been directed by philosophers against the deductivist/falsificationist paradigm in general, and make some tentative suggestions about other ways of approaching the major question: what ought we to consider the desirable outputs of historical investigations to be? What, in fact, ought we to consider 'knowledge' of linguistic change to be? Can we ever be said to 'know' anything at all about it beyond the mere fact of its occurrence?

I must say in advance that I feel a certain discomfort about some of what I'm going to say below, because it suggests attitudes that are hard to justify in terms of the ideology that has dominated most of my argument, and which I still find rather attractive, if not as totally compelling as I once did. But this ideology does have its problems, and in this context they ought to have an airing.

Let us consider the consequences of abandoning two notions that were basic to the argument of chapters 1–3: (a) that the goodness of an explanation is to be judged only in absolute terms, divorced from any consideration of explaining as a speech-act with (happy or unhappy) perlocutionary effects; and (b) that the highest (or even only) goal of intellectual endeavour is D-N explanation and/or falsification of hypotheses, with its corollary that reduction to 'law' is the only source of respectable knowledge. The latter point is probably the more important one; the former may be something of a side-issue, related more to the psychology of linguists than to their subject: though it does provoke some curious reflections on the phenomenology of our evaluation of arguments and explanations, and on some general properties of scholarly discourse.

The fundamental problem as we will see, is that of rationality: is there any sense in which, in the absence of D-N explanations, and even in the absence of (strictly) falsifiable claims, our accounts of language change can be rational? Is there some justification for asserting a non-deductivist, non-falsificationist rationality? If, so, does the knowledge gained through it have any epistemic status?

These questions will prompt a consideration of two topics: (a) the status and value of knowledge (or 'knowledge') that is not agreed on by all rational or competent persons, but is defended by some as being true; and (b) the status and value of non-deductive, non-predictive ('taxonomic', 'descriptive') knowledge in general. We will see that even in the most apparently 'hard' disciplines, a certain irreducible element of personal commitment and metaphysical choice (as well as pure non-predictive description) must probably be said to enter into questions of knowledge – though this does not necessarily lead to irrationalism.

Now to a more precise statement. One way of interpreting what follows is this: I have (correctly or not) argued myself into a position where explanation of language change (in the D-N sense) appears to be impossible, as a matter both of contingent fact and of principle. Therefore any alternatives I try to develop will be simply making a virtue of necessity, or a rather desperate attempt to maintain some kind of intellectual respectability in the face of my arguments that this is unattainable.

Aside from being uncharitable, this would misrepresent my intention. I have already suggested at a number of points that a mature and viable linguistic theory has to be pluralist, in the sense of subsuming complementary aspects of its subject matter (cf. also Lass 1976a: ch. 7 and epilogue; 1976b). The previous chapter was designed specifically to illustrate some of the problems for deductivism raised by the existence of complementations within the domain of linguistics; a slogan deriving from that chapter, and from my earlier arguments (Lass 1976a: epilogue) to the effect that linguistics is of necessity at least partly a form of 'rational metaphysics' might be: deductivism where the subject matter suits it; otherwise whatever else gives results and can be rationally discussed and criticized. That is, it is possible to serve two masters, even if their demands are contradictory – as long as one serves them in different times and different places.

This of course runs afoul of the widespread belief, exemplified by the quotation from Sampson in §4.1, that there cannot be any such complementary approaches to knowledge: only deductive prediction and the falsification of predictions yields knowledge; anything else is 'emotion' or whatever.

Now even though I argued in chapters 2 and 3 that naturalness and function were not respectable notions because they failed to be predictive, I never said at any point that I thought that deductivism was the only source of knowledge, or that explanation in that restricted sense was the only legitimate goal for historical (or any other) linguistics. There was another component to my argument, which will come into focus again in this chapter: that naturalness and function, while not explanatory notions, are not bad just because they are non-explanatory: they are bad because they are irrational, i.e. they simply do not make sense in ANY context, not merely the deductive one.

I do not believe that prediction is the only source of knowledge (though it is an important and in some ways peculiarly satisfactory one). I think that the centrality and hierarchical prominence that have been given to (neo-)positivist methodology as the sole guarantor of epistemic value are disproportionate, and that a case can be made for the validity and value (not to mention necessity) of other approaches. The kinds of 'knowledge', or whatever we may want to call it, that they yield may be quite different from the 'certitude' afforded by deductivism-plus-falsificationism; there is no doubt that they are less satisfactory in some ways, certainly more arguable and less compelling. But even second-best is not the same as universal darkness, and there may well be areas in which second-best is best, because first-best is simply not possible in principle.

But it can also be argued that first-best may not be, in all ways, as good as it seems; I will turn to this in the next section.

5.2 Some criticisms of positivist rationality

Let us return to Sampson's contention that law-derived predictions and their falsifications are the only source of genuine knowledge: or at least higher-order theoretical knowledge, as opposed to 'mere' empirical knowledge (though this may not be such a strict opposition: cf. §5.3). Can this really be supported? Or does it depend (circularly) on an assertion that 'knowledge' is to be defined solely in this way? There are two subquestions here, both of which have been extensively discussed in the literature, so I will make my comments rather schematic:[1] (a) what exactly can we be said to know when we have achieved a D-N explanation? and (b) is the falsificationist programme an adequate foundation for an epistemology?

To begin with (a). I suppose that the output of a D-N explanation is a special kind of conviction, perhaps the strongest available to us: that of 'necessary truth'. That is, if *modus ponens* is valid, then any explanation reducible to it is valid and unchallengeable. But there is something unsatisfactorily *post hoc* about it (quite different from the *post hoc* fudging of functional explanation). And this is that it can by definition yield no more knowledge than we put into it in the first place. We must already know the laws, initial conditions, etc., and the explanation is simply a formalization of (part of) what we know already (cf. §4.5).

This property of D-N explanations forms the basis for Polanyi's exceedingly harsh criticism (Polanyi & Prosch 1975: 55ff). Polanyi claims that (even given their merits) D-N explanations do not have a very strong bearing on the ultimate goal of explanation, 'relief from puzzlement' (53). He claims (55) that:

To define the explanation of an event as its subsumption under a general law leaves unexplained its capacity to relieve puzzlement and isolates it from numerous other, more fundamental, acts which have this capacity. Explanation

---

[1] For more technically philosophical criticism, see Hesse (1966: 155–77, 1974, 1976); Harré (1972: ch. 2); and Feyerabend (1975).

must thus be understood as a particular form of insight – an insight that relieves our puzzlement through the establishment of a more meaningful integration of parts of our experience, achieved through subsumption of a natural law under a more general law.

Thus Polanyi seeks, not to isolate the D-N schema as uniquely insightful, but to suggest that it is merely one (highly specialized and limited) source of insight.

Because of this, he argues, we should not reduce explanation 'to any merely *formal* subsumption' (55, emphasis Polanyi's). If we do this, what happens is that 'the actual subject matter is restricted to a fragment found suitable for formalization' (*ibid.*). This is not necessarily bad *per se*: so long as we don't sweep the unformalized residue under the rug, and assume that insight into the formalizeable is all we need.

A further problem with formal explanation, in Polanyi's view, is that it leads to 'loss of meaning', an isolation of the formalized explanatory schema from the mental act which originally led to it, and thus to an illegitimate granting of explanatory or insight-giving power to a partial substitute for the original ordering act, which is – necessarily – informal and 'integrative'. The D-N schema lacks in the end even the full 'perlocutionary' effect of the original act of insight. Thus (*ibid.*):

. . . formalization, if carried out strictly, produces a result that is . . . in itself, empty of any bearing on the subject matter: but by calling it an 'explanation', one imbues it with the memory of that informal . . . act of the mind which it was supposed to replace. Such a denial of mental powers avoids its ultimate consequences by borrowing the qualities of the very powers it sets out to eliminate.

This is a consequence of Polanyi's insistence that D-N explanation, since it is ultimately tied to strict materialism, i.e. to a kind of Laplacean vision, is essentially MEANINGLESS (25):

. . . the *ideal* goals of science are nonsensical . . . The ideal of science remains what it was in the time of Laplace: to replace all human knowledge by a complete knowledge of atoms in motion. In spite of much that is said to the contrary, quantum mechanics makes no difference in this respect. A quantum-mechanical theory of the universe is just as empty of meaning as a Laplacean mechanical theory. [Emphasis his]

The objection is thus that deductivism – as a TOTAL foundation for an epistemology – is flawed because, in its insistence on complete 'lawfulness', it is ultimately materialist or physicalist; and any totally materialist theory of the world is devoid of interest in terms of uniquely human knowledge (as well as being unacceptable on other grounds).[2]

Perhaps the best way of seeing the source of the D-N paradigm's peculiar attractiveness and power is in terms of its undoubted ability to establish CONNECTIONS: by means of a successful D-N explanation we impose a certain connecting order on our knowledge, by bringing formerly disparate aspects of it into contact. Though there may be nothing (substantively) totally 'new', the old material is differently ordered, or ordered where it was unordered, and the new order is backed up by logical coherence. The criticism is not of D-N itself, but of its inflated claims; there are many other activities, often performed by respectable scientists, that have very similar effects, and may in some cases establish a superior coherence.

Now to a bridge between points (a) and (b) above, the connection between deductivism and falsificationism. Sampson, as we saw, associates D-N explanation with the (potential) falsification of predictions, which seems on the face of it quite reasonable. But (even though Popper was one of the pioneers of the recent theory behind D-N explanation) there is something odd in the conjunction of deductivism and falsificationism as components of the same epistemology. Certainly if we adopt any kind of radical falsificationism (say that of Popper 1968a or 1968b, without neo-Popperian additions like those of Lakatos 1970), we have a conflict. In order for a D-N explanation to be correct, its premises must be true; but if one is a hard-line and consistent falsificationist, there is no way that a 'law of nature' (which will be at least one of the premises in the schema) can be known to be true; therefore part of the power of the D-N schema is vitiated, because the 'laws' are themselves falsifiable hypotheses (this argument comes essentially from Harré 1972). This leads to the following paradox for anyone who claims to be both a deductivist and a falsificationist: an attempted D-N explanation that fails is more 'informative' than a successful one, since it is really only in this case that we know something new that we didn't know before: namely that what we thought we knew was false.

D-N explanation, then, in order to be genuinely successful in producing knowledge, must be divorced from radical falsificationism; since *modus ponens* obviously yields true conclusions only from true premises, and if we stipulate the truth of a natural law we step outside

---

[2] For similar objections to determinism cf. Eccles in Popper & Eccles (1977: 546).

the (deductive) falsificationist paradigm into an (inductive) verificationist one.[3] There is of course nothing wrong with this, since only maniacs are totally consistent; but it points out the interesting fact that no one can work in a real discipline and maintain a single restricting philosophical position at all times without becoming obsessive and ultimately trivializing his work (cf. Harré 1972: ch. 2). This is problematical only for the practitioner who is trying to be 'philosophical', not for the philosopher as outsider.

Some brief comments now on falsificationism itself, the other side of what I have been calling 'positivist rationality'. Whatever its status as an ideal, the Popperian scenario for the growth of knowledge (or its various modifications, such as Lakatos' 'Research Programmes' methodology) neither is nor can be absolutely followed in practice. In the day-to-day conduct of scientific enterprises is it clear that the splendid vision of refutation by *experimentum crucis* rarely if ever materializes (as Lakatos 1970 shows; for criticism even of 'sophisticated' versions of falsificationism like his cf. Feyerabend 1975, especially ch. 16). There are, it seems, no hard-and-fast 'universal' criteria that will force an investigator – even in the interests of rationality – to give up a theory. 'Refutation' is to a considerable extent defined by an interaction between individual convictions and the canons set up by a particular scholarly community for determining the point at which a theory should be discarded (note the emphasis on 'theory': criteria for scrapping individual assertions or claims made within the context of a global theory are usually more clear-cut). This may even, as Feyerabend argues, be a good thing: the idea that the 'supersession' of one theory by another is always due to the superseding theory having a genuinely superior empirical content may be an 'epistemological illusion'.[4]

This is not to say that I adopt an irrationalist position like Feyerabend's, but an assertion that rationality is not necessarily compromised by irrational or apparently irrational convictions, or even

[3] Mary Hesse has argued (1974: 95) that even Popperian falsificationism, set as it is within a system that asserts the impossibility of induction, is itself dependent on inductive confirmation: 'one past falsification of a generalization does not imply that [it] is false for future instances. To assume that it will be falsified again in similar circumstances is to make an inductive assumption.'

[4] Feyerabend (1975: 67) argues that because of problems with observation terms, etc., theories may be inconsistent with the evidence not because they are incorrect, but 'because the evidence is contaminated'. This suggests that 'it would be extremely imprudent to let the evidence judge our theories directly and without any further ado'.

a certain amount of willful 'tenacity' – so long as these are taken as the bases for and stimuli towards the development of rational strategies of public argumentation (strategies of 'criticism', not necessarily 'falsification'). I will return to this point in the following sections.

As a preliminary to the rest of my argument here, I want to stress the following: all forms of scientific (and other) reasoning are flawed, limited, and ultimately necessarily complementary. Rather than contenting (or discontenting) ourselves with the kind of positivist exclusivity claimed by Sampson, we ought to consider the possibilities of a view in which inductive heuristics, analogical thinking and model-building, falsification, deductivism, taxonomy, etc. all have their roles to play (cf. Harré 1972: 57). At any rate, if the output of the deductivist programme is the only kind of 'knowledge' that counts, we need another name for the rest of what any intellectual discipline with an empirical subject matter provides: e.g. refinements of descriptive techniques and categories, discoveries of new objects, development of powerful new metaphors, insightful taxonomies, new ordering principles that organize previously unorganized observations or fragments of empirical knowledge, and so on. A linguistics (or any other discipline) which presented us with nothing but deductive schemata would be impoverished and ultimately sterile, as would one that downgraded all these other activities and hoped to reduce them to 'epiphenomena' of formalized deductive systems. A good moral for the rest of this chapter (as indeed for this book – though it cuts two ways) might be the Nun's Priest's admonition: 'Taketh the fruyt, and lat the chaf be stille.'

5.3 Different kinds of 'knowing': private, community and public rationality

One of the issues raised by the positivist claims for D-N explanation is that of what constitutes 'knowledge'. Sampson provides a very simple and straightforward definition, which skirts many problems; his (non-falsificationist) definition is simply that if we take certain 'laws' as true, and follow the ordinary rules of deductive logic, we attain to a situation where the laws plus specified initial conditions entail our observations, and this entailment constitutes knowledge.

This view can probably be reconstructed as being pretty much the same as the ordinary-language sense of 'knowing a proposition': i.e. *know* is a 'factive' verb which presupposes the truth of its sentential object, and it can be said to stand in a certain relation to *believe*, which does not. Thus 'S believes that p, and p is false', but *'S knows that p, and p is false'. (Other meanings of *know*, e.g. in 'S knows the Linnaean binomial taxonomy' or 'S knows Chomsky's views on innateness' are not at issue at the moment: though we will see later that they have a role to play in defining the kind of knowledge historical linguistics ought to yield.)

Within the deductivist framework, we can take knowledge then as a special case of belief, i.e. belief in true propositions (and in the falsificationist one, which is less important here, belief in true propositions of the form 'p is false'). Thus we can say here that 'S knows that p' $\supset$ ('S believes that p' & 'p is true').[5]

If this is the case, then within a strict version of the epistemology Sampson proposes, no explanatory proposition in historical linguistics (or any other form of linguistics, or other empirical discipline) can be known, since all laws are hypothetical; and only fairly trivial non-explanatory ones can be known – in fact, I suppose, only analytic propositions. This is clearly not a very useful definition of 'knowledge'; since among other things it excludes knowledge of empirical generalizations. I will assume that we can, even in a deductivist/falsificationist framework, use 'true' in a simple (if rather loose) 'correspondence' sense, and be said to know at least that certain empirical facts and generalizations are true (I take it that this is a harmless and necessary sloppiness).

There is for example a sense in which I can uncontroversially be said to know that 'all voiceless stops before stressed vowels, unless preceded by [s], are aspirated in my dialect of English'. (Leaving aside the fact that I have transferred theoretical terms like 'stressed', 'aspirated' to the observation language without comment.) Assuming that my hearing is in order, and that I can legitimately generalize from observations of native speakers, and that I am not using any of the terms in a Pickwickian way, if this statement is p and I believe that p, I know that p.

---

[5] As is clear from the text above, I am not proposing this as an exhaustive definition of knowledge in any philosophical sense (cf. §5.5 below). Nor am I assuming that 'true' is an unproblematical predicate (cf. Putnam 1978: Lecture 1). This is merely one possible definition, and the one relevant to Sampson's claims, and to this part of my discussion. I assume here that 'true' means either (a) true by correspondence (in a Tarskian sense), or (b) true (derivatively) by virtue of valid deduction from true (in sense (a)) premises. (For some discussion cf. Lyons 1977: §§16.2, 17.2.)

Now let us go a step further. On the basis of the generalization above, many phonologists would claim that (therefore) they know e.g. that 'there is a /p/ → [ph] rule in this dialect of English'. Can this be 'known' in the same way as the empirical generalization? The answer would seem to be no, unless '/p/ → [ph]' (where the notation implies a set of higher-order theoretical categories like 'underlying representation', 'rule', etc.) is stripped of any ontological content; in which case it is merely a notational variant of the prose statement of distribution. But if one BELIEVES that distributional regularities of a certain kind are 'in fact' reflexes of a rule of some specific type, and relegates this belief to 'background knowledge', then there probably is a sense in which he can be said to 'know that /p/ → [ph]'. But of course knowing theoretical statements at this level of abstraction is not the same thing as knowing a logically true proposition or knowing a lower-level empirical generalization, since the former must necessarily be stipulated;[6] they are not intersubjectively verifiable by equally competent observers with different beliefs. The truth of '/p/ → [ph]' in this case is metaphysical. But I think we can still claim knowledge of a sort, as I will try to show below.

I now propose a taxonomy of types of belief which may clarify the nature of the metaphysical component in a statement like the 'rule' given above, and which reflects on the critical question of rational canons of acceptability for such claims to knowledge. I begin by distinguishing what I will call Public, Community, and Private rationality. These define forms of belief (and ultimately knowledge) which differ, not in the strength of the epistemic conviction they produce, or even (necessarily) in their degree of 'correctness'; but rather in the social context in which the statement or act of belief occurs, and its degree of intersubjective acceptance.

Public rationality defines the domain of agreement among all competent persons. I assume for instance that there is a public (cross-disciplinary) rationality in which all competent persons will agree that 'affirming the consequent is an invalid inferential move', and so on; that

---

[6] There is of course a sense in which the distribution of aspiration (even as stated by a competent observer) is 'stipulated': at least it is taken, like all universal statements, as potentially corrigible. In cases like this we could define 'true by correspondence' as 'very highly corroborated', i.e. (so far) lacking in counter-observations by equally competent observers, and with a consensus among competent observers that counter-observations are highly unlikely to be made. (In practice this is what we normally mean when we say things like 'all voiceless stops in L . . .', etc.)

there exists, in other words, some kind of general framework defining argumentative validity, the degree (roughly) of evidential support required to make assertions warrantable, and the like. The Private/ Community distinction can be introduced by two examples.

First case: in learned disciplines, and in everyday life, we are (or should be) forced to abide by public criteria in matters of observation and inference. But there is a kind of private conviction (however it comes about) that arises from one's incontrovertible direct experience, where the truth of some proposition is 'made manifest' with such power or numinosity that there is no possibility of denying it – however much it may transgress or appear to transgress the bounds of public rationality. Thus a non-believer may be converted to Christianity, and come to know that the proposition 'Christ rose from the dead on the third day' is true; and he may know it with as powerful a sense of epistemic conviction as he knows that '*modus ponens* is a valid rule of inference', or knows his own name. It is clear that this kind of conviction, while no less powerful, has a different source from that which comes from a successful and correct deduction. But it raises a problem of discrimination.

Second case: say that I come to believe with utter conviction that I am a cockroach. Even though this proposition can be refuted by inter-subjective agreement (my wife and friends all agree that I'm not a cockroach, they know what cockroaches look like, etc.), this has no effect on my conviction. I KNOW what I am. Is this case the same as that of the Christian?

I maintain that it isn't; and this introduces the distinction between purely private conviction and what we might call 'semi-private' or community conviction: what I have chosen to call Community rationality. The difference is this: many of my friends and relations and other competent persons would consider me deluded if I were epistemically convinced of the reality of the Resurrection. But there are many who would not; whereas the chances are that nobody would agree that I was a cockroach. This suggests that there is a kind of line between conviction of a non-demonstrable but possibly true proposition and delusion (conviction of a demonstrably untrue one).

Leaving aside manifestly private convictions of the 'I am a cockroach' type, let us return to the 'Christ rose on the third day' type. There is a large community of believers who are convinced of the truth of this proposition, and can assume its relegation to unproblematical background knowledge within that community; and it can serve for all members as a tacit presupposition for religious discourse, an ordering principle in daily life, etc. Unless all Christians are insane in parallel, there is a genuine intellectual community, many of whose members can lay claim to being 'competent persons' in the public sphere, who nevertheless hold this problematical belief. Outside the community, their 'knowledge' may be taken as in error: they believe that p, but they do not know that p, because p is not true.

Now the Christian believer can simply hold his faith in private, and behave otherwise like a publicly competent person (in a way that the person who's convinced he's a cockroach may not be able to). But if he wants, not merely to hold his faith, but to convince others of its validity (that he knows, rather than merely believes), he must make this claim on public grounds (a mystical experience is not a claim to credibility). In other words, he must argue and attempt to justify his belief as publicly rational, and consonant with (if not, in the ideal case, entailed by) what he and the public at large share in the way of other beliefs about the world and about what constitutes rational argument. And if he does this, he can then properly be held accountable to public standards, and sanctioned (by not being taken seriously, being denounced as a crank or a nut-case) if he fails to adhere to these standards. Obviously, if his claim in the first place is not a purely empirical one, he will not (if he has any sense) try to make his appeal primarily on empirical grounds (the fate of 'natural theology' in the nineteenth century suggests that this is a counter-productive move); what he will try to do is construct well-formed metaphysical arguments that lend credibility to his position. And in this way community (or in some cases even private) convictions can be made into the material for public debate.

This has a bearing on theoretical positions in learned disciplines as well. Since propositions about 'function' in language, for instance, appear to be neither empirically verifiable nor even logically coherent, it would seem to follow that the main source of belief in them is immediate epistemic conviction of the religious type (or a related kind of 'vision', to be discussed in the next section). This conviction is apparently available to a large number of competent people, which I assume takes it out of the realm of simple delusion (though not of course necessarily into that of true propositions: there is certainly a grey area). But it is further the case that if the members of the community of believers want to make a case for others joining them, they should be obliged to proceed in a particular way: above all, they must break out of the protective hermetic circle defined by their particular community as an institution.

And here is where the intersection between public and community rationality enters; and this, in retrospect, seems to be the main theme of this book. Once a tenet of community belief is proposed as potentially suitable for public acceptance – i.e. when the community submits its convictions to a larger public (even within a discipline) – then at least the logical and argumentative standards of public rationality ought to be observed. Any member of the larger public has the right to insist that, if there is to be genuine dialogue, and any hope of conviction, the public 'rules of the game' be observed. It is up to the individual, of course, to decide whether or not to submit his beliefs to public scrutiny; but once he does (e.g. by publishing), he makes an implicit claim on the credence of the public, and it is incumbent on him to play by their rules. One's personal grounds for the acceptance of a position, and one's claims on public confidence in that position, are two very different things; certainly the mere conjunction of personal conviction and expertise do not warrant the presentation of convictions without argumentative warrants, in the way that is typically done (e.g. in the quotations from Jakobson given as examples in §3.1).

But personal grounds for the acceptance of a position are not entirely without interest, and I will comment on them in the next section; it is however public criteria that are of the greatest importance for the growth of a discipline and the preservation of rationality, and I will return to this matter in §§5.5–6.

5.4 Intelligibility: non-'scientific' components

I now turn to the question of why people might join a community of believers such as 'teleologists' (a community which, as I pointed out in §3.6 I have more or less beeen a member of myself),[7] 'functionalists', 'natural phonologists', or whatever. This section and what follows may be taken as a somewhat speculative and value-laden postscript to my main argument. I want to ask whether we have to be content, in the end,

---

[7] The arguments of chapter 3 may be taken as a reconstruction of why I left this particular community; it is always possible for a convert or believer to lose his faith if the force of an argument-against becomes greater than that of his original epistemic conviction, or of the arguments-for. I like to see my own 'deconversion' as a shift from community to public standards, but that may be wishful thinking.

with a vision of ourselves as myopic gropers after illusory certainty, or whether, even out of the conflict between community and public rationality, in cases where neither really wins, there might emerge some grounds for optimism.

If I am right, no historical explanation is or can be deductive, or 'empirical'. We do not have available to us the particular modes of conviction (both of ourselves and others) represented by the concepts 'deductive certainty' and 'refutation'. Assuming the partial aptness anyhow of these terms for some of the knowledge that one can gain in the 'empirical sciences' narrowly conceived (but not all of it: cf. §5.5), what we know must be qualitatively different.

The central question is this: if functional explanations, etc. of language change are non-causal and non-empirical; and if they are riddled with elementary logical fallacies, and full of ill-defined or undefined notions; why, in the face of all this (which I can't have been the first to notice) are they so attractive? After all, those who propose them aren't idiots (and nothing I say below is to be taken as suggesting that they are, or as being patronizing; though it IS to be taken, as is the whole of my main argument, as suggesting that they are in error).

The answer, I think – and this constitutes part of a marginal preliminary defence even of rickety structures like the ones I've been considering – may well be 'psychological'. But the psychology in question is the linguist's, not that of the speaker or community he's supposed to be investigating. I suggest that what really counts, the first reason we have for believing in the potential fruitfulness of a type of explanation, and for holding onto it in the face of a lack of obvious warrantability (or even in the face of evidence that it makes no sense) is some kind of criterion of INTELLIGIBILITY, which serves as a quasi-esthetic control on the evaluation of explanations. I think that we often judge (what we call) the 'explanatory' power of a statement or model on the basis of the PLEASURE, of a very specific kind, that it affords us (cf. Polanyi 1958: ch. 1; Bohm 1969a, 1969b). This pleasure is essentially 'architectonic'; the structure we impose on the chaos that confronts us is beautiful in some way, it makes things cohere that otherwise would not, and it gives us a sense of having transcended the primal disorder.

I think we are all (privately) familiar with this feeling though we have been brainwashed into thinking it in some way 'unworthy'. And this prompts us to try and communicate it in a terminology borrowed from the brainwashing tradition, to talk about 'explanations' when we mean 'models' or 'metaphors', and to claim that we have shown 'why X happened' when what we have really done is linked X up in a 'network' with Y, Z, etc., and thus created a more or less plausible and imaginatively pleasing picture of 'how (*ceteris paribus*) X could happen'. This is all really relatively harmless, as I have suggested elsewhere (Lass 1976a: epilogue); at least it is if we can bring ourselves to see clearly what we actually do, and avoid terminological subterfuge and defensive pretence.

The critical factor is the 'Aha!' feeling that comes from the imposition of order on some domain. One of the main stimuli to being a linguist (or any other kind of researcher) is the desire for order; our domain, when we first approach it, is 'Chaos dark and deep/Where nameless Somethings in their Causes sleep'.[8] If an explanation, model, analogy, or whatever fails to evoke the feeling of 'illumination', then it's a failure, however rational it seems to be; and by the same token, if the feeling is evoked, we are tempted to fight like hell to hold onto the source of it. I will suggest later that this might be all to the good. We feel that we OUGHT, of course, to accept things only on purely rational grounds, but this is not what we do. We require more, or even something else. (Cf. Polanyi 1958: ch. 1 on Kepler's attitudes to his astronomical theory, and Feyerabend 1975 on Galileo and the Copernican theory.)[9]

I suggest that there is nothing particularly reprehensible about acknowledging this, and getting off our metascientific high horses on occasion: as long as we don't simply stop here. We might anyhow try admitting that often when we say we are providing 'explanations', what we are really doing is proposing models or 'metaphorical redescriptions' (Hesse 1966), which we think provide something woollier, but equally important: what we might, without at the moment attempting further definition, call 'insight'. To return for a moment to the domain of human history, and the idea of history as 'myth' mentioned in §1.1, consider this comment (Abelson 1963: 173):

---

[8] *Dunciad* I.55–6. Pope of course means 'causes' in all the Aristotelian senses; this is not an oblique reference on my part to classical causation theory. I merely quote the lines because they seem apposite.

[9] Another psychological motivation – perhaps a less worthy one – has been suggested for functional explanations by Sprigge (1971: 170): a 'satisfying answer' to a function question 'is like an explanation for the thing's existence, inasmuch as it stops us worrying about it' (cited and discussed in Woodfield 1976: 135ff).

... deduction is a method of proof, and not, in history at least, a method of explanation. When a historian proves that an event occurred, he is not *explaining* the action, he is merely justifying his claim that the action took place. Again, when he proves that the action was performed for a certain reason, he is not explaining anything, but merely convincing us that the explanation he has already suggested is a true one. It is in the creative activity of describing the ... pattern in which the action occupies an appropriate place that the work of explanation is performed, whereby a vision is evoked in the mind of the reader that illuminates the historical scene and makes sense out of chaos. [Emphasis Abelson's]

What historiography aims to present, in Abelson's view, is a 'vision'; specifically a vision that illuminates the subject matter in some way. While I think 'explanation' is certainly the wrong word for what Abelson is talking about, the thing he is talking about is, I would maintain, what we should be aiming at. In this sense historiography is not 'scientific history', but something more like an art form: the historian presents a unifying metaphysical vision. But not only this: his second responsibility is to present his vision in such a way that it is not 'mere' poetry, but the material for critical discussion. However metaphysical the initial content of the vision, however 'poetical', the substance of the vision must be made to cohere with empirical knowledge.

The distinction between historiography (of any sort) and science (in the narrow sense), is that the historiographic act both produces the history that really counts, and at the same time produces insights into it. 'Though with a cognitive content a novel need not have ... historiography is like the novel in being itself our experience of what it narrates — whereas science and scientific writing contain but information and rules for obtaining experiences' (van den Haag 1963: 223). Van den Haag's account of 'science' is rather limited, of course, though he is right about historiography; even in the 'hardest' kind of science there remains the possibility of giving public shape to informing metaphysical convictions, and connecting them to the world of public rationality.[10]

[10] Cf. Bohm (1969b: 42) on the role of 'metaphysics' in science. This is particularly interesting as the comment of a physicist:

> 'The proper role of metaphysics is a metaphor which provides an immediate perceptual grasp of the overall order and structure of one's thoughts. It is therefore a kind of poetry. Some "hard-headed" individuals may object to bringing such "poetry" into science ... The point that I want to emphasize ... is that all of us will think more clearly when we frankly ... admit that a lot of "hard-headed common sense" and "factual science" is actually a kind of poetry, which is indispensable to our general mental functioning.'

5·5 Non-explanatory insight: empirical and rational components

The previous section is not to be taken as claiming that 'insight' or 'intelligibility' are holistic, totally visionary or esthetic notions. Insight does of course have a St-Paul-on-the-road-to-Damascus component, but it has a number of others, both more rational and empirically bound. Some of these latter may arise after the fact, as epiphenomena to or developments of, or commentaries on an original 'vision' or Gestalt experience (think of a potential description of one's transactions with a Necker cube); or they may have been from the beginning subliminally perceived, and in fact (unconsciously) part of the source of the vision itself: Kekulé's famous dream of the ring of snakes and the discovery (or invention) of the structure of the benzene molecule may be a case in point.

In this section I want to look at some types of order that can be imposed on experience, either through empirical discovery or the imposition of (partly empirically based) schemata on empirical domains. These all conduce to the sense of 'intelligibility' I have been talking about; and most important, they enter into public discussion in a clear and unambiguous way, and thus avoid the trap of irrationalism (whatever their private sources may have originally been). They fall in general into two types: (a) virtually undeniable 'facts' discovered about some domain, such as statistical correlations, and (b) rather more imaginative projections from facts, such as taxonomic schemata and models as 'metaphorical rediscription': a flawed example of the latter in linguistics is the teratogenesis/functional change dialectic. When type (a) generalizations are discovered, they may be totally accepted intersubjectively, but they can still be argued about: i.e. their 'significance' can be debated. Type (b) structures, on the other hand, can be criticized at a more basic level, in terms of their appropriateness, since they represent rather more arbitrary and less obvious abstractions of principles from empirical data of one kind or another; they can also be criticized in terms of their consonance with the rest of our empirical knowledge, and their internal coherence (this is the type of 'metaphysical' argument I engaged in in chapters 2–3). This should become clearer in what follows.

The main point is that even though all these types of ordering structure will be ones that I have already discarded (§1.7) as non-explanatory (as indeed they are), they can be seen, in a less puritanical (or to use a favourite term of Feyerabend's, 'constipated') framework to have great value in contributing to our understanding.

Once we are willing to admit some kind of epistemological pluralism, we can revert to a more colloquial and less restrictive sense of 'explanation', if we wish, even without admitting that objects like Achinstein's penicillin-rash account (§1.3) or Scriven's paresis example (§4.5) are adequate. We might for instance suggest, as Mary Hesse has, that 'explanation' not be taken as a univocal concept, but as complex and multi-faceted. She proposes defining the explanatory endeavour this way (Hesse 1976: 53): 'Any request for explanation is a request to give more information about a context which will show how different parts of it are related and what further expectations we should have of it.' This has the virtue of enabling us to avoid finding another term for all the modes of insight into and conferring of intelligibility on things that don't come under the D-N heading. Under this rubric, we could admit 'law-like' but non-causal generalizations (at least those which are set in a coherent network of beliefs) as genuinely explanatory, if in a limited sense.

I'm not sure this is in the interests of clarity. I would rather take 'explanation' as univocal, and reserve the fuzzier 'insight' for what Hesse is talking about, since this maintains the important epistemic distinction between 'intelligibility' and 'logical necessity'.

What are the components of 'intelligibility'? Or at least, what are some of the ways in which we can impose order on previously unordered domains, or fit events into schemata which confer coherence, or transcend the singular data?

Some suggestive possibilities are raised in a recent brief discussion by Fischer-Jørgensen (1975: 387). There are, she says, many different kinds of explanations; for instance, 'When a phenomenon or process can be described not as an isolated case, but as an example of a more general phenomenon or process, it is considered as better understood. The possibility of generalization is to some extent an explanation.' This is partly a subjectivist notion, but no less important for that, since generalizations of this type can be intersubjectively acceptable. If something is known to happen frequently, then a new instance takes on a certain 'familiarity', and thus ceases to be isolated: it has a 'place', in that it is referrable to some antecedently specifiable class of frequent occurrences. Thus she says that if some development in a language 'is found to be a common development also in other languages, it is still better understood in the sense that it is an expected development, not an unexpected one' (*ibid.*). This is of course the sense in which markedness and naturalness have been taken to be explanatory notions: but here we must I think not talk about explanation, but about taxonomy. And this is in fact potentially a powerful source of insight, at least if the taxonomy is a sophisticated and highly developed one, that makes considerable sense of its domain: as markedness theory is not, because of its empirical unsoundness. But this does not discredit taxonomy *per se*; indeed, as I shall argue below, taxonomic endeavours are among the highest forms of intellectual activity, and the most potent sources of order.

Another point Fischer-Jørgensen makes is that a 'deeper under-standing is achieved if the single phenomenon can be seen as part of a structure or pattern' (*ibid.*). This is another important kind of 'placement' of phenomena in the world; their identification as points in structures or systems. I will return to this below.

Let us turn now in some detail to various non-explanatory sources of 'information' about the world, or better, perhaps, non-explanatory ways of ordering empirical domains. Perhaps the greatest part of what we do as linguists, and much of our most solid accomplishment, belongs to this sphere, and for the purposes of sketching out a possible future programme in historical linguistics, this material is of great importance.

A useful attempt at organizing the various forms of non-deductive ordering schemata has been made by Abraham Kaplan (1965); he has drawn up a detailed taxonomy of what he calls 'noncausal explanation' types, which, while (for me at least) certainly not explanatory in any strict sense, are nonetheless all examples of the kinds of ordering operations on empirical domains which rank among our most significant achievements.

I will look briefly at Kaplan's analysis, and suggest some examples from linguistics of the types of phenomena he deals with (his examples are from biology and physics). His basic principle is that even if causal prediction is not available or even possible, 'in principle, nothing lies outside the realm of intelligibility' (147). This is of course merely programmatic; but so is every other position that has been taken on this issue. Kaplan's non-causal 'explanations' are as follows:

(i) *Taxonomies*. He claims (148) that taxonomic principles are 'weakly explanatory', and that we gain something when we place entities or phenomena within a taxonomic scheme of some kind. Even 'good' taxonomies (however that is defined: see below) are of course radically different from causal schemata, simply because they do not invoke causes – though one might argue that they are better if they do. (For example, a language taxonomy based on phenotypic characters, like 'all SOV languages' as opposed to 'all SVO languages' is not causal in any sense, though it can be illuminating; but a genotypic taxonomy, based on presumed common origin of certain phenotypic characters, like the 'dental preterite' in Germanic, can be said in some sense to be. The same may be true of evolution-based biological taxonomies.) But even where causal laws are unknown or debatable, or frankly not of interest, investigators in a particular field can still agree on the 'scientific usefulness' of some given taxonomy.

This seems undeniable. It would take an extreme priggishness to dismiss e.g. botanical or zoological systematics as trivial or unrevealing. Anyone who has ever gardened seriously knows what a superb ordering instrument the neo-Linnaean nomenclature is, how in fact it transforms and gives shape to an otherwise confused sensory world – as well as yielding useful practical predictions ('If it's ericaceous – with marginal exceptions – a high soil pH will kill it'). The same thing, to get back to linguistics, can be said (if in a weaker way, because they are more debatable and less developed) of phonetic taxonomies (e.g. Jakobson, Fant & Halle 1951; Chomsky & Halle 1968: ch. 7; Ladefoged 1971; Catford 1977), or taxonomies of case-relations (Fillmore 1968; Anderson 1971), and so on. Whatever the derived explanatory pretensions (and even perhaps successes) of these schemata, their undeniable accomplishment is surely the imposition of structure on otherwise chaotic domains. And this is not a trivial success, but an imaginative and argumentative accomplishment of the highest order. It's time we stopped using 'taxonomic' as a dirty word.

It is important to note here, in the light of the special advantages claimed for the deductivist programme, that the question of the 'truth' or 'falsity' of a taxonomy rarely arises; and when it does, it is usually trivial. (This refers to a taxonomic theory as a whole, not to questions of membership of individuals in particular taxa, which is a different matter, normally resolvable within the framework of the taxonomy itself.) That is, it is possible to produce, for any domain, an indefinitely large set of taxonomies, each of which is 'true' to the extent that it invokes predicates which can be intersubjectively agreed to be legitimately applicable to the individuals in the domain; but which can be critically discussed and evaluated in terms of 'fruitfulness', 'utility', heuristic value, and so on.

Consider for instance a classification of flowering plants in terms of colour. There is no doubt that all competent observers could agree on the accuracy of such a taxonomy (a red rose and a red tulip and a red petunia ... are red); but argument can arise about its utility, its appropriateness, etc. The argument will hinge on considerations like this:

(i)   Given the colour of a flower, you can't tell anything else about the plant.

(ii)   Take roses, which occur in just about every flower colour except blue; a red rose has more characters in common with a white rose than it has with a red tulip or a red zinnia.

Thus we have here a taxonomy that is 'true', but subject to criticism as 'useless' or 'unrevealing' – for scientific purposes anyhow: though it may not be for purposes of bedding-out or flower-arranging. This brings up the important point that one of the main criteria for evaluating a taxonomy (or in the end, perhaps, any 'true' description where there is more than one available) is USEFULNESS FOR A PARTICULAR PURPOSE (cf. Harris 1960: 9, n. 8).

Again, take a more sophisticated and equally true taxonomy of plants according to their ability to tolerate free lime in the soil ('calcicole' vs. 'calcifuge'). Here the taxonomy makes valuable predictions for the gardener or the ecologist; though it cross-cuts other taxonomies in an odd way (one set distinguished in this scheme would be '*Dianthus, Clematis*, and *Rhododendron hirsutum*' vs. '*Rhododendron*, except *hirsutum*'; and so on). Whereas a taxonomy like the neo-Linnaean makes for what appears to be – for the general purposes of systematics at least – the imposition of a greater order, in the sense that each taxon predicts a major clustering of predicates. But there is no sense in which the neo-Linnaean taxonomy is 'real', while the others are 'artificial' or 'false': it is a matter of what is relevant for a particular purpose, and what is most revealing for that purpose.

In biological systematics (since Darwin) there has been a traditional feeling that the 'ideal' taxonomy is phylogenetic, rather than say typological (even though the two may coincide in large part: after all, Linnaeus' criteria were morphological, though he happened most often to select as criterial just those morphological features that now seem to be reflexes of common ancestry; but he might not have). However, as the above examples suggest, this is not a question of 'truth', or of taxonomies that capture in some way the 'essence' of a domain, but a question of utility for particular purposes within the frame of particular theoretical outlooks.[11]

The same kind of discussion of 'true' taxonomies can arise in linguistics as well. Language classification has been, since the nineteenth century, predominantly phylogenetic (unsurprisingly, considering the intellectual climate that historical linguistics grew up in, and the influence of Darwin on men like Schleicher). While typology has also flourished, it has tended to be the genetic criteria that predominated, e.g. in textbook classifications of the world's languages, etc. Typological, areal, and other factors have always been taken to be part of 'special-purpose' taxonomies, in some way not basic (cf. the discussion in Wunderlich 1974: ch. 11). But it has been argued (e.g. by Andronov 1968) that there are cases in which the phylogenetic taxonomy is essentially unrevealing, and that a typological classification may be more to the point: for instance, in cases where, as a result of long and intimate contact, genetically unaffiliated languages become so similar typologically that they may be said to 'change families'. Andronov's example is the typological confluence of Indic and Dravidian on the Indian subcontinent; *'Sprachbund'* phenomena in general provide a case where such arguments are relevant, and conflicting (or complementary) 'true' taxonomies can be debated, without any sort of 'essentialist' truth or falsity coming into the picture at all.[12]

This does not – or does not have to – lead to an instrumentalist view of taxonomies or other theoretical artefacts (like analogical models, where similar conditions may obtain); or at least not to a strong metaphysical instrumentalism, where theoretical predicates have no ontological status 'in the world'. But it does suggest strongly that there may be complementary 'realities', and that one of the purposes of theoretical argument may be to establish a case for one or another in terms of

---

[11] For a useful discussion of the philosophical bases of biological and other taxonomy, and a consideration of the problems I have been discussing in relation to plant classification, see Gilmour & Walters (1963). For some discussion of current issues in biological taxonomy, see Ruse (1973: chs. 7–8). (I am grateful to Sidney Allen for calling the Gilmour & Walters paper to my attention.)

[12] One interesting argumentative possibility concerning taxonomies or other generalizations is their (statistical) significance: i.e. a generalization may be argued to be less worthwhile the more possible it is for the conditions it specifies to have come about by accident. For a sophisticated study of this problem in relation to 'significant generalizations' in linguistics, see Hurford (1977).

'benefit': i.e. in terms of the amount of insight or structure that one selection of predicates yields, as opposed to some other.[13]

(ii) *Mathematical generalizations* (148). These are cases (like many 'laws of nature') where one quantity is formulated as a mathematical function of some other(s): Boyle's Law, the laws predicting the period of a pendulum, and so on. These are clearly predictive (if the value of one variable is known, the other(s) can be computed); but they are not (classically) causal, because they lack the essential properties of unilateral implication (if A causes B, then B can't cause A), and temporal asymmetry (if A causes B, it must precede B). The relations here are, in Kaplan's terms, 'cyclic'.

It is worth pointing out that some of the most interesting recent discoveries in linguistics fall into this class: the kind of 'co-variation' of linguistic-with-linguistic or linguistic-with-social variables now familiar from the work of Labov and his followers. Generalizations of this kind are of considerable methodological importance in the context of this study (as suggested in §2.4), because they constitute what may at first appear to be 'explanations' in the strong sense; though on closer consideration they always lack the crucial empirical relevance (i.e. warrants for causal claims) that are necessary for true explanation.

This is not to devalue the contributions of such work, or to claim that accurate formulations of co-variation are not interesting and significant additions to our knowledge of language and its social functioning. But it is important to realize precisely what kind of knowledge they provide, and to distinguish it from explanatory knowledge. No sociolinguistic (or 'variationist': Lass 1976b) study (regardless of what some people may say, or think) establishes a causal nexus between any social factor and the actuation of a change or the selection of any particular variant; all they do is describe the particular social uses that already-existing variants may be put to, and how they come, within a speech community, to serve some indexical function.

That is, such studies are entirely – and in the best sense – DESCRIPTIVE; as is ultimately all of historical (and I suspect most other) linguistics. What a variationist study does is establish structures, or mathematical formulations of rules that may be said to govern the distribution and deployment of variants in a language. But the

---

[13] On the compatibility of non-unique descriptions with philosophical realism, see Putnam (1978: 50). In a critique of Chomsky as a 'naïve realist', Putnam argues that 'realism is not committed to there being one true theory (and *only* one)' (emphasis his).

correlations are non-causal: within the framework of our knowledge of the world, there is no way we can say that the conjunction of predicates ('Working-Class' & 'Female' & 'Catholic' & '17 Years Old') can CAUSE a particular incidence of [t] and [ʔ], etc. Co-variation is a descriptive, not an explanatory concept. There is no known empirical connection (as well as no temporal asymmetry) between the co-varying items.

This again is not, as should be obvious by now, a criticism: there is little to be gained by trying to explain things causally if they are not caused. Formalization of phenomena like this fulfils important descriptive goals, and these are the primary (perhaps the only?) goals of linguistics. Even 'theory' (in the best sense) is descriptive, not explanatory. For instance, as Hammarström (1978: 27) has pointed out in another connection,

> In T.G. grammar and in other kinds of linguistics it is common that a construction is explained by reference to the rules which generate it. In such cases the construction is thought to be what it is 'because of' its description in terms of rules. It is obvious that this is not a real explanation ... (Where are the 'cause' and the 'effect'?)

This can be extended to the formal results of variation studies (or any other quantitative studies), without in any sense compromising their value, as it does not compromise the value of formalization in generative grammar. It merely recategorizes them as descriptions (arguably better than others).

The important point is that regardless of the presence or absence of explanatory potential, the discovery and formalization of 'variable rules' or whatever is a genuine contribution to knowledge, a powerful incentive to further (explanatory and other) theorization, and a valuable heuristic stimulus; and the theory in which the formalizations are embedded is a powerful and highly useful analytical tool, and a source of new order and new and different conceptual structures, which can only enrich the discipline.

(iii) *Statistical principles* (149–50). It is clear (cf. the arguments in chapter 2) that statistical distributions by themselves are non-causal and non-explanatory in the strict sense (since they cannot predict singular spatio-temporal occurrences). But they can serve as the basis for inferences (for an extended account see Hacking 1976), and if correct they are at least new 'empirical facts' which serve as new explananda. Thus their very existence provides more work in the field. There is no guarantee that given distributions will ever be empirically interpretable, of course, but they are material that provokes attempts at interpretation (all existing regularities demand that we try to account for them), and they are therefore both interesting and important. (Even if markedness theory is as I have argued a failure, it is still an accomplishment, and the debate it has provoked is at least important as anything it has actually shown to be the case.)

(iv) *Temporal laws* (151–2). These are laws of the type where if something happens at time t_i, we can predict that something else will happen at t_{i+k}; but we can't say what will happen at t_{i+j}, where $j < k$. These Kaplan calls 'interval laws'. His example is a psychologist telling a parent that if he does X to his child, next month (next year, 20 years on) the child will do (roughly) Y; but there is no prediction about what the child will do in the next 10 minutes, etc. Much of what we know about the stadial unfolding of language acquisition may come under this heading; and it is no less an addition to the totality of what we know about language because of our lack of understanding of basic mechanisms, individual differences, etc. A (probably unsuccessful) attempt to frame interval laws on the historical dimension can be seen in 'lexicostatistics' or 'glottochronology'.

A related but rather vaguer type of generalization is what Kaplan calls 'genetic laws'; these refer to (unquantified) stages in any kind of ontogenesis. The main difference between these and interval laws seems to be the degree of specificity; perhaps much of what we know about language acquisition (in terms of the correlation of psychomotor maturation, lateralization, myelinization, etc. and language development) comes under this heading rather than the former one.

(v) *Purposive laws* (152–3). These refer to the 'reasons why' people or other organisms do things, i.e. to motives for action; and for this reason they are probably not relevant to language change. At least I can think, as is obvious by now, of no linguistic change that can legitimately be taken as involving purpose; indeed, the notion of linguistic change as an 'act' seems bizarre. Language change is not something that people 'do'. This is why, in general, I think that 'hermeneutic' strategies are of no interest for the study of language change (though they may be for synchronic studies of language use: cf. Itkonen 1974). I see no evidence that language change can be the object of hermeneutic '*Verstehen*', and therefore no evidence that 'immanent reflection' – however valuable it may be in sociology, psychology, or even in history – can be of any use. (But see Itkonen 1978 for some counter-arguments.)

This schematic survey of someone else's taxonomy has merely been intended as a kind of programmatic focus on the importance of a number of sources of what can reasonably be called 'knowledge' of significant things about language, and which do not involve positivist forms of prediction, causal explanation, or falsification of empirical hypotheses. It would be a great, probably irreparable, loss if we were to dismiss them all as of low status or minimal importance, merely grist for the D-N mill.

5.6 In conclusion: new hope for the Laodiceans

I return to some reflections on the relation between creative irrationality and rational progress, and the tasks of historical linguistics. It would seem that if historical linguists can be said to 'know' anything in the sense of having something like a criterion for 'true interpretation of a historical event', this must involve a global, 'coherence' notion of truth, not (strictly) a 'correspondence' notion.[14] Anything like a rigorous correspondence theory of truth is ruled out because the 'facts' with which true statements are supposed to correspond are at least as much historiographical facts as any interpretation of them. In this sense, history is, as I have suggested, something rather more like 'rational art' than science: the interpretive act of giving shape to history at once (partially) creates it and renders it intelligible (or at least takes the first steps toward the latter). The interpretive historian's job, on this account, is to give form to things, not to show that they must have occurred (they probably did anyway, and whether they did or not they didn't have to). If the search for nomic necessity in language history is a lost cause, we might as well be content with insight: so long as we do not lapse into irrationalism or bigotry (see below).

Let us assume that we are forced to accept the general position I argued for in chapter 4, that explanation is inappropriate; i.e. that my arguments were to be bolstered by others, or, indirectly, by the failure of counter-arguments. And that the only view of the nature of change that

---

[14] For discussion of the role of 'coherence' considerations in a non-deductivist but realist theory, see Hesse (1974: especially chs. 1, 2, 12).

we could reasonably accept was one like that suggested by Postal (1968: 283):[15]

> It seems clear . . . that there is no more reason for languages to change than there is for automobiles to add fins one year and remove them the next, for jackets to have three buttons one year and two the next, etc. That is . . . the 'causes' of sound change without language contact lie in the general tendency of human cultural products to undergo 'nonfunctional' stylistic change.

(A view which I find sympathetic, as one might expect.) Would this reduce the study of language history to vacuity? Only if one adopted a position in which disciplines like for instance art history and music history, or art criticism of any kind, were vacuous as well (which I don't believe). These surely are not 'explanatory' disciplines, and the element of 'functional motivation' involved is minimal. But they are rich and significant sources of knowledge of a sort: at the very least what Putnam (1978: 90) characterizes this way: '. . . being aware of a new interpretation of the facts, however repellent, of a construction that can – I now see – be put upon the facts, however perversely – is a kind of knowledge. It is knowledge of a possibility. It is *conceptual* knowledge' (emphasis his). But their richness goes beyond this; they yield not only interpretations, but new structures, new patterns. Disciplines of this type are engaged primarily in the explication of pattern and structure, and the unification of experience, not with the establishment of logically or empirically necessary relations between elements in their domains.

This casts some light on the function of explanatory (or pseudo-explanatory) devices like functional explanation. Even if language change (except at the utterly trivial and quasi-mechanical level of the invention of new lexis for new concepts) is purposeless and essentially meaningless, functional explanation attempts to make it intelligible; it imposes order on chaos, and most of us hate chaos the way nature does vacuums. Functionalism, to take one example, is an anarchy-barring move; we dislike anarchy, so we legislate it out of existence by inventing laws. This is entirely laudable; as is the fact that the invention is at least lucid enough to be subject to the kind of criticism that I have been

[15] Postal restricts the strong version of this claim to 'primary change', i.e. change which 'interrupts an assumed stable . . . system' (283). He finds it 'somewhat more plausible that such stylistic changes may yield a grammar which is in some sense not optimal, and that this may itself lead to "functional" change to bring about an optimal state' (*ibid.*). Note however (a) that the major changes are still 'uncaused', and (b) that optimization only 'may' occur. It is certainly possible to accept Postal's main view without this qualification; and the arguments of chapters 2–3 above suggest that we may have to.

levelling at it in this book. In this case, the attempt to impose order was a failure, and we are back, I think, with something very like Postal's view.

But this doesn't mean that we have any right to stop inventing myths (even causal ones, if we want), and trying our best to defend and argue for our own, and attacking what others produce (or attacking our own, and defending those of others: see below). What is incumbent on us is to do this while adhering to the strictest standards of public rationality that we can, even when much of the material we are attacking or defending is (apparently) beyond rationality.

This can prevent us from lapsing into irrationalism; we must avoid irrationalist programmes, with 'anything goes' as the sole methodological commandment (as Feyerabend 1975 claims to be advocating). Even the production of apparently irrational visions of the world may be related to rationality; indeed, I have suggested (§5.4) that one of the sources of our myth-making is the basic appeal of a rational, ordered vision of empirical reality. This appeal captivates us even to the extent that we pretend (though we shouldn't) that irrational or sloppy formulations are rational and lucid.

What I am advocating is the conduct of a rational 'metaphysical research programme' (Popper 1976: §37), in which non-empirical positions are argued, as far as possible, according to the canons of reason, and criticized, and the worst idiocies pared away. I hold critical rationality of this kind to be self-justifying; and I hold further that it is one of the vital forces for the maintenance of civilization (in the best sense of the term). Its importance lies not so much in the 'solid knowledge' (if any) that it yields, but in the clarification of thought that results, or can result from it, and above all in the activities and attitudes that it engenders.

Perhaps I can clarify this by pointing to a very dangerous and ultimately, I think, immoral position with respect to scientific endeavours, taken by a philosopher and scientist whom I otherwise respect. Polanyi (Polanyi & Prosch 1975: 59f) describes the scientist's relation to his hypotheses as 'one of passionate personal commitment. The effort that led to a surmise committed every fiber of his being to the quest; his surmises embody all his hopes.' In this view, 'every step taken in the pursuit of science is definitive ... in the vital sense that it definitely disposes of the time, the effort ... used in taking that step'.

Polanyi goes on to characterize the true (and, unfortunately, in his conception, the proper) temper of the scientific enterprise (against

Popper and other falsificationists) as follows: 'To think of scientific workers cheerfully trying this and trying that, readily changing course at each failure, is a caricature of a pursuit that consumes a man's whole person. Any questing surmise necessarily seeks its own confirmation.' Surely one can exhibit a certain tenacity without being this committed. If this is true of most scientists (we know it's true of some), it's a bad way to do science, and one has even less reason than one might suspect anyway to trust scientists (the same goes for linguists). Certainly, in my own experience, being forced to 'change course', aside from being deflating in the most salutary possible way, is both exciting and fulfilling: it's only the intractibility of nature with respect to theories that makes any kind of realism tenable, and it is at least possible to feel a genuine sense of having made progress when one has got rid of a bad hypothesis. Polanyi's vision of the 'committed' scientist seems to come perilously close to being a portrait of a fanatic: if we take it as normative, it can lead to an irrationalism as deplorable as Feyerabend's.

The alternative vision I would propose is one of a constant critical scepticism – directed as strongly toward oneself as toward others. Self-criticism and scepticism forestall commitment, and lack of commitment prevents the development of the wrong kind of intellectual passion. Commitment and intellectual passion vested in particular ideas – rather than in the critical enterprise and the attempt to find better ideas – are a vice and a peril. (Ideology kills.) If the kind of attitude I espouse here leads us to become latter-day Laodiceans, I'm all for it.[16]

---

[16] The attitude toward the Church of the Laodiceans that emerges from St John's message (*Rev.* 3:15–16) shows precisely the dangers of a NON-Laodicean attitude: 'I know thy works, that thou art neither cold nor hot ... so then because thou art lukewarm and neither cold nor hot, I will spue thee out of my mouth.' Surely we ought to avoid this kind of arrogance and self-righteousness toward those who disagree with us (as often does not happen in day-to-day life in the linguistic community: cf. Labov's characterization of Harris and Hockett as showing an undesirable 'playfulness' in their work, and his conviction that 'confrontation with the hard facts of the physical world' will lead to unambiguous 'right' answers – provided one plays the game his way: Labov 1971: 492f). It is very important for us to stop being solemn, and taking ourselves and our own rectitude so seriously. Dante's condemnation of the Laodicean type (or 'trimmer') in *Inf.* III. 22ff is a further classical example of uncivilized polemic, and furnishes another excellent model of what we ought to avoid.

References

Abelson, R. (1963) 'Cause and reason in history', in Hook (1963: 167–73)

Achinstein, P. (1968) *Concepts of Science: a philosophical analysis.* Baltimore: Johns Hopkins Press

– (1971) *Law and explanation: an essay in the philosophy of science.* Oxford: Clarendon Press

– (1975) 'The object of explanation', in Körner (1975: 1–75)

Andersen, H. (1973) 'Abductive and deductive change', *Language* 46.765–93

Anderson, J. M. (1971) *The grammar of case: towards a localistic theory.* Cambridge University Press

– & Jones, C. (1974a) 'Three theses concerning phonological representations', *Journal of Linguistics* 10.1–26

– (1974b) *Historical Linguistics. Proceedings of the First International Conference on Historical Linguistics, Edinburgh 2–7 September 1973.* 2 vols. Amsterdam: North-Holland

Anderson, S. & Kiparsky, P. (1973) *A Festschrift for Morris Halle.* New York: Holt, Rinehart & Winston

Andronov, M. (1968) *Two lectures on the historicity of language families.* Annamalainagar: Annamalai University

Anttila, R. (1972) *An introduction to historical and comparative linguistics.* New York: Macmillan

– (1976a) 'The reconstuction of Sprachgefühl: a concrete abstract', in Christie (1976: 216–34)

– (1976b) 'The metamorphosis of allomorphs', in Reich (1976: 238–48)

Ayala, F. J. (1976) 'Biology as an autonomous science', in Grene & Mendelsohn (1976: 312–29)

Bach, E. & Harms, R. T. (1968) *Universals in linguistic theory.* New York: Holt, Rinehart & Winston

Batliner, A. (1975) 'Wie natürlich sind die Assimilationen im Altnordischen?', in Dahlstedt (1975: 362–72)

Baumrin, B. (1963) *Philosophy of science. The Delaware Seminar, vol. 2, 1962–1963.* New York: Wiley

Becker, C. L. (1955) 'What are historical facts?', *Western Political Quarterly* 8.327–40

Beckner, M. (1967) 'Explanation in biological theory', in Morgenbesser (1967: 148–59)

Berger, P. L. & Luckmann, T. (1967) *The social construction of reality : a treatise in the sociology of knowledge*. New York: Doubleday

Bever, T. G. & Langendoen, D. T. (1972) 'The interaction of speech perception and grammatical structure in the evolution of language', in Stockwell & Macaulay (1972: 32–95)

Bhaskar, R. (1975) *A Realist theory of science*. Leeds: Leeds Books

Blackburn, S. (1973) *Reason and prediction*. Cambridge University Press

Blanshard, B. (1962) *Reason and analysis*. La Salle: Open Court Publishing Company

Bloomfield, L. (1933) *Language*. New York: Holt

Bohm, D. (1969a) 'Some remarks on the notion of order', in Waddington (1969: 18–40)

– (1969b) 'Further remarks on order', in Waddington (1969: 41–60)

Borger, R. & Cioffi, F. (1970) *Explanation in the behavioural sciences*. Cambridge University Press

Botha, R. P. (1971) *Methodological aspects of transformational-generative phonology*. The Hague: Mouton

– & Winckler, W. K. (1973) *The justification of linguistic hypotheses*. The Hague: Mouton

Bruck, A., Fox, R. A. & LaGaly, M. W. (1974) *Papers from the parasession on natural phonology*. Chicago Linguistic Society

Campbell, A. (1959) *Old English grammar*. Oxford: Clarendon Press

Campbell, L. (1975) 'Constraints on sound change', in Dahlstedt (1975: 388–406)

Cassirer, E. (1944) *An essay on man*. New Haven: Yale University Press

Catford, J. C. (1974) '"Natural" sound changes: some problems of directionality in diachronic phonetics', in Bruck, Fox & LaGaly (1974: 21–9)

– (1977) *Fundamental problems in phonetics*. University of Edinburgh Press

Chen, M. (1974) 'Natural phonology from a diachronic viewpoint', in Bruck, Fox & LaGaly (1974: 43–80)

– (1976) 'Relative chronology: three methods of reconstruction', *Journal of Linguistics* 12.209–58

Chomsky, N. (1972) *Language and mind*. New York: Harcourt Brace Jovanovich

– (1976) *Reflections on language*. London: Temple Smith

– & Halle, M. (1968) *The sound pattern of English*. New York: Harper

Christie, W. M. (1976) *Current progress in historical linguistics. Proceedings of the Second International Conference on Historical Linguistics, Tucson, Arizona, 12–16 January 1976*. Amsterdam: North-Holland

Coates, R. A. (1977) 'The status of rules in historical phonology', unpublished PhD thesis. University of Cambridge

Cohen, D. (1974) *Explaining linguistic phenomena*. Washington: Hemisphere Publishing Corp.

– & Wirth, J. R. (1975) *Testing linguistic hypotheses*. Washington: Hemisphere Publishing Corp.

Collingwood, R. G. (1946) *The idea of history*. Oxford: Clarendon Press

Cooper, C. (1687) See Sundby (1952)

Croce, B. (1921) *History : its theory and practice*. New York: Harcourt, Brace & Co.

Dahlstedt, K-H. (1975) *The Nordic languages and modern linguistics, 2*. Stockholm: Almqvist & Wiksell International

Derwing, B. L. (1973) *Transformational grammar as a theory of language acquisition*. Cambridge University Press

Dingwall, W. O. (1971) *A survey of linguistic science*. College Park: University of Maryland Linguistics Program

Dorian, N. C. (1973) 'Grammatical change in a dying dialect', *Language* 49.413–38

Dray, W. H. (1964) *Philosophy of history*. Englewood Cliffs: Prentice-Hall

– (1966) *Philosophical analysis and history*. New York: Harper

Dressler, W. U. (1972) 'On the phonology of language death', *Chicago Linguistic Society* 8.448–57

– (1975) 'Methodisches zu Allegro-Regeln', in Dressler & Mareš (1975: 219–34)

– & Mareš, F. V. (1975) *Phonologica 1972. Akten der zweiten internationalen Phonologie-Tagung, Vienna, 5–8 September 1972*. Munich/Salzburg: Fink

Dunne, J. W. (1929) *An experiment with time*. London: Black

Eddington, A. (1958) *The philosophy of physical science*. Ann Arbor: University of Michigan Press

Eliade, M. (1961) *Images and symbols*. London: Havrill Press

– (1963) *Myth and reality : world perspectives*. New York: Harper

Eliasson, S. (1977) 'Cognitive processes and models of language', in de Mey, Pinxton, Porian & Vandamme (1977: 60–72)

Elton, G. R. (1969) *The practice of history*. London: Fontana

Emeneau, M. B. (1958) 'Toda, a Dravidian language', *Transactions of the Philological Society* 15–66

– (1970) *Dravidian comparative phonology: a sketch*. Annamalainagar: Annamalai University

Eustace, S. S. (1972) 'A note on *arse* and *ass*', *Journal of the International Phonetic Association* 2.79–80

Eysenck, H. J. (1970) 'Explanation and the concept of personality', in Borger & Cioffi (1970: 387–410)

Feyerabend, P. (1975) *Against method*. London: NLB

Fillmore, C. J. (1968) 'The case for case', in Bach & Harms (1968: 1–90)

Fischer-Jørgensen, E. (1975) *Trends in phonological theory: a historical introduction*. Copenhagen: Akademisk Forlag

Fisiak, J. (1978) *Recent developments in historical phonology*. The Hague: Mouton

Foley, J. (1973) 'Assimilation of phonological strength in Germanic', in Anderson & Kiparsky (1973: 51–8)

Gardiner, P. (1959) *Theories of history*. New York: Free Press

Gilliéron, J. (1921) *Pathologie et thérapeutique verbales*. Paris: Champion

Gilmour, J. S. L. & Walters, S. M. (1963) 'Philosophy and classification', in Turrill (1963: 1–22)

Goyvaerts, D. & Pullum, G. K. (1975) *Essays on the sound pattern of English.* Ghent: E. Story-Scientia

Grene, M. (1974) *The understanding of nature : essays in the philosophy of biology.* Boston Studies in the Philosophy of Science XXIII. Dordrecht: D. Reidel

– & Mendelsohn, E. (1976) *Topics in the philosophy of biology.* Boston Studies in the Philosophy of Science XXVII. Dordrecht: D. Reidel

Habermas, J. (1968) *Erkenntnis und Interesse.* Frankfurt: Suhrkamp

Hacking, I. (1976) *Logic of statistical inference.* Cambridge University Press

Hale, K. (1971) 'Deep–surface canonical disparities in relation to analysis and change: an Australian example', duplicated. Cambridge, Mass.: MIT Press

Halle, M. (1975) 'Confessio grammatici', *Language* 51.525–35

Hamblin, C. (1970) *Fallacies.* London: Methuen

Hammarström, G. (1978) 'Is linguistics a natural science?' *Lingua* 45.16–31

Harms, R. T. (1968) *Introduction to phonological theory.* Englewood Cliffs: Prentice-Hall

Harré, R. (1972) *The philosophies of science : an introductory survey.* Oxford University Press

Harris, Z. S. (1960) *Structural linguistics.* University of Chicago Press

Haugen, E. (1950) *First Grammatical Treatise : the earliest Germanic phonology.* Supplement to *Language* 26, 4

Hempel, C. (1959) 'The function of general laws in history', in Gardiner (1959: 344–55)

– (1966a) *The philosophy of natural science.* Englewood Cliffs: Prentice-Hall

– (1966b) 'Explanation in science and history', in Dray (1966: 95–126)

– & Oppenheim, P. (1948) 'Studies in the logic of explanation', *Philosophy of Science* 15.135–75

Hesse, M. B. (1966) *Models and analogies in science.* Notre Dame: University of Notre Dame Press

– (1974) *The structure of scientific inference.* London: Macmillan

– (1975) Comment on Achinstein (1975), in Körner (1975: 45–54)

Hjelmslev, L. (1963) *Prolegomena to a theory of language.* Trans. F. J. Whitfield. Madison: University of Wisconsin Press

Hockett, C. F. (1958) *A course in modern linguistics.* New York: Macmillan

Hogg, R. M. (1971) 'Gemination, breaking and reordering in the synchronic phonology of Old English', *Lingua* 28.48–69

Hook, S. (1963) *Philosophy and history.* New York University Press

Hooper, J. B. (1975) 'The archi-segment in natural generative phonology', *Language* 51.536–60

– (1976) *An introduction to natural generative phonology.* New York: Humanities Press

Huizinga, J. (1944) *Homo ludens. Versuch einer Bestimmung des Spielelements der Kultur.* Basel: Burg-Verlag

Hurford, J. R. (1977) 'The significance of linguistic generalizations', *Language* 53.574–620

Itkonen, E. (1974) *Linguistics and metascience. Studia Philosophica Turkuensia,* Fasc. II. Turku: Kokemäki

- (1975) 'Transformational grammar and the philosophy of science', in Koerner (1975: 381–445)
- (1976a) *Linguistics and empiricalness: answers to criticisms.* University of Helsinki, Department of General Linguistics
- (1976b) 'The use and misuse of the principle of axiomatics in linguistics', *Lingua* 38.185–220
- (1978) 'Short-term and long-term teleology in linguistic change. *Publications of the Linguistic Association of Finland* 2.35–68
Jakobson, R. (1929) 'Remarques sur l'évolution phonologique du russe, comparée à celle des autres langues slaves', *Travaux du Cercle Linguistique de Prague* 2
- (1961a) 'The concept of the sound law and the teleological criterion', in Jakobson (1961c: 1–2). [Reprinted in Lass (1969: 8–9)]
- (1961b) 'Phoneme and phonology', in Jakobson (1961c: 231–3). [Reprinted in Lass (1969: 6–7)]
- (1961c) *Selected writings*, I. The Hague: Mouton
Jakobson, R., Fant, C. G. M. & Halle, M. (1951) *Preliminaries to speech analysis.* Cambridge, Mass.: MIT Press
- & Halle, M. (1956) *Fundamentals of language.* The Hague: Mouton
Jespersen, O. (1894) *Progress in language, with special reference to English.* London: Swan Sonnenschein
- (1964) *Language: its nature, development and origin.* Reprint. New York: Norton
Jones, C. (1973) 'Pleasant interludes: some arguments for treating the structure of medial consonant clusters as a function of the constraints on initial and final groups', *Edinburgh Working Papers in Linguistics* 3.74–80
Joos, M. (1957) *Readings in Linguistics*, I. University of Chicago Press
Jordan, R. (1934) *Handbuch der mittelenglischen Grammatik. I Teil: Lautlehre.*[2] Rev. Ch. Mathes. Heidelberg: Winter
Jung, C. G. (1955) *Synchronicity: an acausal connecting principle.* London: Routledge & Kegan Paul
Kac, M. (1978) *Corepresentation of linguistic structure.* London: Croom Helm
Kaplan, A. (1965) 'Noncausal explanation', in Lerner (1965: 145–55)
Keller, R. E. (1961) *German dialects: phonology and morphology.* Manchester University Press
King, R. D. (1967) 'Functional load and sound change', *Language* 43.831–52
- (1969) *Historical linguistics and generative grammar.* Englewood Cliffs: Prentice-Hall
Kiparsky, P. (1965) 'Phonological change', unpublished PhD thesis. Cambridge, Mass.: MIT
- (1971) 'Historical linguistics', in Dingwall (1971: 576–649)
- (1975) 'What are phonological theories about?' in Cohen & Wirth (1975: 187–210)
Koerner, E. F. K. (1975) *The transformational-generative paradigm and modern linguistic theory.* Amsterdam: John Benjamins B.V.
Koestler, A. (1974) *The roots of coincidence.* London: Pan

- & Smythies, J. R. (1969) *The Alpbach Symposium 1968. Beyond reductionism: new perspectives in the life sciences*. London: Hutchinson
Kohler, K. J. (1974) 'Contrastive sentence phonology', *Journal of the International Phonetic Association* 4.87–91
Körner, S. (1975) *Explanation*. Oxford: Basil Blackwell
Kuhn, T. (1962) *The structure of scientific revolutions*. University of Chicago Press
Kurath, H. (1956) 'The loss of long consonants and the rise of voiced fricatives in Middle English', *Language* 32.435–45
Labov, W. (1963) 'The social motivation of a sound change', *Word* 19.273–309
- (1966) *The social stratification of English in New York City*. Washington: Center for Applied Linguistics
- (1971) 'Methodology', in Dingwall (1971: 413–97)
Labov, W., Yeager, M. & Steiner, R. (1972) *A quantitative study of sound change in progress*. 2 vols. Philadelphia: U.S. Regional Survey
Ladefoged, P. (1971) *Preliminaries to linguistic phonetics*. University of Chicago Press
Lakatos, I. (1970) 'Falsification and the methodology of scientific research programmes', in Lakatos & Musgrave (1970: 91–196)
- & Musgrave, A. (1970) *Criticism and the growth of knowledge*. Cambridge University Press
Lass, R. (1966) 'Man's Heaven: the symbolism of Gawain's shield', *Mediaeval Studies* 28.354–60
- (1969) *Approaches to English historical linguistics*. New York: Holt, Rinehart & Winston
- (1973) Review of P. Reaney, *The Origin of English surnames*. *Foundations of Language* 9.393–402
- (1974a) 'Linguistic orthogenesis? Scots vowel quantity and the English length conspiracy', in Anderson & Jones (1974b: II, 311–52)
- (1974b) 'Strategic design as the motivation for a sound shift: the rationale of Grimm's Law', *Acta Linguistica Hafniensia* 15.51–66
- (1975) 'How intrinsic is content? Markedness, sound change, and "family universals"', in Goyvaerts & Pullum (1975: 475–504)
- (1976a) *English phonology and phonological theory: synchronic and diachronic studies*. Cambridge University Press
- (1976b) 'Variation studies and historical linguistics', *Language in Society* 5.219–29
- (1976c) Review of Dressler & Mareš (1975). *Journal of Linguistics* 12.346–58
- (1977) 'Internal reconstruction and generative phonology', *Transactions of the Philological Society* (1975) 1–26
- (1978) 'Mapping constraints in phonological reconstruction: on climbing down trees without falling out of them', in Fisiak (1978: 245–86)
- & Anderson, J. M. (1975) *Old English phonology*. Cambridge University Press
Lehmann, W. P. (1952) *Proto-Indo-European phonology*. Austin: University of Texas Press

– & Malkiel, Y. (1968) *Directions for historical linguistics : a symposium*. Austin: University of Texas Press

Lerner, D. (1965) *Cause and effect. The Hayden Colloquium on scientific method and concept*. New York: Free Press

Lewis, C. S. (1947) *The abolition of man*. New York: Macmillan

Lightfoot, D. (1979) *Principles of diachronic syntax*. Cambridge University Press

Lindblom, B. (1978) 'Phonetic aspects of linguistic explanation', *Studia Linguistica* 32.137–53

Linell, P. (1974) *Problems of psychological reality in generative phonology*. Reports from Uppsala University, Department of Linguistics 4

Lorenz, K. (1977) *Behind the mirror : a search for a natural history of human knowledge*. London: Methuen

Lyons, J. (1977) *Semantics*. 2 vols. Cambridge University Press

Macaulay, R. K. S. (1976) Review of Trudgill (1974). *Language* 52.266–70

– & Trevelyan, G. D. (1973) *Language and employment in Glasgow : a report to the Social Science Research Council*. 2 vols.

Macbeth, N. (1974) *Darwin retried*. London: Garnstone Press

Martinet, A. (1955) *Économie des changements phonétiques*. Bern: Francke

– (1975) 'Formalisme et réalisme en phonologie', in Dressler & Mareš (1975: 35–42)

Mayr, E. (1968) 'Cause and effect in biology', in Waddington (1968a: 42–54)

Mellor, D. H. (1975) Comment on Salmon (1975), in Körner (1975: 146–52)

Mey, M. de, Pinxton, R., Porian, M. & Vandamme, F. (1977) *CC 77. International Workshop on the Cognitive Viewpoint*. University of Ghent

Miller, J. E. (1975) 'The parasitic growth of deep structures', *Foundations of Language* 13.361–89

Milroy, J. (1976) 'Synopsis of Belfast vowels', *Belfast Working Papers in Language and Linguistics* 1.111–16

Monod, J. (1972) *Chance and necessity : an essay in the natural philosophy of modern biology*. London: Collins

Moore, T. (1976) 'Languages are clouds *and* clocks', *York Papers in Linguistics* 6.21–32

Morgenbesser, S. (1967) *Philosophy of science today*. New York: Basic Books

Nagel, E. (1961) *The structure of science*. New York: Harcourt Brace Jovanovich

– (1965) 'Types of causal explanation in science', in Lerner (1965: 11–32)

Ohala, J. (1974) 'Phonetic explanation in phonology', in Bruck, Fox & LaGaly (1974: 251–74)

Ohlander, S. (1976) *Phonology, meaning, morphology*. Göteborg: Acta Universitatis Gothoburgensis

Parsons, T. (1965) 'Cause and effect in sociology', in Lerner (1965: 51–73)

Paul, H. (1920) *Prinzipien der Sprachgeschichte*.[5] Halle: Niemeyer

Polanyi, M. (1958) *Personal knowledge*. London: Routledge & Kegan Paul

– (1967) *The tacit dimension*. London: Routledge & Kegan Paul

– & Prosch, H. (1975) *Meaning*. University of Chicago Press

Popper, K. R. (1961) *The poverty of historicism*. London: Routledge & Kegan Paul

– (1968a) *The logic of scientific discovery.* New York: Harper
– (1968b) *Conjectures and refutations : the growth of scientific knowledge.* New York: Harper
– (1973) *Objective knowledge : an evolutionary approach.* Oxford: Clarendon Press
– (1976) *Unended quest : an intellectual autobiography.* London: Fontana
– & Eccles, J. (1977) *The self and its brain.* Berlin: Springer International
Postal, P. M. (1968) *Aspects of phonological theory.* New York: Harper
Putnam, H. (1978) *Meaning and the moral sciences.* London: Routledge & Kegan Paul
Reich, P. A. (1976) *The second LACUS Forum, 1975.* Columbia, S.C.: Hornbeam Press
Rescher, N. (1963) 'Fundamental problems in the theory of scientific explanation', in Baumrin (1963: 41–60)
Ringen, J. (1975) 'Linguistic facts: a study of the empirical scientific status of transformational generative grammars', in Cohen & Wirth (1975: 1–42)
Ruse, M. (1973) *The philosophy of biology.* London: Hutchinson
Salmon, W. S. (1975) 'Theoretical explanation', in Körner (1975: 118–84)
Sampson, G. (1975a) 'One fact needs one explanation', *Lingua* 36.231–9
– (1975b) *The form of language.* London: Weidenfeld & Nicolson
– (1976) Review of Koerner (1975). *Language* 52.961–6
Samuels, M. L. (1965) 'On the role of functional selection in the history of English', *Transactions of the Philological Society* 15–40
– (1972) *Linguistic evolution.* Cambridge University Press
Saussure, F. de (1959) *Course in general linguistics.* Trans. W. Baskin. New York: McGraw Hill
Schachter, P. (1969) 'Natural assimilation rules in Akan', *International Journal of American Linguistics* 35.342–55
Schane, S. A. (1972) 'Natural rules in phonology', in Stockwell & Macaulay (1972: 199–229)
Scheffler, I. (1963) *The anatomy of inquiry : philosophical studies in the theory of science.* New York: Knopf
Scriven, M. (1959) 'Explanation and prediction in evolutionary theory', *Science* 130.477–82
– (1963) 'New issues in the logic of explanation', in Hook (1963: 339–61)
Sedlak, P. (1969) 'Typological considerations of vowel quality systems', *Working Papers on Language Universals*, 1. Stanford: Language Universals Project
Sigurd, B. (1975) 'Linearization in phonology', in Dressler & Mareš (1975: 185–208)
Simpson, G. G. (1964) *This view of life : the world of an evolutionist.* New York: Harcourt Brace & World
Smuts, J. C. (1961) *Holism and evolution.* New York: Viking Press
Sprigge, T. L. S. (1971) 'Final causes', *Aristotelian Society Supplement* 45
Steinberg, R. M. (1977) *Fra Girolamo Savonarola, Florentine art, and Renaissance historiography.* Athens, Ohio: Ohio University Press

Stockwell, R. P. & Macaulay, R. K. S. (1972) *Linguistic change and generative theory. Essays from the UCLA Conference on Historical Linguistics in the Perspective of Transformational Theory, February 1969.* Bloomington: Indiana University Press

Sturtevant, E. H. (1947) *An introduction to linguistic science.* New Haven: Yale University Press

Sundby, B. (1952) *Christopher Cooper's English Teacher (1687).* Lund: Gleerup

Sütterlin, L. (1913) *Werden und Wesen der Sprache.* Leipzig

Teilhard de Chardin, P. (1965) *The phenomenon of man.* London: Fontana

Thompson, D. (1942) *On growth and form.*[2] Cambridge University Press

Toulmin, S. (1958) *The uses of argument.* Cambridge University Press

Trudgill, P. (1974) *The social differentiation of English in Norwich.* Cambridge University Press

– (1978) 'Creolization in reverse: reduction and simplification in the Albanian dialects of Greece', *Transactions of the Philological Society* 32–50

Turrill, W. B. (1963) *Vistas in botany* IV. London: Pergamon Press

Vachek, J. (1964) 'On peripheral phonemes in modern English', *Brno Studies in English* 4.7–100

– (1966) *The linguistic school of Prague : an introduction to its theory and practice.* Bloomington: Indiana University Press

– (1969) 'On the explanatory power of the functional load of phonemes', *Slavica Pragensia* 11.63–71

van den Haag, E. (1963) 'History as factualized fiction', in Hook (1963: 212–26)

Verner, K. (1877) 'Eine Ausnahme der ersten Lautverschiebung', *Zeitschrift für vergleichende Sprachforschung auf dem Gebiete der indogermanischen Sprachen* 23,2.97–130

Vincent, N. (1978) 'Is sound change teleological?' in Fisiak (1978: 409–30)

von Bertalanffy, L. (1968) *General system theory.* Harmondsworth: Penguin Books

Waddington, C. H. (1957) *The strategy of the genes.* London: Allen & Unwin

– (1968a) *Towards a theoretical biology, 1 : prolegomena. An IUBS Symposium.* Edinburgh University Press

– (1968b) 'The basic ideas of biology', in Waddington (1968a: 1–32)

– (1969) *Towards a theoretical biology, 2 : sketches. An IUBS Symposium.* Edinburgh University Press

– (1977) *Tools for thought.* London: Jonathan Cape

Wang, W. S-Y. (1969) 'Competing changes as a cause of residue', *Language* 45.9–25

Weinreich, U., Labov, W. & Herzog, M. (1968) 'Empirical foundations for a theory of language change', in Lehmann & Malkiel (1968: 95–195)

Wisdom, J. O. (1970) 'Situational individualism and the emergent group-properties', in Borger & Cioffi (1970: 271–96)

Woodfield, A. (1976) *Teleology.* Cambridge University Press

Wunderlich, D. (1974) *Grundlagen der Linguistik.* Hamburg: Rowohlt

Wyld, H. C. (1927) *A short history of English.* London: John Murray

Index

abduction 37
Abelson, R. 2, 158f
Abercrombie, D. 36n
Achinstein, P. 5ff, 9n, 11, 11n, 14, 112, 161
Allen, W. S. 165n
analogy 71, 72f
Andersen, H. 37
Anderson, J. M. 16n, 25n, 40n, 163; & Jones, C. 38
Andronov, M. 165
Anglo-Frisian Brightening 72
Anttila, R. 70, 71
argument, uniformitarian 53ff
Aristotle 1, 64
Armenian 41n
arse/ass, history of 77f
Arvanitika 87n
assimilation 35ff, 41n, 131
autonomy of language 115ff, 119ff
Ayala, F. 141, 142

Bantu 31
Batliner, A. 41n
Becker, C. L. 47n
Beckner, M. 88n
behaviourism 102f
Berger, P. L. & Luckmann, T. 132n
Bever, T. G. & Langendoen, D. T. 70n
Bhaskar, R. 105n
biosphere 3, 134
Blackburn, S. 55n
Blanshard, B. 112
blocking devices 81
Bloomfield, L. 18n, 94, 102, 120
Bohm, D. 110n, 157, 159n
Botha, R. 69, 81, 157
'boring universals' 16f
boundary-conditions 39n, 130, 134
Breton 85
bring, history of 71ff

Campbell, A. 71
Campbell, L. 66ff, 69, 70, 71, 75, 77n, 79, 99

Cassirer, E. 8n, 34n, 130n
Catford, J. C. 41n, 163
causality ch. 4, *passim*; biological 103ff; principle of 100ff
causes, ultimate vs. proximate 104
Celtic 84
change, linguistic, as therapeutic 66, 67; as stylistic 170; indeterminism in 114ff; in progress 28, 95; non-necessity of 131; under autonomy thesis 126ff
Chen, M. 35, 36n, 79n
Chomsky, N. 108n, 120, 121, 121n, 125, 126, 166n; & Halle, M. 17n, 25, 31n, 35, 36, 42, 43, 44, 163
Clark, R. 22n
'clincher cases' 68f
closure 105n
Coates, R. A. 21, 46n, 58n, 92n
Cohen, D. 9n
Collingwood, R. G. 59n
commitment 100, 171f
Comte, A. 130n
communicative efficiency 68, 136
competence 121
complementarity 131ff, 136, 146, 150f
conspiracies 81f
constant conjunction 23
conventionalism 50, 59ff
Cooper, C. 37n
correlations, statistical, explanatory force of 23; as sources of insight 166f
creolization in reverse 87n
Croce, B. 47n
Curtius, G. 18
CV, as optimal syllable structure 32ff, 70n

Dante 172n
Darwin, C. 110, 110n, 113, 164, 165
derivations, 'abstract' 9
Derwing, B. L. 108n, 121n
Descartes, R. 102
description 31, 167ff
determinism 99, 102; arguments against

182

For EU product safety concerns, contact us at Calle de José Abascal, 56–1°,
28003 Madrid, Spain or eugpsr@cambridge.org.

www.ingramcontent.com/pod-product-compliance
Ingram Content Group UK Ltd.
Pitfield, Milton Keynes, MK11 3LW, UK
UKHW010046140625
459647UK00012BB/1642